## INTRODUCTION

Welcome to readers old and new. A famous author once said, "The best part of writing a book is finishing it". I so understand that observation after several years of effort on this project and still such a long way to go. Although the number of people downloading my book feels impressive, many folk of mature years, indicated their keenness to savour my recollections but were only comfortable with traditional print. Hence this "The first 40 Years." I hope my readers will bear with me that this volume finishes in 1982. I will strive for a second volume to cover the subsequent third of a century but it's a big ask at my age.

For people new to my autobiography, I saw my first Albion game in the early days of the War, probably in 1940. I so wish I could rhapsodise at length about my first 90 minutes but my memory fails me completely. My first clear memory was in May 1942 so in a way the book starts there- hence the title. Going to the Hawthorns during the war laid down the ground rules that shaped my 'career' as a dedicated Albion nut case!

Since then, I've seen over 2,000 WBA games in nearly three quarters of a century and witnessed pretty much everything. Albion winning the Cup, losing the Cup, winning promotion, missing promotion, relegation and near relegation, in and out of the Third Division and playing in Europe. Note my cautionary "pretty much everything." In response to the email wags, no, I didn't see Jesse Pennington play. Nor did I see the Charge of the Light Brigade. But I do have so many unique memories to share and I'm eager to commit them to print to add a human angle to the bare facts.

I must emphasise that this book is not an Albion history. I can't better the experts so I'm not going to try. Instead, this volume features the life and times of one WBA supporter from the era of Flat caps right up to hopefully Bronx hats though that ultimate ambition is still years away.

Once again, I'm grateful for my proofreaders Katrina Baker and Steve Carr. Any errors remaining are my own. I think I am grateful to my slave-driving publisher Simon Wright, though he is sometimes a harder task master than Tony Pulis on a training field.

Happy Reading

*TERRY*

## Early Years 1941-1945...

I was born within walking distance of the Hawthorns. The aura felt strong, being just two years after West Bromwich Albion created football history by becoming the first, and to date, the only team to win the FA Cup and promotion to the top tier in the same season. Equally, I was born just two years before another Wembley Final. Thus it's not difficult to understand just why I had an upbringing steeped around the fortunes of the "Baggies".

From the age of eight (the earliest I can recall), I have trundled the paths to and from the Hawthorns. As any supporter knows, once that hypnotic needle filled with the "football drug" is injected into your system, that's it. You're hooked. The "fix" becomes a necessity that is way out of proportion to life's really important happenings.

But nevertheless it's always there, nibbling and gnawing away at your innermost thoughts. The key difference being older and wiser, is the relief of a comfortable seat affording a perfect sightline. Now that holds far greater appeal than those early years when a packed ground meant tumbling up and down the terraces, whenever the action moved anywhere near the goalmouth. Oh happy days!

For me, those terrace scenes remain so vivid. Thousands of men wearing flat caps, boys like myself clad in short trousers (only 14 year olds and above wore "longs"), not too many women, clouds of cigarette smoke, buying a penny programme, glancing at the teams, and crumpling a piece of history into a coat pocket, without any thought that in years to come it would become the focus of outstanding memories of previous generations.

So many memories of childhood are forgotten, mercifully in many instances, but in the magical world of football, it's amazing just how many fans can remember their embryonic days of "going to the match", even if the rest of their upbringing remains a veritable blank. I'm no different, and while it would be ridiculous to suggest that I have a perfect recollection of those so long ago years, I do have some very powerful images of those times and can recall certain events very clearly indeed. I believe that's because children of my generation were bought up and survived a period that can and never will be forgotten - the Second World War.

Attending Oldbury Road Junior and Infants School was never much of an attraction for me. I moved onto Smethwick Hall Secondary Modern School but that didn't appeal either. Sadly, my strongest memory of the place is that some light-fingered soul decided that my lapel badge with the inscription *"West Bromwich FA Cup and Promotion Winners"* would be a treasure for him to keep. Even now, I miss that badge.

Like most kids I just wanted to be out on the streets or in one of the local parks. Inevitably Mom and Dad asked, *"Where have you been all day?"* As if they didn't know! There were no distractions and not too many alternatives. No television or personal computers, no shop windows full of mega-drive video games and mobile phones.

Family entertainment meant sitting around a coal fire listening to a wireless set that boasted the Home Service and Light Programme wavelengths as its majority output. That was a routine life until that fateful date of September 3rd 1939 when the outbreak of the war to end all wars was declared.

Initially, it meant little to me. But in 1940, when German bombers began blitzing Birmingham and its suburbs, I soon realised that something was very wrong; especially when my mother tried to explain why my favourite foods were in short supply. This led to the introduction of ration books, and clothing coupons. These were issued to combat the shortage of virtually every daily commodity such as meat, cheese, butter, bread, etc. When any item was purchased, the appropriate number of coupons was detached from the ration book. And if the prescribed monthly allocation of points were all used on the first day of the month, that was it. No more until the start of the next four weekly cycles. Naturally these restrictions led to a flourishing 'black market'. Some 'wide boys' realised if they could lay their hands on restricted foodstuffs, they could make a significant profit. This led to a two-tier economy where people with money could obtain goods not available officially. Another visible sign was that many shops in what was once a typical bustling busy High Street were boarded up with the familiar notice "Closed for the Duration." How long is the Duration? No one knew. It is hard to describe the elation and excitement when on a single memorable occasion; one of the remaining shops advertised *"Toffee Apples on sale tomorrow."* Every kid's favourite treat leading to dozens patiently queuing to snap up what had almost been a forgotten delicacy.

It's not difficult describing how kids occupied their time when not playing football. Summer would be practising whatever dormant cricketing talent I may have had- but not 'up the Park.' No, it meant using a lamppost in nearby Chatwin Street as the wickets, which left angry residents complaining if a tennis ball, slog- bashed a window (or as did occasionally happen) shatter the glass. We'd immediately down our bat and scarper home as fast as our legs would allow knowing that the ball wouldn't be returned by mostly unsympathetic residents. No sense of humour some people!

That wasn't the only way to lose a ball. On the other side of the street was a huge concrete reservoir filled with water just in case the Fire Brigade needed a handy supply. It was surrounded by a high wire fence with warning notices not to climb over. It was a very high fence and a challenge I wouldn't risk. So if our ball was lustily struck "for six" and landed in the reservoir, it was game over with fingers pointed at the batsman. Collectively, we'd simply have to beg our parents to buy us another ball.

Summer evenings would often be spent in the Empire where manager Ernie Spencer introduced a weekly talent show (for want of a better phrase). The audience were invited to sing, dance, or tell jokes. Let's just say I can't recall any genuine hidden talent.

In those days, films were shown on a continuing basis. Pay to get in and you could sit there as long as you liked watching the same films.

But as the years passed slowly, crowds became so large that at the end of a film you'd hear the announcement *"would patrons that have seen the show please leave to allow those queuing to get in."*

Even at my tender age, I couldn't help noticing how intently adults would listen to the news bulletins; all wondering just how long this imposition would remain in force. It was during this `unreal' period that I have my first memories of football in general and Albion in particular.

History tells us that the League was suspended between 1939 and 1946. With players being called up for National Service, it was impossible for clubs to rely on their own players for fixtures, so a joint meeting of the Football League and the Football Association decided to suspend all such contracts until definite decisions could be implemented.

Within weeks, permission was given to resume competitive football based around 13 restructured regional Leagues, to ensure that journeys to away matches would be completed on the day of the fixture. The Baggies actually participated in both the Football League South and the Football League North, and in common with every other club, faced the worrying problem of finding sufficient players to make up a team. Often it depended simply on what players happened to be in the vicinity at the time. The great English International Tommy Lawton remarkably once played two games on a Christmas Day - Everton in the morning and then Tranmere Rovers in the afternoon. It's also on record that one Bradford City player turned out for no less than eight different clubs in just nine weeks!

Under these conditions, Albion subsequently fielded a variety of guest players. I can remember seeing Gilbert Merrick and Don Dearson of Birmingham City turning out, as did the Brentford outside left Leslie Smith, another international who later enjoyed a distinguished career after leaving Brentford to join Aston Villa.

My first ever live game was during the 1940-41 season. I honestly cannot remember my first ever match but I can recall one early fixture that still haunts me! It was May 25th 1942 against a team wearing claret and blue shirts and they won     4-3. Yes, it was that team from Aston who ensured, for me at least, that they'd forever be our greatest rivals. As a curly haired schoolchild in short trousers I screamed, groaned, and cursed at the injustice. No swearing, that was for grown-ups! Villa's Frank Broome scored a hat- trick and as far as I was concerned, every goal was offside and Villa was very lucky to win. Not that I was biased of course! The game was billed as a friendly as were many at the time for instance against such unlikely-sounding opponents such as Hednesford and Revo Sports. In fact, in one friendly against the RAF the immortal W. G. Richardson scored all the Throstles goals in a 6-1 win but, sad to say, I can't remember any of them.

At the tender age of eight, the memories became more focused, not just war memories, but also my regular trips to the Hawthorns. I ran there. I ran to the ground via Smethwick High Street, over the railway bridge, and up Halfords Lane, just to ensure that I'd be able to claim "my" space on the Smethwick End terrace right behind the goal. I ran even though kick-off was at least two hours distant. For me, the time would soon pass. I simply needed to be there... and quickly.

For the first time, I was identifying my own favourite players. With no TV and no great interest in the opposition, I only knew those who wore the famous blue and white stripes. My favourites were players such as Cecil Shaw, Jack Sankey, Billy Gripton, Cliff Edwards, Ike (Nobby) Clarke, Sammy Heaselgrave, Len Millard and Peter McKennan. These gentlemen and others introduced a wide-eyed youngster to the raw emotions of the game - delight, ecstasy, despair, and abject disappointment – mandatory staples for any supporter.

Others were to follow such as young Len Millard, in the early stages of a glorious career, which would ultimately lead to a fine marking job on Tom Finney in the FA Cup Final of 1954. Another favourite was Sandy McNab; a ferocious tackling red-haired Scotsman who was small in stature but big in heart, who bore comparison to Billy Bremner, Alan Ball, or Paul Scholes.

Billy Elliott was a fast raiding winger who had the marvellous knack of disguising his intentions, much to the chagrin of his opponent. Billy would set off at top speed and, once in full flight, he miraculously gave the distinct impression that he was about to check his run by dragging his foot over the ball. He rarely did, and simply carried on regardless leaving more than one full back lying on the turf suitably nonplussed, and Baggie fans wondering at his skill. To this day, I have never seen this touch of magic repeated and if it hadn't been for a certain Stanley Matthews, the name of Billy Elliott would almost certainly have been seen in a lot more International programmes. Without question, Billy was worthy of many more than his two England caps.

Sammy Heaselgrave was more than a great favourite. He was also a family friend who made many visits to see my parents. I remember once he asked me if I was going to the match on Saturday. I shyly answered, "Yes". Sammy said he would do his best to score a couple of goals, just for me. The result? A 2-2 draw against Northampton Town, and yes, 'Uncle Sammy' did keep his word as he netted both goals. What a pity he didn't say he would try to score a hat trick!

Sammy was born in Smethwick and was a regular in my parents' sweet shop. Even to a schoolboy, he wasn't a tall fellow. Sammy was probably best described as dapper, with a neat, trimmed hairstyle and a cheery disposition. He was a frequent customer to Mom and Dad's Sweets/Chocolates/and Cigarette shop directly opposite the 'Smethwick Empire' Picture House.  He was always happy to chat with the family and fellow customers, with endless variants of *"When do you think the war will end?"* to the latest events at the Hawthorns.

Leaving Albion after 13 years loyal service and 57 goals, he went on to play for Northampton Town and as a guest player 'down the road' at Walsall. I was sad to see him go. Sammy was not an average footballer. After all, how many players, after retiring from the game, were knowledgeable enough to become a solicitor? He was and being true to his roots, the name of 'Heaselgrave-Solicitors' would be prominent in Bearwood Road for years to come.

I mentioned earlier that the family shop was directly opposite a cinema. What memories come flooding back of 'going over the road' to see flickering black and white pictures. Modern readers will find it difficult to comprehend that unless an adult accompanied children, they were refused admission. If a parent didn't fancy the film, the problem was finding a way around it.

Answer? Simply ask a complete stranger *"Can you take me in please?"*

Many refused but when someone said, "Yes", I'd gleefully hand over 6d (2 and a half new pence), they'd buy the ticket. Job done?

Not quite! After buying the ticket we'd be told, *"Remember you have to sit together- no wandering off on your own."* No way. Once inside, kids would find themselves a seat as far away from their benefactors as possible and settle down hoping the film was worth the time and expense involved.

Even then the fun wasn't over. At the end of the film, there was a clattering of seats as patrons rushed to the nearest exit before the playing of the National Anthem, Unpatriotic? No, we just wanted to get home and the quicker the better!

Most of the population smoked. It was considered to be good for your health at the time and it was one way of relieving daily stress. Many children smoked and even more were aware that I lived over a shop. If I'd given in to virtual non-stop pleas, I'd be the most popular kid for miles around.

The question? *"Can you nick me a few fags, I can't afford to buy 'em."*

The answer? *"Yes I could but I won't."*

My parents were VERY trusting. If I came home to discover they'd gone out, I simply had to put my hand through the letter box, grab hold of a piece of thick string, and firmly pull. This was attached to the inside handle knob so 'Bingo'- the door was unlocked. One firm push and in we went! Can you imagine such a scenario these days? Thought not!

Football was an essential distraction for me from the desperate realities of the war. Children learned to grow up very, very quickly as the chilling implications of constant air raids created universal fear and trepidation. Everyone was issued with a gas mask, to be carried at all times, although this instruction was often ignored. If air raid wardens heard gas bombs were being dropped, they'd grab their rattle and run up and down streets swinging it around, to remind people to take their gas masks with them into the nearest community Air Raid shelter. These masks varied in size, ranging from adult to children with babies being accommodated in a box type package. Gas warnings were thankfully rare, but bombings of cities and industrial areas were common. Whenever an Air Raid warning sounded in the middle of the night, that hideous screeching high-pitched siren awaked residents. Air raids were truly frightening. Frantic scrambling ensued as Mom and Dad urged my bleary-eyed sisters and me to dress immediately.

As we rushed pell-mell from our house, we were only half-aware of a pitch black sky criss-crossed with searchlights beams and floating tethered whale-shaped barrage balloons. Those dirigibles were to become a familiar friendly sight as part of England's defences.

We crammed into the shelter, hoping to find a spare bed or chair available. An orchestrated "*sing along*" attempted to drown out the drone of the bombers, and more ominously, bombs exploding on your neighbourhood. This feeling really was terrifying. No war film can adequately replicate living through the trauma of hearing bombs being dropped. Singing songs from the 'Top Twenty' of the era acted as some kind of distraction. It was all we had. Tunes such as *'Run rabbit, run rabbit, run run run"* made famous by Flanagan and Allen, and Vera Lynn's classic (long before she became a Dame) "*We'll meet again, don't know where, don't know when"*

Eventually the "All Clear" siren would sound to confirm it was safe to leave our refuge, and venture out with one question in everyone's mind. "Will our house still be standing?" Many were destroyed, but mercifully we remained lucky. Yes we sometimes found doors and windows jammed and other superficial damage, but compared to others less fortunate who had been made homeless, these problems were trivial.

Even so, next day you'd find me and other kids scrambling around what remained of homes just reduced to rubble, hoping we could find pieces of the bombs that had caused carnage, homelessness and, worst of all, a loss of life. *"I've got some, I've got some"* we'd frequently yell only on closer examination to prove that the prize was simply a piece of shattered guttering, kettle, saucepan or cutlery. Just occasionally, I did find genuine gleaming shreds of shrapnel, which I kept as a souvenir until the novelty wore off. One night there was a muted scare. A land mine was tangled in its parachute in the Council House telegraph wires. Had it exploded, the damage to people and property would be immense. I didn't need any warnings to keep clear but "Keep Clear" I was told anyway at maximum volume. I'm not certain how the mine was eventually disabled in that awkward position, but however it was, everyone was truly grateful.

If you didn't live through the war, you couldn't begin to understand the emotions when peace was finally declared on May 8th 1945. VE-Day (Victory in Europe) meant a day and night of all-out rejoicing. Street parties were organised and people dressed in whatever would pass as fancy dress, but it was the bonfires that captured the imagination and took centre-stage. While adults sang and danced, most of the kids thought it strange we were being allowed to stay up late to kick a ball around the streets. My first experience of football under lights!

The sense of relief was utterly overwhelming. No more blackouts and shouts of *"Put that light out"*. Complete strangers hugged each other in the streets and the parties went on long into the night.

The historic year which ended a terrible era held more memories for me. Football memories. Even at 12, I needed an escape mechanism. I remember reading that Albion lost at Stamford Bridge to Chelsea 7-4. Impossible! How could my beloved Albion concede seven goals in one match, whoever they were playing? There was instant revenge a week later when the Pensioners came to the Hawthorns for the return match and left on the end of an 8-1 thrashing, Nobby Clarke became the first player I ever seen score four goals in one match.  I just wish I had clearer memories of such a stonking!

Memories are curious institutions, with often random or unusual incidents clinging on determinedly inside my brain.  I can remember none of Nobby's goals yet I have a first-class recollection of a strange incident just a month later against Southampton.

Playing the same side in successive matches was normal during this period. Fresh from defeating the Saints 2-1 on the South Coast, the same opposition then visited the Hawthorns. Goals were flying into their net, five compared to their two with just five minutes left.  Baggies striker Arthur Rowley who was a well-built stocky character, challenged the keeper in the air. From my vantage point behind the pitch level wall at the Smethwick End, I had a perfect view as the pair rose …and then came down again straight into the left-hand goalpost.  The post was apparently weaker than Arthur because it just snapped in two under the strain.

Astonishment all round and much head scratching in front of the collapsed goal-frame. What's to be done? Abandoning the game with so little time remaining didn't seem fair. Equally, it's impossible to finish the game with just one post and a crossbar. In an era when making do or improvisation was commonplace, a solution was quickly found. Send out two men with a plank, push the two 'shattered halves together, stand them upright and finish the game courtesy of the two 'craftsmen' holding up the post! And it worked with thankfully no awkward rulebook-testing moments like the post-holder accidentally blocking a shot or tripping up the goalkeeper.

Other high scoring wins included a 5-0 drubbing of Tottenham Hotspur, when a certain Ray Barlow scored a hat trick, but much more of him later. Plus there were 5-2 wins against both Plymouth Argyle and Southampton plus a 4-1 against Fulham. Best of all was a 6-0 whitewash of Newport County when 'Nobby' Clarke scored his nineteenth goal of the season.

On October 20th, I was part of the largest crowd I had ever seen when England played Wales in a Victory International Match at the Hawthorns. The England team contained many of the top players of the era such as Bert Williams, Frank Soo, Neil Franklin and Joe Mercer. Plus the player, who it could be argued, was the greatest player in the world at the time, the supremely talented "Wizard of the Dribble", Stanley Matthews.

Left back Harry Kinsell represented Albion, but it wasn't to be a happy debut due to a very unusual incident. After clashing with Coventry City's George Lowrie both players were taken to the touchline by the referee who issued a stern 'calm down' warning. Message received and understood. No further aggro. They carried on playing. The official attendance was given as 54,611 but I know this was incorrect because I was one of many who slipped in without paying due to having insufficient "pocket money." It wasn't unknown then for a friendly operator to let kids clamber over, or under, a turnstile for whatever you could afford!

There was an awful tragedy in 1946 at Burnden Park, Bolton in an F.A Cup match against Stoke City. The attendance was given as 65,419, but it was later estimated that nearer 85,000 turned up. In a ground that was already packed to capacity, thousands arriving late tried to gain admittance at the Railway End. A father and son, who sensed danger, picked the lock of an exit gate to escape the crush. As a result, hundreds more piled in through the opening.

Under the weight, two barriers in the stand collapsed and those in front were crushed. The game wasn't even abandoned. All those who had perished were placed on the sidelines with a coat over them. Thirty minutes later, with new narrower touchlines marked out with sawdust; the players were expected to continue playing. I can still see the headlines on the front of the newspapers..."33 CRUSHED TO DEATH AT BOLTON." How supremely ironic that people who had survived everything that a major war could throw at them would lose there lives such a short time later at a football match.

There was a happier memory of that season in the FA Cup. Albion were paired with Cardiff City. At Ninian Park, the teams drew 1-1 and, as these were the days before floodlights, it meant the match at the Hawthorns would have to be played on a Wednesday afternoon. This dismayed the school authorities who feared that I and other 'Barmy' Throstles fans would much prefer to see the game as opposed to sitting on a hard school chair listening to a teacher! On Monday, the headmaster announced that if anyone tried to see this match, they would find school inspectors at the turnstiles to prevent absentees gaining admittance. Of course, this was absolute nonsense, aimed at deterring the faint-hearted. The determined or those who detested arithmetic (I was both) were not put off, although I did feel apprehensive as I handed over my pocket money at the turnstile. Throughout the game, I was concerned about being hauled away and marched back to school though it never happened. The Baggies' 4-0 victory was well worth the rollicking from both parents and teachers that inevitably followed.

## 1946-47

The new season would be a proper one, allowing me to see the "Throstles" playing in the Second Division with unfamiliar teams rolling up at the Hawthorns. Sadly, it would inevitably mean several of my "heroes" moving on with replacements coming in. Even so, it had to be an exciting, challenging, and unknown prospect for any teenager. Maybe there would be a chance to see the big names in action, players such as Matthews, Finney, and Lawton.

The "big kick off" on August 31st saw Swansea Town v Albion at the Vetch Field. As a matter of interest, the fixtures for the whole Football League programme were exactly the same as the corresponding day of the short-lived season of 1939/40. A crowd of over 29,000 turned out for Swansea - the match all Albion fans hoped would herald the start of a promotion-winning season. Well, it was a winning start and indeed the first dozen games were so encouraging that my dreams were already turning to next seasons magical First Division. Seven of those games were won, two drawn with only three defeats.

Much of my optimism was brought about with the acquisition of Albion's new hero with the Midas scoring touch, Dave Walsh. Dave joined from Linfield in the close season after scoring over 60 goals for the Irish outfit, and he certainly made a dramatic start, scoring twice in a 3-2 win over the Welsh side. Two days later, I was among the large contingent of supporters who travelled to Highfield Road in Coventry to see him repeat the performance. This time we were on the wrong end of a five-goal thriller. To this day, his record of scoring in his first six consecutive matches remains a club record.

It was also during this spell that I witnessed one of the finest displays of wing play I had ever seen. Unfortunately the player in question wasn't wearing an Albion shirt. His name was Johnny Kelly, a player of breath taking brilliance on his day, and, unfortunately for the Albion, this was one of his days as Barnsley thumped the Baggies 5-2. Kelly didn't score, but his twisting, darting runs had defenders looking on in despair. Clearly they had no idea how to stop him.

A few days later came my first ever visit to St. Andrews and a taste of a meaningful local derby. It wasn't a happy visit - we went down by a single goal with over 50,000 cramming into a ground that, for years, had the reputation of being one of the worst in the country. A reputation that haunted them for nearly fifty years until David Sullivan's soft porn empire rescued them.

I have one more everlasting memory when Albion played a Bank Holiday Monday match at the Hawthorns. The visitors were Chesterfield. Early in the second half Albion were losing 2-0. What a turnabout! Two goals from Walsh and another from Frank Hodgetts saw the 'Throstles' run out 3-2 winners. Such was my enthusiasm with this magical happening that I actually compiled a match report for an English lesson. It must have impressed the teacher, as I was asked to read it at morning assembly as a reward for my efforts.

The worst winter in living memory started with heavy snowfalls in February 1947. Schools were closed, which was a bonus. Traffic came to a halt as ten-foot high snowdrifts blocked the roads. Families struggled to keep warm as fuel stocks ran out, due to the coalmen being unable to keep up deliveries in their horse and carts. My Dad struggled on foot to work daily from Smethwick to Cadburys in Bournville along footpaths and roadways covered in deep snow. Small wonder he was absolutely shattered when he finally arrived back home at the end of his shift. Despite Cadburys being an enlightened employer, it was simply expected that workers would turn up on time, snow or no snow.

You can imagine the chaos this caused for sport. I vividly remember spending a day snow- shifting with other volunteers in a vain attempt to make the Hawthorns playable. But to where exactly do you move the snow?  We quickly ran out of "safe" areas. No point in dumping it on the terraces or the pavements or on the roads outside. The drifts outside the ground already towered above everyone; some were thirty foot tall or even higher.  It was simply impossible and with hindsight, the whole exercise was pointless and badly thought through.

No football for five weeks and supporters were denied the chance to see the great Irish International Jack Vernon who had joined the club from Belfast Celtic.

When he did make his debut, it was unfortunately away at Upton Park in a 3-2 defeat, but it wasn't long before he became another of my boyhood heroes along with Walsh, Clarke, Millard and Billy Elliot.

When football finally resumed in mid-March, the Baggies still had 15 games to play.  The season was extended until the end of May with WBA finishing in comfortable mid-table. There was even an end-of-season flourish with an impressive three wins in four games comprising a 4-2 win at Bradford, a 5-1 drubbing of Nottingham Forest and a last match 3-1 defeat of Manchester City. All in all, I was filled with enthusiasm and Mom and Dad were probably sick to the teeth hearing that Albion would easily win promotion next season.

Let me share a few points of "football trivia" with you. The great Stanley Matthews controversially left Stoke City for Blackpool for a fee of £11,500. Derby County broke the British transfer record with the purchase of Billy Steel from Morton for a staggering fee of £15,500 and the incredible skills of one of England's most controversial players, Len Shackleton, were moved to Newcastle United from Bradford for another "staggering" fee of £13,000. It didn't take long before he started repaying his fee as on his debut he scored six goals against Newport County. In those days, everyone looked forward to playing County!

That horrendous winter left its mark on the family, who decided to move house to Selly Oak, Birmingham I didn't want to leave Smethwick although deep down I recognised the logic. Dad would be a mere 10 minute walk from Cadbury's. He would save bus fares (he never owned a car) or worse the prospect of walking in snow when the buses couldn't move.

I am sad in many ways about what I was leaving behind. Gone would be the days of watching Smethwick Highfield FC on Londonderry Playing fields. I was leaving 'lifelong' teenage mates who together with yours truly formed a parks football team called Bowden Wanderers. Why not Albion Wanderers? Simple answer, the lad with the casting vote lived in Bowden Road and his parents more often than not stumped up the pounds, shillings, and pence to buy a new case ball when required. (He who pays the piper calls the tune!) Our designated home ground was West Smethwick Park. Each day we'd turn up, practice and look around to see if we could find enough kids to challenge us.

If not, it'd be upping sticks, going down to Victoria Park next to the Council House and asking kids if *"they'd gissa game?"* No organised fixtures of course. They were only for grown-ups!

It was during these embryonic years that I first came across Trevor Long. Younger than me but he already stood out as a footballer. He joined the powerful works team of Mitchells and Butler as a winger, who presumably never went short of good honest beer. I lost touch with him after that but I was pleased he went to have some kind of footballing career with Wolverhampton, Gillingham and then Non–League with Yeovil.

My eventual unwanted move over the border into the big city of Birmingham was delayed thanks to a compromise that allowed me to live with my grandmother at Bearwood during the week and go home at weekends. I did this for a few months, but accepting the compromise was an unhappy one and reluctantly moved full time to my new home.

So farewell Smethwick Hall Modern and instead welcome Selly Oak's Raddlebarn Road. Somewhat nervously, I was greeted by the Headmaster at School Assembly, He wished me well while my new found school-mates asked *"do you play football?"* (Is the Pope a Catholic?) After a few playground 'trials', I was chosen to make my debut proudly wearing the blue and gold coloured shirts in the inside-right position. My performance was reasonable though I did recall with horror when I managed to replicate one of my many Albion scoring heroes by skiing an open goal opportunity high, wide and not very handsome!

I quickly realised why the reputation of the School of being one of the best team's around was spot on.

Two brothers, Ray and Malcolm Spencer stood out. Ray was literally in a class of his own, confirmed when the Head proudly announced he'd been chosen for the England International School side. There were cheers and congratulations all round. But with the brutal honesty of kids, I felt compelled to say *"if you make it as a professional and play against the Albion, I won't be supporting you."* Friends? Only if it doesn't impact on WBA.

Ray signed for a certain Aston Villa in 1950. He spent eight years at Villa Park but strangely he never made a first team appearance. Can anyone possibly envisage that scenario today? Eight years at a club, never chosen to make a debut but still retained? He eventually moved on to Darlington but not before I saw him playing against Albion in a Central League game. True to my word, while wishing him well my allegiance to the Blue and White Stripes had to take precedence. *"Sorry, Ray!"* My school mate went on to play 150 games for either Darlington or Torquay, so good for him.

I felt strange being among the 'foreign' football fans of Aston Villa and Birmingham City. In those days, replica strips didn't exist and the team you supported was a mystery unless it came up in conversation. But needless to say, it wasn't too long before I began to encroach on the football chat with stories that the 'Throstles' were a much better team than anything the City of Birmingham could produce! The move meant the start of thousands of trips to and from Birmingham to the Hawthorns.

On that score visiting the City centre was poles apart from any previous visits to Villa Park and St Andrews. Now I couldn't help compare the large stores with the modest shops in Smethwick High Street and Cape Hill where the likes of Peacocks and

Woolworths took centre stage. I was both fascinated and excited by the hustle and bustle of the Bull Ring. I marvelled at the buskers and the 'magicians.' If possible, I always put a few coppers into a cap held by a blind man. He simply stood in the same location every week silently holding his white stick.

## 1947/48

Although the Baggies started well with victories in their first four games and only 2 defeats in the first fourteen, they were unable to maintain a promotion charge. They finished 7<sup>th</sup>. Dave Walsh was way out in front with 22 goals from a club total of 63. The season however wasn't without its memories, mainly revolving around individual players.

Peter McKennan, who had played for Albion during the war years, joined the club permanently from Patrick Thistle, and he soon became one of my great all time Albion favourites. He had all the attributes. Big and strong with a thunderbolt shot, he could withstand the fiercest of tackles. But for me, his greatest asset was the ability to totally embarrass opponents with his skill.

In today's game, he would probably be considered a luxury, the type of player appreciated by the fans but not the manager. Many times I gaped open-mouthed as he literally 'took the mickey' out of the opposition, challenging them to take the ball from him before disappearing in the opposite direction. Magical skills but strangely he only made a handful of appearances before being transferred to Leicester City in exchange for John (Jackie) Haines.

I simply can't resist sharing a memory that even now leaves me grinning like a Cheshire cat. It was October 18th and Albion were playing at Chesterfield, an exotic ground for me and the chance to visit a different part of the country. With money being tight, up to then I'd been restricted to travelling only to local grounds such as Villa Park, St Andrews, Molineux and Highfield Road.

"Can I go, please?" was my fervent plea to Mom and Dad. It did the trick, they gave me the money and

I was set to visit Chesterfield, a Derbyshire town best known as having a church with a crooked spire. With my war memories still fresh, I imagined the spire's twists were due to bombing. It was only much later that I learnt the church spire has leant for over 400 years.

So it was all systems go in the company of mainly elderly Albion supporters who determinedly followed the team up and down the country. We set out from Bearwood on a 'Gliderways' charabanc. Although the word "charabanc" remained in common usage until the 1960's, this was far from the open-top lumbering liable-to-turn-over vehicles of the 1920's. Gliderways were one of the biggest names in the West Midlands coach industry but even such a big player was short of vehicles due to post-war shortages. Basically, you took what was given and were grateful. After all, petrol rationing remained in force and using precious red diesel for such a frivolous purpose felt dubious for many people.

Coaches of the era had room for only 25-30 passengers but boasted solid wood interior trim and floral patterns on the seats. Speed was limited to about 50mph at best, downhill with a following wind. A radio was an unheard-of luxury in such a vehicle, never mind reclining seats, toilets etc.

We intrepid travellers drove close by the 'Crooked Spire', perhaps not as spectacular as the 'Leaning Tower of Pisa' but definitely a unique piece of architecture. That's far more than can be said for Saltergate – it was, putting it mildly, a dilapidated, sad looking wasteland compared to the Hawthorns. Once inside, I followed the ritual of buying a programme costing two old pence. But there was another version on sale outside the ground, an unofficial 'pirate' programme that some wide-eyed character put together and sold for one penny. The contents were simply wretched. I didn't fall into the trap but many others did.

For some unknown reason, I paid for a seat. Obviously Mom and Dad had given me too much pocket money, allowing me to sit in comfort among the privileged few. Enter an Albion fan that'd obviously enjoyed supping a pre-match pint, or three. He plonked himself down next to me, and immediately started to chat (in rather slurred tones) about the chances of a Baggies win. He did most of the talking, I simply listened, but I did ask him what he thought of the Crooked Spire.

Came this classic response delivered in a thick, slurred Black Country accent: *"Funny aye it. Yow'd have thought the foreman would have sin what was wos gooin' on when they wus building it, wouldn't ya?"* No response from me! Some 60 years later, my wife Dot and I wore Albion shirts to visit the famous Leaning Tower of Pisa where we posed for photographs. During those moments, I recalled that Baggies fan who believed it was a neglectful foreman who was responsible for Chesterfield's crooked spire. Pisa was a happy memory but if forced to choose, it would be a poor second to my first-ever visit to that small Derbyshire town and a 2-0 win thanks to goals from Billy Elliott and Dave Walsh.

Also during this season, I witnessed one of the best goals I have ever seen in 75 odd years of support. The Baggies were at home to Cardiff and were 2-1 up courtesy of goals from McKennan and Walsh, and appeared to have had the game won. Enter the Cardiff left winger, a certain Duggie Blair, and his performance will live with me forever. He turned the game on its head with a magical strike. Blair had already scored once with a staggering 30 yard strike that left keeper Tom Grimley watching helplessly.

Let Alan Hoby of the Sunday People take up the tale. "*Cardiff won an enthralling match 3-2. But the story of the way they won is the story of Duggie Blair. Picking up the ball in an incredible dribble, he beat six men in 50 yards, and just as he looked to be losing the ball, he coolly lofted it with his left foot into the roof of the net.*" Back then, I was always reluctant to praise the opposition, but the sheer poetry of this winning goal couldn't be denied, especially as it had come in front of a staggering amount of ecstatic Welsh supporters. Many people claim that the goal scored by Ryan Giggs in a FA Cup Semi-Final replay at Villa Park in 1998 was the best goal ever. It's all a matter of personal opinion, but for me that Blair's wonder effort would top that by some distance. My only complaint was that an Albion player didn't score it!

The narrow defeat merely emphasised there would no escape from the Second Division for another year. By way of consolation, we had the satisfaction of enjoying another end of season goals bonanza. A crushing 6-0 home win over Bradford with a Haines hat trick was followed by the last away game at Cardiff City. There was a paragraph in the City match day programme that after all these years still makes me smile. It simply said: "*The City players are fit and confident*". They may have been fit but they were hardly confident after Albion recorded their best away win of the season in a 5-0 victory!

Other items of interest included Millwall's ground being closed for seven days due to crowd trouble (nothing new in football). The transfer fee record was smashed when Len Shackleton (yes, him again) moved from Newcastle United to Sunderland for a fee of £20,500. As can be imagined, the Geordie fans weren't too happy with this deal but they had gained promotion to the First Division, which acted as some consolation.

**1948/49 Promoted to the First Division**

Our third attempt at emulating Newcastle's success and, at last, we finally made it. Early results didn't provide much optimism as after a first day win over Nottingham Forest, courtesy of a Dave Walsh goal, a further five matches elapsed before we won again with a convincing 5-0 win over Lincoln City - a hat trick from Walsh and two from Haines doing the damage. But this was the start of a tremendous run with nine wins and three draws rocketing WBA up the table. From then on, it was to be neck and neck with numerous highs and lows before promotion was guaranteed. And what memories!

This season saw the emergence of one of Albion's greatest ever players - Ray Barlow. Ray was a phenomenal player, arguably the finest ever to win just a single England International cap and who was only denied more honours by the consistent performances of Portsmouth's Jimmy Dickinson. No one will ever convince me that Dickinson was a better player. In those days, it was hard to lose your place if you were an England regular, no matter how well other players were performing. That was of course sometime in the future but even in his early Albion days; it was obvious Ray had all the skills necessary to reach the top of his profession.

Another budding star was Joe Kennedy, definitely the finest centre half I have ever seen and quite astonishing in the air. Again, in years to come, Joe was to challenge Billy Wright for his place in the England team. Whenever Kennedy faced the great John Charles, recognised as one of the world's truly outstanding players, we witnessed epic confrontations. On more than one occasion, Joe would emerge the victor against the aptly named "Gentle Giant."

Many of the clubs competing in Division Two that term would today be described as being of modest means. A number of them including Lincoln, Grimsby and Bradford Park Avenue are no longer League clubs. Similarly Bury, Chesterfield, Plymouth, Brentford et al were enjoying some of the best years of their history.

In November, I was off to see Albion take on the might of Bradford Park Avenue. It was my first visit to Bradford, of which I knew little apart that it had a lot of textile mills. It was raining; it always seemed to be raining in the white rose county. The 'Throstles were on a crest of a wave. Nine wins and three draws in twelve games meant they were pushing hard for promotion. Another two points at Park Avenue surely?

There were always a goodly number of Albion fans willing to travel to away games, budgets permitting. I went on my own before linking up with kids of my age on what was termed a 'Football Special'. The journey by steam train started at Birmingham's New Street Station before picking up fellow Baggies at Rolfe Street, Oldbury, Tipton, Dudley Port and the other Black Country LMS stations. (No British Rail in those days, it was the famous but private London Midland Scottish region).

The wartime blitz had left its mark on New Street. Sections of its glass roof had been shattered, leaving passengers praying for a dry day. Their plight was worsened by clouds of smoke that billowed and swirled overhead before depositing ash on anyone who hadn't been quick enough to get through a carriage door as soon as the train pulled into the platform.

Arriving at Bradford the first thing to do was to find a fish and chip shop. Here I discovered when trying to place my order and then chat with a local, there was a language barrier. Cue complete culture shock as West Yorkshire and Brummie accents just didn't gel. In haste, I covered my embarrassment by concentrating on my fish and chips (eaten out of a torn up copy of the 'News of the World').

Sadly, Albion's display matched the miserable weather. A windswept, sodden open terrace in itself was bad enough (a seat in the stand next to the famous Dolls' House was beyond my means). Far worse was an equally miserable 90 minutes for Albion fans, counterbalanced by sheer joy from the Avenue supporters. A white flag was metaphorically hoisted and a goal from Jackie Haines was the only crumb of comfort to the four netted by the Avenue.

How did Albion fans react to this setback? There was no orchestrated chanting or singing, as this was a decade or more into the future. No, we just cheered or groaned, as we felt necessary. But we did swing our heavy wooden rattles as vigorously as our strength allowed. I still have mine, splashed and smudged in blue and white paint and covered with a faded picture of the 1955 team. Loud rattles were the key weapons for air raid wardens during the war.

Once the bombing stopped, they became surplus to requirements and were snapped up by any football fans that enjoyed making as much noise as possible. Rattles were marvellous during a game for celebrating an Albion goal, or even better, a win. Disembarking after an away win at New Street was the perfect excuse for maximum volume. It's fair to say that non-football lovers didn't share our enthusiasm. They'd glower and stare before crossing the road while, at the same time, yell at us to stop behaving like children! They didn't need to tell us anything after that miserable soggy trip to West Yorkshire.

Albion did extract revenge for their comprehensive defeat. Four goals from Dave Walsh in a 7-1 drubbing sent them packing to back to inevitably soggy Bradford. Even so, who would have dreamt that this well-rooted League club, the side who developed the skills of Vic Buckingham and Derek Kevan for us, would fold completely in the early 1970's?

As the race for promotion hotted up, Albion were locked in a three-way struggle with Fulham and Southampton for two promotion places. The Baggies were actually outsiders in the race as Fulham were way out in front with the Saints being second favourites. Much to my delight, they began to fall away. Every point dropped was greeted with relief and renewed confidence among supporters that we could reach the First Division at their expense.

Four successive victories, highlighted by that 7-1 drubbing of Bradford at the Hawthorns, set us up. And then after a 2-0 win against Barnsley, thanks to goals from Dave Walsh and Ray Barlow, victory at Leicester would clinch promotion. But City would scrap because they needed one more point themselves to avoid relegation.

It was to be a truly unforgettable Thursday afternoon against the losing FA Cup finalists Leicester City. Every Baggies supporter who could get there, adults and children alike, descended on Filbert Street. Trains and coaches were overflowing; excitement wasn't only in the air, it was in the stratosphere. With no thought of making the match all-ticket, the first challenge was just to get through the turnstiles before they were closed. Once inside, the next job was to obtain a view of the pitch. No segregation of course but there was smoke everywhere - in your eyes, up your nose and on your clothes. This was normal of course in the 1950's when smoking was billed as being a healthy activity but far more intense when crammed in like cattle.

This was a rip-roaring full-blooded battle with no quarter asked and the brave decision Albion's manager Jack Smith to play new boy Kennedy up front paid even greater dividends than even he could have anticipated. Joe, along with Ray Barlow, partnered Dave Walsh.

Twelve minutes gone and Walsh found the net. Cue apoplectic cheers and hundreds of rattles going into overdrive. Just 14 minutes later (count 'em!) and surely I was dreaming as Joe Kennedy demonstrated that in years to come just why he'd become one of the finest headers of a football in the game.

2-0 up and while the looks on the faces of City supporters demonstrated their abject despair, I was already dreaming of taking on the best that Division One could offer. I knew all too well that a 2-0 lead doesn't always guarantee victory and that fear was never far away. Urged on by their desperate supporters, Leicester fought back, buoyed by the managers' decision to swap positions for five of his team. But as goalkeeper Jim Sanders pulled off some fine saves to frustrate Leicester, my sense of anticipation grew minute by minute. When a rare breakaway gave Barlow a chance at the far post which he put away from a narrow angle, that was promotion secured. A 3-0 victory and I was delirious with joy. Rattles had never been so vigorously whirled in joyous celebration.

There were delirious, unforgettable scenes at the final whistle as I, together with hundreds of other Baggie fans, sprinted onto the pitch. The first on the scene lifted all the players shoulder-high in celebration and carried them back to the dressing room. Today, that would be considered a criminal offence but, in those days, it was simply the way things were done.

I desperately wanted to be at Grimsby to see my West Bromwich Albion crowned as Champions but I couldn't afford to travel and all I could do was to sit at home listening to a very disappointing 1-0 defeat. Ah well, the main thing was that promotion had been achieved. Meanwhile, in their third game in four days, Leicester grabbed the point they needed to avoid relegation.

The total attendance for the Football League that season was 41.2 million, in what later became known as "The Golden Age of Football." It was a quite astonishing figure that can never be beaten. The interest is best illustrated by the 30,000 devotees who turned out at Newcastle for a friendly between United's first team and their reserves.

## 1949/50 The First Division at last!

The prospect of seeing the big name teams and players at the Hawthorns generated an unbelievable upsurge in attendances. A fraction under 50,000 jammed into our famous old ground for the visit of Charlton Athletic. Thanks to a solitary goal by Cyril Williams, they all went home happy. Home and away matches against the Brummie Blues maintained the 50,000 average. With both sides winning their home game and further boosted by a draw at Old Trafford, the Baggies had 5 points out of 8 and already bore the solidity of an at least mid-table outfit. This was highly encouraging for new boys in such elevated company. The quality of First Division players felt almost oppressive. Every team seemed to have household names to draw upon.

Arsenal had the bandy legged "Gentleman" Joe Mercer, who was a wonderful wing half (midfielder). They also had a giant central defender by the name of Leslie Compton, brother of the legendary Dennis Compton who himself played football and cricket for England. Leslie holds a record that still stands today, that of being the oldest player to win his first international cap at the age of 38. I was no admirer as he was a rugged (the polite word for dirty) player who took no prisoners and never pulled out of a tackle even if he had no chance of winning the ball. On the South Coast, Portsmouth fielded Jimmy Dickinson, a wing half who rarely really let his country down but who unjustly kept Ray Barlow out of the England team. Football writers throughout the land were united in this view. Only the selectors didn't agree.

In the North, silver haired Wilf Mannion was the star at Middlesbrough as well as being a brilliant inside left for England. Bolton had striker Nat Lofthouse who never shirked a challenge and scored goals for both club and country. Similarly, Liverpool possessed the classy Billy Liddell and Bob Paisley, a player who eventually became the most successful manager in their long, proud trophy-winning history. Lucky Blackpool had the two Stans - Matthews and Mortenson. Both players would attract huge crowds wherever they played. Every football lover wanted to see these true legends in action.

The season progressed in steady, if unspectacular style. In October, there were two huge 'back to back' local derby games, Villa at home and Wolves away. With pride at stake, it finished honours even, 1-1 in both matches. Eddie Wilcox saved the day against the Wanderers and reliable Billy Elliott scored against Villa in front of 53,000 at the Hawthorns. There were 56,000 at Molineux 'enjoying' the action. At the end of the day, all that mattered was that we hadn't lost to avoid any Mickey-taking on the Monday.

Visiting 'new' away grounds became more frequent for me. One was my first visit to Maine Road's Manchester City. Maine Road sat within Moss Side which had a reputation of being a rough, tough and downbeat area. Just one look at the place and I wasn't about to argue. Imagine the opening credits on the original episodes of Coronation Street and you are somewhere close. Bleak, bare back to back terraces. No trees, no colour and still much evidence of bomb damage from the War.

I'd been warned repeatedly that rain was always guaranteed in Manchester so I'd travelled prepared. Ironically, the only rain all day came as we pulled back into New Street Station, reasonably content after a Billy Elliot goal earned a point in a 1-1 draw.

While the Baggies were having some useful home results, away from the Hawthorns, scoring was a problem. There were some very comprehensive home victories such as Stoke (3-1), Burnley (3-0), Everton (4-0), Fulham (4-1), and Portsmouth (3-0). On our travels, it was a vastly different story and there were far too many trips where we left downhearted.

The F.A. Cup paired Albion with Cardiff City and after a 2-2 draw at the Hawthorns; the replay was lost by a single goal so all that was left was reaching a respectable League position. The Baggies scored only 5 times in 9 games, then considered to be a highly paltry number. Albion needed a new goal scorer quickly. In the last match of this depressing sequence, we suffered another agonising 1-0 defeat at Villa Park with the goal coming in the 87th minute.

At that time, many fans cycled to games. You'd pedal to the ground (weaving in and out of traffic to avoid getting a wheel caught in a tram line) find a house owner willing to store bikes in their back yard or garden, exchange your bike for a small fee and collect it at the end of the match.  This sounded simple but I witnessed at first hand a couple of the pitfalls, one of which was immediately after that teeth-grinding defeat.

One Baggies supporter, who was loudly moaning and groaning at the sheer injustice of the result, decided someone else ought to suffer too. He ignored his ticket number, picked up a smart looking bike with an Aston Villa pennant, and before anyone could stop him, peddled away as fast as his legs, crowd, and traffic allowed!

On another occasion, I saw one fan waving his ticket only to be shown the only uncollected bike, which was a just-out-of-the-canal rusting heap.  Even Steptoe would have refused it. His reaction had to be heard to be believed, with language surely far worse than any he'd screamed from the terraces.

Before the next match, another derby at home to the Wolves, a young forward who was to become a legend joined the Baggies from Port Vale - Ronnie Allen. It's well documented that when Allen arrived at the Hawthorns, he was refused admission. No one recognised him but that quickly changed as in the Wolves game in front of 60,000 plus, he earned the Baggies a share of the spoils with a cracking goal. What a prospect. He could play in any forward position because he was a genuine two-footed player.

I "saw" my first ever abandoned game that season. Blackpool, including the dynamic duo of Matthews and Mortenson, were the visitors and were 2-1 ahead after 70 minutes of farce. No one could see the action or the dynamic duo and why it was allowed to continue for so long only the official could answer. Reporters employed a runner to ferry touchline information to them when it appeared the teams were lining up to kick off because a goal had been scored! As the conditions were no worse after 70 minutes, Blackpool had a point with their protests about the abandonment but everyone else was simply relieved. Subsequently, they had even more reason to feel aggrieved because when it was eventually replayed, a Ronnie Allen goal beat them 1-0.

It's grim up North. A modern cliché but one I instinctively link to a visit to Burnley that season. At the time, Burnley was probably no grimmer than anywhere else – everywhere was grim post-war! No recollection of the game (a goalless draw) but what did grab my attention was a goat tied to the front door of a terraced house. I deliberately closed my eyes and then opened them again. No, I was right the first time -a goat tied to a front door, happily chomping away. My imagination ran away with me. Did it normally live in the back yard and the front door allowed him a change of scenery? What did the neighbours think?  Such thoughts were far more entertaining than the match. It's grim up North.

Yet again, we enjoyed another promising end of season run, with 4 wins and 2 draws. Dave Walsh inevitably finished as top scorer with 15 goals with Ronnie Allen netted 5 from his eleven appearances. It augured well for the future.  Albion finished in a creditable 14th position and that was encouraging for a promoted side,

Other points of interest? Liverpool received over 100,000 applications for just 8,000 Cup Final tickets. They decided that the fairest way would be to hold a ballot. Read and digest this carefully - only people living within 25 miles of the city boundaries could apply!  To round off, hooligans threatened the referee at matches at Plymouth and, where else, but Millwall!

## The Early 50's

One of the most fascinating aspects about recalling previous eras is how it also automatically triggers other recollections.  Memories such as patrons  (note 'patrons' not 'customers') queuing at cinemas eager to see black and white British made war films (in the mould of "The Dam Busters" and "The Wooden Horse") or to enjoy the halcyon MGM days of Hollywood musicals such as "Singin' in the Rain" and "An American in Paris". We queued at the Birmingham Hippodrome to pay a shilling (5p) to sit in the balcony to admire the pop stars of the day such as American favourites Frankie Laine, Guy Mitchell, The Four Aces etc, Or British stars such as Dickie Valentine, David Whitfield and Eve Boswell.

Talking of music, how can I forget that as I enjoyed musicals Dad decided that I should take piano lessons? He was an enthusiastic player who enjoyed tinkling the ivories and also composed his own songs. He entered one called 'Penelope Jane' in a BBC song writing competition. He posted another to famous war entertainer George Formby in the hope he'd use it. It wasn't accepted but I've never forgotten the lyrics.  I proved this during an interview on BBC Radio Birmingham to chat about the contents of this book. Presenter Carl Chinn, an Aston Villa supporter and University professor, asked if I could sing it for the delight (or despair) of his wireless –sorry radio listeners.

How could I resist? So after 70 long awaited years, Dad's 'masterpiece' received it's one and only mass audience broadcast.  Eat your heart out Mr Formby! As for the piano lessons, I wasn't overly keen at first but I did manage to pass a standard exam before deciding enough was enough. Looking back, I wish I'd continued. Who knows I could have become a second Russ Conway and gone on to entertain millions – only joking!

This era featured my first of a countless number of visits to London's West End to enjoy the magic of the theatre. There were happy days at Perry Barr watching the world's best Speedway riders take on the `Brummies' with regular crowds of 20,000, making Saturday night a regular meeting place. It would also be the decade (which I certainly wasn't anticipating with any great enthusiasm) of being `called up' to do National Service for King and Country.

There was the first 4-minute mile run by Roger Bannister. This was a breath taking floodlit televised 5,000 metres race at the White City between Chris Chattaway and Russian Vladmir Kuts when Chattaway broke the world record. Then there was the astonishing feat of Czech wonder runner Emil Zatopek who after winning two gold medals in the 1952 Olympics decided at the last minute to run in the Marathon. The result? After asking fellow competitors during the race if he was adopting the right tactics, and whether the pace was OK, he simply left them in his wake to win his third goal medal!

*"Aren't we going a bit slow lads? I've never run 26 miles before?"*

*"No Emil, this is about right mate."*

*"Well I'm desperate for a leak so I'll push on if it's all the same to you lot"*

I couldn't overlook England winning the Ashes at the Oval aided by the immortal Denis Compton. Many, many more memories, too numerous to mention, but over-riding everything are football - related memories. Watching the Throstles lift the FA Cup at Wembley, being privileged to have seen some of the world's greatest players in action and so on.

Being amazed, and dismayed, as Hungary became the first continental team to beat England at Wembley with a staggering 6-3 win. But I'm getting ahead of myself, so let's concentrate for now on the summer of 1950 when England competed in their first ever World Cup. What an eye-opener!

While today the World Cup is by far the world's biggest football occasion that certainly wasn't the case in 1950 with Brazil hosting the first Championship since the War. It was become infamous as the most disorganised and ramshackle tournament in the events history!

Countries who had qualified withdrew. France (who had been knocked out!) were then invited to compete and accepted but, when they were handed a travelling itinerary, which would have seen them criss-crossing the vast sprawl of Brazil, they too pulled out. Portugal, another eliminated country, were offered a place and surprise, surprise, they also declined. Against this background the tournament, consisting of only thirteen countries, got underway with a split into unequal groups. One group consisted of just two countries.

England were in Pool One along with Spain, Chile, and the expected whipping boys -The United States of America. At the time, I knew little or nothing about the strengths or weaknesses of European or South American football. What I had been led to believe from newspapers was that England were certainly one of the best, and most feared, teams in world football.

In their first match, England beat Chile 1-0. This was wholly predictable and could only enhance their reputation as one of the tournament favourites. With big names such as Bert Williams, Alf Ramsay, Billy Wright, Stanley Matthews, Tom Finney, Stan

Mortenson and Wilf Mannion within their ranks, what could possibly go wrong?

What then transpired was the most humiliating result in England's football history. They fielded the same team that had beaten Chile, apart from Matthews, and completely outplayed the United States but still managed to go down to a single goal defeat which, even to this day, ranks as probably the biggest World Cup upset of all time. No one back home could believe the result. In fact, without the benefit of today's telecommunication expertise, some newspapers were convinced it was a typing error from the news agencies and printed it as a 10-1 English win! Along with the players it felt as if the match had been played in a dream state but the result was only too true.

And after England again lost 1-0 in their final game, this time to Spain, they were on the boat home. The myth that our players were the best in the world had been shattered. In best ostrich-head-in-the-sand tradition, England's failure was shrugged off as *one of those things"*. Being a patriotic biased young Albion-loving teenager, I concluded that if there had been a few Albion players in the England team we would have won the trophy without any bother!

Back in Brazil, there was no provision for a Final. The four group winners went on to form a final pool. Fortunately for the organisers, the last match of the tournament did decide the championship, with Brazil, the overwhelming favourites, with 13 goals in just five games, being beaten 2-1 by Uruguay. They had been so confident of winning the trophy that they had a victory song written in advance. Brazil, like England, returned home sadder and wiser.

## 1950/51

Sadly another modest season with a 16$^{th}$ place finish. Scoring was still a problem and only Ronnie Allen with ten, Ray Barlow with eight, and Fred Richardson, a signing from Barnsley, who was as strong as a horse, who notched eight were anything like regular goal scorers. Ronnie was scoring his goals from the flanks; he hadn't yet been converted to a centre forward while four of Ray's goals came when he donned the number nine shirt.  I was hugely frustrated that Dave Walsh was sold to Aston Villa. He'd scored 100 goals in his comparatively short time at the Hawthorns and his transfer to Aston Villa, of all clubs, made no sense.  Releasing popular strikers cheaply at the wrong time has become something of an art form for the Baggies over the decades –Walsh, Kevan, Regis, Bull, Thompson, Phillips etc.  In this era, the only way of relieving our frustrations were to moan at other regulars and as they wanted to moan back at you, it wasn't terribly satisfactory.

One outstanding memory came at Tottenham on a wet and windy day in March. I travelled by train but got separated from my mates and eventually found myself standing with the home fans without any cover. To round off a thoroughly miserable day we lost 5-0. That really was a desperate day. Not for the first time, I wondered why 22 men kicking a leather ball in near tropical conditions, managed to retain such a magnetic attraction!

## 1951/52

This was a dramatic period for me as, along with numerous other 18 year olds, I was called up for two years National Service. This was a legacy from the War, with 18 year olds having to learn military skills in case hostilities were renewed in the future. Like everyone else, I hated the idea and was desperately hoping that my name would be conveniently forgotten. Albion's indifferent start did nothing to help my glum mood. In my final match, before my papers required me to be at her Majesty's Service, the Baggies were hammered 6-1 at Burnley. Despite disliking the idea, very few people dodged National Service. Memories of so much sacrifice just a few years earlier were still too fresh to realistically resist.

I reluctantly travelled to Devizes for 3 months basic training in the Royal Army Pay Corps as part of Intake 81. Now I was a number, specifically 22593444. Private J. T. Wills. The old cliché about never forgetting your army number is completely true. Learning to cope with a new identity was one of the more difficult adjustments I had to make.

There were many other indignities such as my frankly horrible, ill-fitting khaki uniform. These were teamed with ugly black boots that required polishing every day with a tin of 'dubbin' and dusters plus a rifle, which the army insisted, was completely cleaned each day. There was a daily inspection and if your rifle was found to have any dust upon it, you were on a charge. In addition, I was forced to have a haircut by a barber who took no prisoners and knew only one style. *"Long hair, off with it!"*

I had to learn square-bashing, a daily grind of learning to march in perfect synchronisation. Up, down, and across a Parade ground we trooped, normally under the gimlet eye of Lance Corporal Hardaker. He was a thoroughly evil sod, who enjoyed 'bullying' raw fresh- faced recruits from 5.30am till lights out. He was not very tall, had no distinguishing features, and if it hadn't have been for the single stripe on his uniform, he'd have been instantly forgettable. Looking back, I realise it was merely his way of instilling discipline into a very reluctant bunch of conscripts. But, at the time, there was more than one who would have been happy to see him on the wrong end of a rifle range bullet! A 'Little Hitler', you'd better believe it!

Mercifully, after a few weeks, I was granted my first 48-hour weekend pass and it was straight back to the Hawthorns whether to watch a First team, or Central League match. The visitors were Portsmouth and were demolished 5-0. Great to see but I so much resented having the Army effectively choosing which games I could get to. The following week, the Baggies demolished Liverpool 5-2 at Anfield and where was I – back in Devizes.

Maybe I should have counted my blessings. I was given a posting – an 18-month stint in Hong Kong. I'd never even been to Scotland, let alone crossed seas and Oceans. Hong Kong – it's the other end of the earth and no Albion games at all!

Before this epic journey, I had to spend a few weeks at Tilehurst in Reading. No Albion to watch but as a very minor consolation, Reading did have a football team so why not try to get to see a Third Division South game? The fixtures didn't appear to offer any hope. Home games regularly clashed with Army duties but deciding to risk all, I decided to sneak away despite being on guard duty. Normally that wouldn't be a problem as guard duty simply meant being there in an emergency and what could possibly happen in Tilehurst?

It wasn't my lucky day. Returning to camp, to my horror I found a smouldering Guardhouse. Something had triggered a fire and I hadn't been there to take action and warn anyone. What would be my fate for such a dereliction of duty - locked up and shot at dawn? I was placed on a charge and when, with boots polished, and buttons gleaming. I was marched into a room to face the prosecution, I feared the worst. Mercifully, I received a lenient sentence - warned as to my future actions and confined to barracks for two weeks. Lucky, lucky me.

A week of embarkation leave gave me precious little time to bid farewell to family and friends before sailing from Southampton on the troopship Dilwara. The sailing date of February 6th was significant. King George VI died on that day and exactly six years later, a plane crash at Munich Airport shocked the football world and, in my opinion, spawned the birth of the worldwide adulation now lavished on Manchester United.

But, as a perfect send-off, a goal from George Lee was sufficient to beat Middlesbrough at Ayresome Park. And, as the statistical among you will be only too aware, that was the last time we managed to beat the Teesiders on their home turf for more years than I care to remember.

Six weeks later, after a horrendous journey on this elderly multi-refitted lumbering troopship Dilwara with its top speed of 14 knots, we finally disembarked. During that period, we'd travelled slowly through the notorious Bay of Biscay fighting a rolling sea all the way. Life became very unpleasant. Put a plate on the table and it would immediately go crashing to the floor. Most of the reluctant soldiers weren't overly concerned about eating as they were jostling for space in the sick bay. Even though my sailing experience was limited to Cannon Hill Park, I was pleasantly surprised to be largely unaffected by the ships lurching and rolling.

After the notorious "Bay", the sea and the weather relented but the Army didn't. There was no escaping Army discipline, step out of line and you were in trouble. A mate of mine, George Faulder, decided to indulge in a spot of sun bathing. Stripped to the waist, he fell asleep and when he awoke he resemble a boiled lobster. "Sunburnt" was an understatement. The Army's response? Yes, he was given lotion to slap on but was placed on a charge for a self-inflicted injury!

There were some perks including shore leave on the famous Rock of Gibraltar, a visit to Malta and a slow journey through the Suez Canal with soldiers bearing arms. Relations at the time with the Egyptians were very strained and no chances were being taken. There was more leave in blistering sun- drenched Aden when, believe it or not, as we approached the ship to continue our 'cruise', there were women with babies in their arms pleading *"You buy my baby please - I have no money"*. Absolutely astonishing! Yes, I intended to take some souvenirs home but a baby from the Yemen would be somewhat inappropriate!

Then there was a visit to Colombo to be photographed proudly holding pineapples plus a week thrown in at Nee Soon Barracks in Singapore. The very same barracks made famous by "*The Virgin Soldiers*", Leslie Thomas's classic book about National Servicemen. He was in the Pay Corps too!

Despite my callow youth, even I was aware that Singapore was the home of the world famous 'Raffles'

Hotel. I grabbed the first opportunity to ditch uniform for civilian clothes and take a closer look at a hotel aimed at people who most certainly had a far greater income than that of a National serviceman! Yet another first for me in what was becoming an endless stream of new experiences was a ride in a trishaw. This was a carriage fitted to a bicycle complete with a driver and we relaxed as he chauffeured us around the city to look at the sights.

The final leg of our epic voyage saw us finally reach Hong Kong. Despite the abundance of revelations to date, the extraordinary Hong Kong skyline had all us young men pushing and jostling for a better view as we entered the harbour. Even now, that extraordinary vista is impossible to forget.

Our 'home' was Victoria Barracks, situated in the heart of this far flung other world and what a massive culture shock for a teenager who'd never been further afield than Newcastle or Sunderland. All around us, the streets were a constant hubbub with the hustle and bustle of seemingly never-ending crowds. Strolling around, you'd hear the shuffling of 'Mah Jong', a game similar to dominoes but more of a wooden card game, for 24 hours a day. How it's played, I hadn't the faintest idea but the sound forever remains embedded after listening to it for months on end. In addition, there were street vendors, peddling goods of every description and the amazing number of people who lived and worked from sampans and junks moored in the harbour.

And how to deal with the eye-popping sight of women in dresses split to the top of the thigh? Back home, ladies always dressed modestly in drab post-war colours so for many of my fellow draftees, they just stared and stared despite the bromide in their tea.

Another adjustment required was for public transport. Hong Kong trams were both antiquated and crowded. Crowded to an astonishing, often dangerous level but there was no British reserve or queuing here. You literally had to force your way into the tram – pushing, shoving, elbows jabbing and then reverse the process when you arrived at your stop. I was by then an experienced user of the tube in London but that was strictly amateur class compared to Hong Kong.

Chinese food never appealed so whether 'feasting' in the Barracks or in the British Serviceman's Club, it was invariably good old fish and chips that proved the main attraction. But one thing definitely off the menu was rice. Boiled, steamed, or fried it was always there- staring you in the eyes seemingly defying and daring you not to choose it. Enough for a lifetime was, most definitely, enough!

Victoria Barracks was situated just a hundred yards from a restricted area – Wanchai. The area was deemed "off limits" to us servicemen because of the area's reputation for criminal activities and prostitution. For most, the lure was too strong to resist despite the abundant patrolling M.P's (Military Policemen) and the prospect of catching something rather unpleasant from the ladies of the night. Many were caught, many others needed medical treatment and no, I wasn't among them! There were often "interesting" sights when entering or leaving the Star cinema which, although being In Wanchai, wasn't out of bounds.

Over the water was Kowloon, some 50 miles from the border of Mainland China. There was only one way to visit this 'upmarket' location and this was to use the world-renowned 'Star Ferry'. For a few Hong Kong cents, we would grab a seat on the ferry, or stand if full, to drink in the colony's impressive 1950's skyline. When I look at modern pictures of Hong Kong, what I was then admiring now look like ugly blocks of council flats. But I was young then and the world was a different place.

A lady member of Toc H spoke to us looking for volunteers to help with their projects. Dating back to World War One, Toc H is a charity that helps needy people. Despite the old saying in the Army of *"never volunteer for anything"*, I was one of a dozen soldiers who did exactly that. Our little group used the ferry to Kowloon before being transported via antiquated private transport to a homeless children's shelter very close to the Chinese border. We did whatever we could to improve their living conditions by repairing broken fences, painting discoloured walls and generally tidying up but what impressed the children most of all were the sweets or chocolates we'd bought with us. We mingled with the kids, picked them up, had photographs taken and I often wonder just what happened to them after we left?

Albion's progress could only be followed via press reports and the frustratingly intermittent reception of a communal radio housed high in the rafters of our barrack room. Over the festive period, Albion played their customary three games in four days. They lost 3-2 away at Bolton on Christmas Day but reversed the score at the Hawthorns on Boxing Day, courtesy of a hat trick by Ronnie Allen. That put me in a very good mood.

So much so that when my mates asked me to join them at a local dance hall, despite not being able to dance a single step of a waltz or quickstep, I immediately agreed. If you wanted a dance in Hong Kong, which I didn't, the procedure was to pay the local girls for allowing you the privilege.

Being a strictly non-dancer saw me sitting alone for most of the time. To show willing, I found myself ordering a selection of local drinks. I hadn't the faintest idea what was in them but what I do know is that apart from downing far too many, I apparently handed over a few dollars to a lovely girl to teach me the dances as they came along. Can't remember how good, or more probably bad, my first dancing steps were but the hazy memory of that one off night' still sits in the back of my mind.

How did I get back to the barracks? I hadn't the faintest idea but when I awoke next morning, I was told I'd shared a taxi with those who'd managed to stay clear headed. And. believe it or not, that was my one and only experience of being 'drunk'.

I did everything I could to stay in touch with events at the Hawthorns. I had the Saturday night Sports papers, the Argus and the Blue Mail plus the Albion News posted to me, while I spent a small fortune writing off for every away programme.

During Easter, there were another three games in four days. Derby were defeated 1-0 but of greater interest was a double over a certain Wolverhampton Wanderers. At the Hawthorns, goals from Frank Griffin and Johnny Nicholls clinched a 2-1 win, which, while in itself was cause for celebration, was bettered next day at Molineux as Ronnie Allen hit a hat-trick and Johnny Nicholls joined in the fun with a goal to seal a 4-1 win. What could be better than that? Being there to see it! I was constantly irked that some unknown supporter had taken `my' regular space on the Smethwick End terraces. Lucky Sod! Ronnie Allen's 32 goals, aided by Johnny Nicholls five from his first twelve appearances, left the Baggies 13th in the league with the promise of better things to come.

Although there were supporters of many other teams in the Platoon, none were as football barmy as me. They were all envious when I received so much post from home. We received letters from home twice weekly and mine was normally much bulkier than my mates, due to the mass of press cuttings sent by my mom. She realised just how important they were to me.

Receiving letters was exciting in itself. You'd congregate in the Barrack Room at a fixed time. An Officer, accompanied by an NCO, would handle the correspondence. One by one, he'd call out the name and number of the lucky recipients before handing over the letters. Each man in turn would stretch out luxuriously on his bed to devour the news from home.

Fortunately there was plenty of football to see in this far-flung colony and, although all branches of the services entered their own teams in the local league, I rarely went to see them unless they were playing my adopted team, South China. They were the outstanding team in the colony and I suppose they could be likened to Manchester United. Subsequently, I sadly became a `glory hunter' – following them whenever service duties permitted. And although the standard had to be open to debate, they did possess some quality players who could be great entertainers when the mood took them.

South China's great rivals were more simply named Eastern, and whenever the teams met, the rivalry could, on a smaller scale, be compared to that of Albion v Villa. The most noticeable difference being there wasn't a rosette, rattle, or flat cap in sight! In their place were army berets, caps worn by the 'Top Brass' and thousands of Cantonese sporting large coolie hats to protect heads from the sun.

After capturing the league title, South China faced Eastern in the Cup Final. Okay, it wasn't Wembley but it was a packed house in hot sunshine. South China had 90 per cent of the play, it was one-way traffic and they were in total control but it proved the point, for me at least, if you can't put the ball in the net you're more than likely to be on the end of a sucker punch. Or in this case two punches –the final score was South China 1 Eastern 2. Ouch!

It's strange, with the vast number of Chinese now playing the world's most popular game, that very few have made their mark in English football although the number is slowly rising.  It's open to debate of course but when nostalgically recalling the performances of South China's outside left, who had the "magical" name of Mok-Chuen Wai, I often wonder how he would have fared in the English game. He possessed all the requisite skills. Fast, tricky, an accurate distributor and the ability to have the crowd rising to their feet whenever the ball went anywhere near him.

Lapsing into Walter Mitty mode, I'd compare him to a 1950's Willie Johnston and visualise the Brummie Road singing; *"Mok-Chuen.'Mok-Chuen Wai."Mok-Chuen Wai, on the wing!"* The words don't fit the tune I know. Could he have transferred his South China skills displayed on a sun drenched Hong Kong, to a miserable winter's day at the Hawthorns? Probably not, but I'd have liked to have seen him given the chance.

## 1952/53

This was a great season for Baggies fans and how I regretted missing the opportunity to see the moulding of the club's most successful team ever. The "Argus" told me that manager Jack Smith had resigned and his place taken by Jessie Carver. He'd been a centre half with Newcastle United and Blackburn Rovers, building a reputation on the continent via a number of clubs. At the time, he was coach at Juventus but he decided to leave Italy and return to England to take over at the Hawthorns. What was intriguing about his appointment was the introduction of what, at the time, were revolutionary training methods

Out went the traditional lapping of the pitch to keep players fit. Instead, they were actually training with footballs, working on individual skills and learning the art of creating attacks, from the full backs forward. Techniques now taken for granted but then considered revolutionary. Results certainly indicated the success of these changes. Seven of the first nine games were won starting with a 4-1 victory at Tottenham and a 1-0 win at home over Newcastle.

Strangely, Carver only stayed at the Hawthorns for six months before deciding to move back to Italy, but his philosophy on how he felt football should be played was carried on by his successor Vic Buckingham. Buckingham had been a member of the wonderful Spurs team under the stewardship of Arthur Rowe.

The nucleus of the team that were to bring honours to the club was beginning to take shape. Right back Stan Rickaby stepped in to replace the injured Jim Pemberton and played so well he went on to gain an England cap against Northern Ireland

Left back was the dependable Len Millard. Len was a quietly spoken Black County man. Ever reliable, I considered he was also worth an England call up. Behind them was the reliable goalkeeper Norman Heath.

Jack Vernon had left the club to return home to Ireland and this led to the eventual formation of what, by popular opinion, was the finest half back line in the club's illustrious history - Jimmy Dudley, Joe Kennedy and Ray Barlow. Initially, it was Jimmy Dugdale taking over from Vernon but circumstances decreed he was to be another ex-Baggie who would serve rivals Aston Villa so successfully after joining them.

According to my numerous reports, Kennedy and Barlow stood out in virtually every match. They had the look of sheer class in everything they did but Jim Dudley was also an outstanding player who did just as much for the team in a more refined role. His style was to get on with the game with the minimum of fuss and while a Scotland under 21 International caps came his way, I still wonder just why the Scottish selectors had ignored him for the highest honour?

The forward line, and in the 1950's it was just that, five forwards, consisted of Frank Griffin, Paddy Ryan, Ronnie Allen, Johnny Nicholls and George Lee. They were evolving into a potentially lethal unit and helped the Throstles reach a creditable fourth in the division, their highest placing since gaining promotion. Sadly, I could only look on from 8,000 miles away, cursing at my misfortune.

In the steaming sun, I read and re-read details of several memorable, not to mention bizarre, results. In a crazy match at Hillsborough on Boxing Day, Albion won 5-4 with the aid of two own goals but a day later capitulated 1-0 at the Hawthorns. In the FA Cup, there were even more 'fun and games'- After beating West Ham 4-1 away in the third round and feeling confident of making further progress, Chelsea came to the Hawthorns and ground out a 1-1 draw. Amazingly, it took three replays at Stamford Bridge, Villa Park and Highbury before Chelsea ended the saga with a comfortable 4-0 win- damn them, they must have been lucky!

The Final that year was described as "The Matthews Final" as Blackpool beat Bolton 4-3 with the great Stanley Matthews winning the one honour he wanted above any other. He did star but was it the Matthews Final seeing as his teammate, Stan Mortensen, did his fair share by scoring a match winning hat trick? Alongside other football 'lovers', some more 'loving' than others, I listened to a crackling match commentary on the antiquated barrack room wireless set with just one thought. I would have gone berserk if Albion had been at Wembley and I hadn't been there. Little did I realise that this dream lay in store just one year later.

That was a minor moan as I realised the time spent in Hong Kong was, despite my negative initial feeling, a tremendous experience. I represented the Corps at football and cricket and even had a crack at hockey and tennis. I also learned how to play table tennis, (never 'Ping Pong'), courtesy of Leung, a local lad who worked in the NAAFI. He was a tremendous player and, under his tuition, I became reasonably proficient although I certainly couldn't replicate his ability to play in the renowned Asian style- holding a bat with the 'penholder ' grip. But for all that I still couldn't wait for my duty to end and to get back home to England, the Albion, and those familiar flat caps.

## 1953/4 Hong Kong to Wembley!

As the days passed, I realised that it wouldn't be long before my newfound friends would shortly become old acquaintances. Among them was Walter ('Wally') Watt, the canny Scotsman who had the misfortune to support Falkirk! 'Taffy Thomas' not particularly interested in football, but how he loved his rugby. George Faulder, a Fulham fan, who in Civvy Street worked as an assistant in a posh London upmarket clothing store, plus many others. Together we enjoyed days out at 'Tigerbalm Gardens' where giant animal statues lay in the shadow of a Giant Pagoda. We travelled to both Repulse Bay and Silvermine Bay to relax and bask in glorious sunshine following cooling swims in a calm sea. Not much of that back in West Bromwich or Birmingham!

Then there was the Corps annual sports day and being a member of a winning team. Nothing so grand as an athletic sprint triumph but how many other Albion fans have won a gold medal in a platoon tug of war team in Hong Kong?

Finally the big day arrived. We packed our kit bags with souvenirs and bade farewell to those left behind including Leung *and 'Sew Sew'*. Who was *'Sew Sew*? Very few of us wanted to darn holes in those horrible grey thick army socks and our saviour was *'Sew Sew'*, a Chinese lady, who sat cross-legged outside adjoining Barrack Rooms offering to do the necessary for a few cents. She must have made a fair income as she always seemed to be sewing or darning.

Lorries took us back to the docks where we boarded the 'Empire Trooper'. Surprisingly, as we stood on deck taking a last look from 'The Fragrant Harbour', I actually felt sad. The startling views, the sun, the frantic pace of life in Hong Kong – I'd more than tolerated them, to use modern idiom I'd actually "embraced them."

Apart from my sadness, I also had a worry. The Army had a strict limit on the amount of luggage we could take home in the official kit bag. Thus all my expensively assembled Albion programmes had to be separately parcelled up into a (hopefully) secure suitcase and passed to an independent shipping company for transit back to the UK. The inevitable happened. Somewhere between the Far East and Southampton they disappeared. The case never reached the UK and the memorabilia painstakingly collected was lost forever. I still wonder what happened to them.

As we cruised in this 30-year-old ship oh so slowly back to the UK with games coming and going, I was always fretting to hear the football results on the ship's tannoy system. Albion had started the season in fine style, which only increased my impatience. Desperate to hear them as soon as possible, I struck up a friendship with a lad who worked in the ops room who promised, unofficially, to pass them on as soon as they were received and before broadcasting them to all and sundry.

He was a Geordie, which naturally meant he followed the Toon Army. How very apt as in mid-September the Baggies were at St James Park.

*"Well, how did we get on yesterday?"* I asked.

*"You won 7-3"* came the spluttered response.

This result remains one of Albion's finest ever performances. With a hat trick from Nicholls, two from Allen, and a goal apiece from Griffin and Ryan, it resulted in the whole team being applauded off the pitch by 58,000 Geordies. Were the Baggies really that good? I was soon to find out.

Entertainment was provided most nights courtesy of screening various black and white films. In the absence of anything else more entertaining, hundreds of national servicemen squatted shoulder-to- shoulder on a very crowded deck to watch. One film gave me a blinding inspiration (Ok an idea) to leave a unique message to mark what was likely to be my one and only sojourn to the Far East. So the next day I penned a message, put into a bottle and tossed it overboard! What was the message? *"If found, please contact Terry Wills travelling from Hong Kong to the Hawthorns"* I added my address to confirm finding. Predictably, nobody did find the bottle, which probably ended up in the same place as my Albion programmes.

The Empire Trooper eventually docked at Southampton. We travelled to Aldershot for a couple of days and then mercifully were officially demobbed. In what was probably an idle threat just to calm us down, there were dire warnings that any breach of regulations would delay our de-mobilisation. We former soldiers exchanged typical "stiff upper lip" cheerio's as we would now go our separate ways never to meet again. Only a select few had a telephone at home and although we promised to write to each other, the promises were rarely kept.

I had a joyful reunion with my parents and younger sisters Pat and Christine. There were awkward introductions to my new sister Yvonne who I'd never previously met as she'd been born while I was overseas. Fortunately, she was young enough to quickly adapt to this tall, sunburnt adult being her big brother.

My life had changed dramatically and it was a strange feeling. Army life does instil a sense of discipline and the need to obey orders however ludicrous. But no more. No more looking at Part 2 Orders. No more square bashing. Never again having to queue up, with buttons polished, to receive a wage packet and having to salute the Officer who handed it to you. No more uniforms, or spit and polish, no having to quote your Army Number (22593444, you never forget it!). No more coolie hats. No berets.

But what I did have was the freedom to return to the Hawthorns. And so I did on October 3rd 1953. The once mundane was now so exciting. Rarely had I taken so much pleasure from a no. 36 tram into the city and then a '79' bus to the Hawthorns. Even Hockley and Handsworth looked attractive. I even used proper money – shillings and pence.

I was back on the Smethwick End in "my" place. Precious few of the regulars remained from two years ago but I made the most of every face I recognised, chatting at length about the team and players I'd missed so much. With strangely apt symmetry, Middlesbrough was in town, who'd also been in opposition in my last game before being called up. I realised I'd missed the accents too - Black Country English or Brummie English. Deeper tones leavened with a variety of industrial language that was second nature to National Servicemen. I could never quite get used to the chattering, high pitched, squealing excitement from Chinese fans.

I'd hoped for a victory on my return and I got one. 2-1 was a narrow-sounding win but Albion's newfound passing style was a wonder to behold. I immediately determined I was going to maximise my new-found freedom by travelling to see every game home and away that I could afford to attend.

Even though the season was only two months old, it was clear that either the Albion or their disliked local rivals Wolverhampton would become League

Champions. The rest of the First Division was already trailing unhappily in their wake. A contrast in the playing styles of the leading pair made for endless discussions in pubs, shops and barbers, usually prompted by the latest views from journalists.

The diverse playing styles made a fascinating contrast with pundits, professional and amateur, arguing long and loud over the merits of each team's chances of winning the title. It was West Bromwich Albion, now under Vic Buckingham, who were predictably the purists. There was no better example of their art than on Christmas Day. The red and white Scousers were in town but were sent packing 5-2. Liverpool had lost every away game that term so another heavy defeat wasn't a shock but even so their whole side were bamboozled by one Albion goal which featured 25 passes.

Next day, and for the first time, I stood on the famous Kop at Anfield for the return match. A 0-0 draw against the bottom side didn't sound impressive but in contrast to their shocking away form, the then red and white Liverpool side (an all red kit was not adopted for another decade) were decent in front of their own. Only twice had the enormous Kop terrace seen their side beaten. Liverpool were regular scorers, indeed the Baggies were the only side to stop them scoring in 19 matches, home or away.

At this time, the Kop was famed for its size rather for its vocals and tacit intimidation of the opposition. This was the original huge covered terrace, which in these less safety-conscious days, had room for 30,000 people. That's more people on one terrace than some clubs could fit into their entire ground. In 1953, the Kop seemed filled with noisy, passionate and enthusiastic supporters. Chatting to one who had seen his beloved team hammered at the Hawthorns, he was convinced that Albion would be the League Champions.

In sharp contrast to the Baggies' easy-on-the-eye style, Wolves were the 1950's answer to a Tony Pulis Stoke team except they were better at it. The Molineux men played long ball and often simply out-muscled their opposition. Wolves had many quality players such as Billy Wright, the Captain of England, Bill Slater, Ron Flowers, Peter Broadbent, Roy Swinborne and the extraordinary Bert "The Cat "Williams in goal. All of them, together with goal-scoring quick wingers Johnny Hancock and Jimmy Mullen were household names. But they played to orders, heaving the ball forward at great speed.

With no other club able to live with the Midlands pair, the games between the League's top two were eagerly awaited. The first match was at Molineux and 56,000 crammed in for the 'battle of the giants', including the England selectors. The Baggies held a two-point lead and had ambitions of doubling their advantage. What an atmosphere. What a game. No segregation of the fans. We stood together, shoulder to shoulder, hurling encouragement and abuse in turn at the respective teams. My agonising recollection was of a second-half header from Ronnie Allen beating the keeper, hitting the inside of the post and rebounding straight into his hands. Biased I may have been but it was the home fans screaming for the final whistle to end their agony. At the end of a pulsating battle, a solitary fortunate goal from Jimmy Mullen turned out to be the winner.

At least one journalist agreed with my assessment of Mullen's winner. Dick Knight in the Birmingham Gazette wrote, "*Was it a fluke? It could have been. But whether it was or not, it was a goal that deserved to win such a vital game. And in fact I thought Albion deserved to take at least a point back with them."*

Ivan Sharpe of the Sunday Chronicle also offered some succour to disappointed Albionites. "*The last hour of the contest left the impression that Albion were worthy leaders and the better equipped team. Well, who were the stars? Barlow and Kennedy in the Albion half back line who, if ever they get into the England team, will probably remain there".*

All very flattering- but at the end of the day it meant first blood to the Wanderers. It was a set-back but no more. Ronnie Allen was in top form and just a week after the Wolves defeat he cracked home another four in a 6-1 blitzing of Cardiff City. Confidence restored all round!

Later, an excellent opportunity presented itself to get one over a member of the old gold contingent. Albion had a top-of-the-table match at Huddersfield and, as was customary during the era, all Football Specials to Northern grounds, always stopped at Wolverhampton High Level station to pick up any stray Baggies fans unfortunate enough to live in the town.

Anyway, when we boarded the train at New Street station, one of the passengers was a Wolves supporter. He was making a very early start for their home game and although only 10 o'clock, he was well on the way to oblivion thanks to an excess of alcohol. Buoyed by Dutch courage, he slurred to all and sundry that we had no chance against the Town, and Wolves were a much better team anyhow

Just the usual banter, but by the time we reached Coseley, he was dead to the world. Like the 'gentlemen' we were, we decided that it would be a shame to interrupt his slumber so soon. Wolverhampton High Level came and went and so did many other stations.  It was only when we were approaching Huddersfield that our reluctant companion awoke.  In the spirit of true kinship, we invited him to join us at Leeds Road. Curiously, that idea didn't appeal. He became somewhat agitated and roundly abused us simply because we hadn't woken him at Wolverhampton. Oh dear, no sense of humour. He might have got back to Wolverhampton for kick-off if Inter-City Concorde travel had been around at the time but as it wasn't, God knows what he did for the rest of the day. We didn't see him on the return journey. I was happy enough as we won 4-0, thanks to Allen and Nicholls.

The New Year brought with it the FA Cup with suggestions that Albion wanted to win both League and Cup in the same season.  Impossible surely – no club had won the double that century.  Albion were drawn at home – in fact, they were to be drawn at home at every possible opportunity. The Gods were smiling on them surely and given the Baggies' continuing good form, maybe the impossible could become possible.

Chelsea and Rotherham were easily seen off in the first two rounds. In the last 16, Albion had the rather larger barrier of renowned cup specialists, Newcastle. The interest in the match was intense, with many supporters travelling from the Northeast to see their side continue their march on Wembley.  Over 61,000 people ultimately crammed in. Normally the Hawthorns had no restrictions on movement. You paid your money and stood wherever the fancy took you.  After the teams had changed ends, either before the kick-off or at half time, many fans would change with them.  Smethwick Enders would make their way round to the Brummie Road or vice versa. My regular spot was in the Smethwick End but I was always anxious to stand behind the goal Albion was attacking. There was no chance of doing that for the big Cup match such was the crowd density. Most supporters were inside the ground more than an hour before kick-off. If you were fortunate enough to have a clear uninterrupted view of proceedings, you hung on grimly to that spot.

Despite the crowd density, one of the great rituals of the era continued as usual. Pancho was unique, very popular and frankly an eccentric Baggies fan. Before every home game he would enter the pitch from the Birmingham Road End, wave to the crowd and then walk on his hands the full length of the pitch. That in itself was difficult but he achieved this wearing a Mexican Sombrero hat! We became firm friends, frequently photographed by the press before setting off on a 'Puffing Billy' steam train to grounds up and down the country. Another familiar face was the official Albion mascot "Little" Johnny Tromans, who remained "*Little*" even when he was a teenager. He regularly collected for Dr Barnados, including the coin used to decide choice of ends. These were simpler times when the football club had yet to cotton to the thought that a club mascot could be a chargeable activity.

Little Johnny and 'Pancho' in their respective ways were part of Albion culture during the era. There is a large photograph of them both on display within the East Stand. Happy days indeed.

Newcastle had won the Cup in both 1951 and 1952 and fought determinedly. Another brilliant Ronnie Allen hat trick was just enough to put the Geordies out, including what Ronnie subsequently described as his best ever goal. His stunning volley into the roof of the Smethwick End net was a masterpiece of timing and power.

After such a pulsating game, the Quarter Final seemed almost mundane. Spurs came and were easily conquered 3-0 thanks to *"On the Spot"* Nicholls (2) and *"Legs"* Barlow.  That was it! Just one step away from Wembley and all that stood in our path was the team that gave us Ronnie Allen - Port Vale.

Not that it would be easy although they were a Third Division North side. Their "Iron Curtain" defence was formidable – only 7 conceded in the previous 19 games, quite extraordinary in the goal-fest 1950's. They were Champions-elect and come seasons end, won their Division by eleven points, remained unbeaten at home, lost only three games away and conceded a mere twenty-one goals in 46 matches. Even more significantly, Vale had knocked out the cup-holders Blackpool, Matthews and all, in Round 5. All highly impressive, but I was confident that they wouldn't be good enough to stop Albion clinching their first Cup Final spot in 19 years. Going to Wembley was my dream, my almost nightly dream. Please don't wake me up.

This pairing of 'David and Goliath' had captured the public's imagination and it was obvious that tickets for the Villa Park semi-final would be at a premium. As usual, they were issued on a first come, first served basis to non- season ticket holders. They were to go on sale on a Sunday morning and I immediately made plans to avoid the remotest possibility that I could miss out. I wasn't a season ticket holder myself due to lack of funds and National Service dictating that I'd miss the first two months of the season.

The day before, Albion played Blackpool at the Hawthorns and after goals from Ronnie Allen and 'Paddy' Ryan had sent them packing in a 2-1 defeat, I simply dashed out of the ground to claim first place in the queue at the Smethwick End turnstiles.  People thought I was mad, one in particular, with a sympathetic glance, merely saying *"you're barmy"* as he made his way home.

Sleeping was virtually impossible. I had nothing with me so I only had the cold pavement to lie on. Some fellow supporters had had the foresight to arrange for family members to bring pillows and blankets to ease their discomfort. Mercifully it wasn't raining but it was cold.  Thankfully, some kind souls delivered sandwiches, flasks of tea and best of all, braziers. Once stuffed with wood and coal, their warmth was a magnet to the patient queue. Predictably, the local press turned up asking *"why?"* Everyone indulged them, the distraction was welcome but all were privately thinking, *"If you were a passionate football supporter, you wouldn't need to ask why."*

This was to be a long night. Queuing was second nature in austere post-war Britain but even so, overnighters were far from common.  As was normal in the 1950's, we talked to each other at great length. Everyone was agreed though that a small club from the Potteries was not going to stop the mighty Albion getting to Wembley.  Didn't the League table prove we are the best club in the country?  Also we regularly burst into song to maintain spirits and keep fatigue at bay.

There was a price to pay for drinking large amounts of tea during a cold night.  I was a stubborn model of abstinence but many others weren't slow in coming forward. Let's just say that the front gardens of houses in Halfords Lane received enough 'manure' and 'water' to ensure seeds or flowers would wonder what had hit them!   What with the nocturnal garden visitors and a long line of noisy supporters standing outside their house all night, the patience of the residents must have been severely tested.

A great tradition of any British queue is a need to know just how people are in that line. Making sure that those around me acknowledged I was first in line, I took a stroll down Halfords Lane. The dim outlines of weary supporters, two or three deep, continued for hundreds of yards, past what is now the Hawthorns rail station and beyond. There were simply thousands in that queue. For me, I was reassured that my time investment was a wise one. I knew that I'd get a ticket when the office eventually opened but would those at the back?

As that time grew closer, fatigue led to many impatient cries of "*Come on, come on, open up.*" Finally the golden moment and cheers, especially from me, my patience had paid off and I collected the prized possession. Time for bed but I couldn't resist eagerly bearing the ticket aloft to show those patiently waiting at the back of the queue what it looked like!

Then the supreme irony, as who did I see but the character that 17 hours earlier had told me *"I'm barmy".* I didn't bear him any malice but I did wonder whether he missed out on a ticket and if so whether he'd changed his opinion.

Cup fever also hit the Potteries. Vale made their tickets available before and during a reserve match with Mossley and, as a result, recorded a freak 30,000 attendance for the "stiffs". All 25,000 tickets were sold that night with thousands more disappointed.

A week later, following reams of press speculation as to the result, that time was nigh. Nervously, I caught cross city buses to Villa Park praying that we wouldn't be let down and dumped out of the cup by a Third Division team. The moment of truth had arrived.

Over 68,000 people crammed into Villa Park. Most people stood on one of the enormous open terraces at either end of the ground. Surprisingly, Albion fans had been allocated the Witton End and not the larger Holte End terraces. Seating was limited to the narrow Witton Lane stand and its magnificent Leitch-designed counterpart on the opposite touchline. Both stands were adorned with huge "Mitchells and Butler" adverts.

Perhaps Albion were over-confident, possibly Vale were better than expected, but whatever the reasons it was far from being a vintage performance. Vale took the lead just before half time and I was becoming distinctly uneasy. So too were the Albion side who weren't getting anywhere against the "Iron Curtain." Vale's wingers were under orders to defend whenever they didn't have the ball, an unorthodox tactic for the time, but it was effective.

Finally the Baggies had a stroke of luck. Jimmy Dudley floated what appeared to be a harmless cross into the box. A deflection off the back of a defenders head made a routine catch suddenly impossible to reach. There was the ball resting in the back of the net in front of delirious Baggies fans.

With the scores tied, Albion at last began to get on top without really displaying any real conviction. But then it happened. A defender fouled George Lee and the referee awarded a spot kick despite protests from Vale that the foul was two yards outside the penalty box.

What a responsibility for Ronnie Allen, a penalty against his old team, a spot kick that could take the team to Wembley, and a penalty that had me, and every Baggie fan, praying his nerve would hold out. It could and it did. The ball was in the net, players and supporters hugged each other in joyous celebration.

Ronnie had done it - we had done it. Wembley beckoned but there were still several anxious moments to endure. Vale thought they'd equalised right at the death but their effort was disallowed. Whew! We were in the Cup Final.

But before that, there was the little matter of the Wolves and the race for the First Division Championship. It's an old adage that once a team has booked a place at Wembley, their league form suffers. Albion couldn't permit any slips without handing the title to their rivals.

A few days later, WBA made the long journey to tackle Sunderland at Roker Park where they lost painfully 2-1. No one felt the pain more than goalkeeper Norman Heath who, when rushing from goal to foil Ted Purdon, was involved in a nasty collision. The popular 'keeper was carried off, never to play again, while the ten men toiled in vain to retrieve the game.

Albion still had a two-point lead but the next game was the 'big one' - the vital return match at the Hawthorns against the Wolves. Both teams were weakened by the absence of key players. In those days, if there was an international fixture, clubs couldn't postpone the match, they simply had to bring in whoever was available. Albion missed Ronnie Allen and Johnny Nicholls while Wolves were without Billy Wright and Ron Flowers, all lining up for England against Scotland. In theory, the absences balanced out, but in reality the Baggies were short of experienced cover for their big stars. Midfielder Ray Barlow reluctantly stood in for Allen.

It was a bad tempered affair, not helped by a crunching tackle on Barlow by Bill Shorthouse that virtually left him a passenger and the Baggies down to ten men. With the main strikers missing and one of the reluctant deputies just a passenger, it was hard to imagine Albion scoring but they could at least shut the opposition out. A bitter struggle was inevitable and sadly for the majority of the nearly 50,000 supporters, Wolves again won by a single goal. Would Albion have won all things being equal? No one, of course, will ever know, but I feel sure that if Allen and Nicholls had played there would have been a vastly different score.

The result was hugely deflating for both supporters and players alike. With just five games remaining, all the momentum was with Wolverhampton. The whole world seemed to be against the Albion team as Ray Barlow explained." *we lost a silly goal to Wolves and ended up losing 1-0 and the League pretty much went with it, because the confidence went out of the side. We knew we could have finished Wolves off and we didn't do it."*

Incidentally, the England versus Scotland fixture, which weakened both teams, was won by England 4-2 and among the scorers were Ronnie Allen and Johnny Nicholls. Great for England but I would have much preferred to have seen them knocking the ball into the back of the Wolves net.

Meanwhile, Cup Final fever was reaching epic proportions with every fan fervently hoping, no, praying they'd be able to lay their hands on the most wanted ticket in the game. A Wembley Cup Final... Albion's allocation of 12,000 tickets, primarily for the terraces with the equivalent face value of 17p, was pathetically small. The Baggies supporters could have filled Wembley by themselves. Over 70,000 supporters swamped the club with their postal orders. It was simply a lottery and I was among the majority who received the shattering reply *"We are sorry that your application has been unsuccessful."*

They were nowhere near as sorry as me. I was absolutely devastated. After following the team all over the country, it seemed that this counted for nothing and I would miss out on achieving a lifetime's ambition. Feeling sorry for myself, I (along with many others) wrote a letter to the Birmingham Evening Mail pouring out my woes. Incredibly my plea generated a wonderful response from George Smith from Gloucester.

George was an Albion fan, had two tickets, and was willing to let me have one if I met him outside Wembley Stadium. Sheer unrestrained relief, I could look forward to the Final, with all its attendant glamour. Yet even then after such marvellous fortune, I wanted more. I still believed winning the double was possible.

Sadly, team fortunes worsened and a series of defeats, plus more injuries, had everyone fearing that the Baggies might end up with nothing. Disappointingly, we won only one of the last seven League games, an Allen penalty seeing off Manchester City, and the last two matches were depressing beyond belief.

The Easter programme saw Albion facing Villa in successive days. After a 1-1 draw at the Hawthorns, we travelled to Villa Park or, if you prefer, *"the Last Chance Saloon."* A win gave us a slight chance, but anything that could go wrong that afternoon did go wrong. More players were injured and we were thrashed 6-1. A final day 3-0 defeat at Fratton Park meant we'd finished runners up to Wolverhampton Wanderers, four points adrift. Those two defeats to the Molineux men were the difference.

Now we had Wembley on our minds but with none of the swagger that the team and supporters had possessed just a few weeks earlier. Apart from losing first choice 'keeper Norman Heath, Stan Rickaby had been ruled out permanently. There was some surprise when out-of-form midfielder Joe Kennedy was slotted in at right back as his replacement. Proud Preston felt more and more formidable the nearer the big day became. After all, Preston had Tom Finney.

Finney for years had been adjudged the equal of Stanley Matthews and, like Matthews, was also regarded as a national treasure. Twelve months previously, the football world had enjoyed the so-called 'Matthews Final' as Blackpool beat Bolton 4-3. Neutral supporters craved a repeat performance and it's fair to say that, with this depth of feeling and because of Albion's sad loss of form, Preston were the clear favourites.

For a whole generation of Albion supporters, the 1954 Cup Final was their first ever visit to the twin towers. To help them get there, British Rail laid on 10 Football Special "Day Excursions to London". Four of them ran from Wolverhampton while another picked up in Witton and Aston – perhaps as a gentle reminder to the neighbours. A Day Excursion meant exactly that – most of the Specials didn't leave Euston until 1.00am or 2.00am. .

In a mood of anticipation and nervousness, we were on the first Special out of New Street for the equivalent of £1.20 (third class, of course). My feelings of excitement remained tempered, as I was currently ticketless. My overwhelming concern all week had been that my benefactor wouldn't be there with 'my' ticket and I'd be marooned outside Wembley.

We arrived at Euston, caught the tube to Wembley Park and then, almost dreamlike I was walking up Wembley Way. This really was wonderful. I'd travelled a fair distance around the world.

Experienced, at first hand, differing customs and cultures, seen strange and unusual buildings but all of these memories faded into the distance as I made that magical walk along Wembley Way for the first time.

There was so much hustle and bustle; numerous souvenir stalls were selling outsize rosettes and souvenirs. Everyone looked excited. We were there at the Mecca of football and most important of all, to see OUR team, West Bromwich Albion, attempting to win the most prized trophy in football.

Nervously, I made my way to a rendezvous with Mr Smith. My fears of not getting on my hands on a ticket were simply too awful to voice. Mercifully, he kept his promise and after a short conversation, in which I repeated my thanks ad nauseam, he handed over the prized ticket for entrance 23, Turnstile A. I still have the stub today.

Now nursing a new concern that the generous Mr Smith might change his mind, I scuttled towards Turnstile A to gain quick entrance. There I was! I picked my spot on the terracing high above the Players Tunnel entrance. Heavens, this ground was big!

The pre match community singing was far from synchronised but for the traditional "Abide With Me" everyone joined in, whether they could sing in tune or not. Somehow, that didn't matter.

The comparison between the Hawthorns, Villa Park or indeed any other ground, seemed even more pronounced when, at long last, the teams emerged from their from the dressing rooms onto the pitch. From my position, they resembled tiny toy soldiers.

It was first blood to Albion courtesy of an Allen goal. Preston equalised and at the interval, the teams were equally matched. North End's superstar Tom Finney had been generally well held by Len Millard.

Then disaster as Preston's Charlie Wayman was allowed to score a goal that was beyond dispute. It was simply 'miles' offside. Protests were of no avail and no amount of curses from supporters would change the referee's decision. Apparently, I swore in Chinese, an instinctive throwback to my Hong Kong experiences. Clearly, National Service had taught me something.

Then it was the Preston fans' turn to feel aggrieved. Tommy Docherty baulked Ray Barlow as he charged into the box and the decision to award a spot kick wasn't universally popular. It looked like a classic *"I've made a mistake that I need to even things up"* decision.

So another pressure spot kick for Ronnie Allen. Although it wasn't one of his best, he levelled the scores and it was all to play for. Among those who couldn't bear to watch was Baggie keeper Jim Sanders. The photograph of him turning his back on Allen's penalty became an iconic image.

Nerve endings were jangling both on and off the pitch. Every player was fearful of making a fatal error and this showed with the tentative play. With little time remaining, the next goal would most likely be decisive. And it was.

Three minutes to go and Joe Kennedy slid the ball forward to Frank Griffin. Cutting in, he took the ball on, squeezed a shot across the goalmouth from a narrow angle and there it was, spinning around in the back of the net.

There was pandemonium on the terraces. Arms punched the air, hats flew in all directions. I cleared my immediate area with a non-stop series of feverish 'rattle waving.  Even the players hugged each other in a most ungentlemanly manner.

We were nearly there. I was raving almost incoherently *"Defend for your lives, give nothing away and the Cup will be ours. ....Blow the whistle ref, blow the bloody whistle. Time's up, blow, PLEASE!"* Most everyone else around me was also bellowing furiously. After several more nervous nail-biting minutes, referee Luty did indeed blow for the last time. Albion had won the most famous Cup competition in the world.

There can be no finer feeling for a supporter than seeing your team running around Wembley showing off a trophy, beginning celebrations that would last for weeks. The 90 minutes had flown by. It wasn't a great game but set piece occasions rarely match the hype.

Many hours later when I finally got home, my folks had pinned the Sports Argus on the front window. Its uplifting banner headline read "ALBION'S CUP." A STREET AHEAD BUT VICTORY BY A WHISPER"

Naturally, there was an open-top bus parade. As if to remind the Brummies who was the premier club in the area, the victory procession started at Birmingham Snow Hill railway station.  The coach, with its precious cargo, wended slowly through the streets, past the Hawthorns and onto West Bromwich Town Hall.  Many locals had waited for hours to see the famous FA Cup return to the town. As Captain, Len Millard was expected to make a speech. With thousands hanging onto every word, he said *"Next time, and I hope it's next season, we can do the double we fought so hard for this season".*  It was exactly the right words to choose and supporters, many who'd waited for hours, were ecstatic.

Nobody wanted to leave this triumphant scene but eventually crowds started to drift away.  My thoughts were already turning to next season, wondering what lay in store for the FA Cup winners. I'd had a lifetime of memories in just seven month. Whatever was in store, I wanted to be there … for the whole season this time.

Forced to choose between your team winning the FA Cup or England winning the World Cup, what would you pick? Yes, ideally both of course but that's about as likely as two Non-League sides reaching the Champions League Final. For me, I would not surrender the first-hand experience of the Baggies capering around Wembley with the Cup, despite my patriotism.

And yet… why not both? The summer of 1954 offered just that. Just months after my soiree at the Twin Towers, England was competing in the World Cup in Switzerland and of course England are the best side in the world. (Losing to the USA four years earlier was just a one-off freak).

Putting personal bias aside, for me it just seemed common sense. Identify the outstanding League team, which was the near double-winners West Bromwich Albion and select their most consistent English players – namely Allen, Barlow and Kennedy. The England selectors looked elsewhere and chose the same old names … and ended up with the same old result. England lost in the Quarter-Final to Cup Holders Uruguay.

Hungary remained firm favourites to lift the trophy. Hardly surprising seeing that in two friendlies, they'd crushed England 6-3 at Wembley and 7-1 in Budapest (Two more freak results of course). But in the Final, they were beaten 3-2 by West Germany, amid accusations of appalling refereeing and doping.

There was confirmation that 1954 was a time of plenty for Baggies supporters with the end of rationing in July. With the world physically and financially exhausted, the end of the war actually meant more rationing, not less. Eight long years of struggle to obtain food, clothing and fuel came to an end. Sweets and chocolate were among the final items to become unrestricted. Initially it was difficult to take in. You'd still see people queuing or checking with shop staff that they realised coupons were no longer required.  I had a sweet tooth so sweets and chocolates topped my most craved-for list. Recalling pre -war days when my family owned a sweet shop, how heavy would I have become with unrestricted access? It didn't bear thinking about.

## 1954-55

I found a job in the Birmingham Steel and Tubes warehouse, a small firm employing only a dozen people. Naturally, I was the only Baggies fan, which led to many an argument whenever we faced the Villa or Blues. My weekly wage, at around £4 per week, was modest but a big improvement on serviceman's pay of 28 shillings per week (equivalent of £1.40). My earnings were sufficient to cover costs for most away matches. It was my first ever job and very close to home though it was a humdrum, doing nothing in particular, way of making a living. It didn't last but alternatives were plentiful.

I considered various options and even went for an interview at a butchers shop in Pershore Road. Heaven knows why. I'd always been concerned about animals being reared for slaughter, so much so I later became a vegetarian. Eventually, I found a job in Bridge Street, Birmingham working for Pearce and Cutler who are a well-known glass firm. Their manager was a football lover which I originally considered a bonus until I discovered his team wore claret and blue.

I had very high expectations for the new season. We had the same players, with the same ability, plus the experience of winning a trophy so what could stop us? Thanks to some sadistic planning by the Football League, the Baggies opened 54-55 with away trips to Sunderland and Newcastle; the two longest trips in the whole season and WBA had them both in 5 days. Both matches were lost quite heavily. The stars in stripes did recover in some style with 16 points from the next 18 and climbed to within a single point of top spot. But we eventually had to be content with a mid-table placing, mainly thanks to an alarming 96 goals being conceded. Stand-outs games for me were few in the League. It was the Cup (as ever) and the one-offs, which linger longest.

For instance, as the FA Cup Holders, we were duty-bound to play in the FA Charity Shield. In the 1950's, this was normally a low-key affair played in October, with the emphasis on fundraising. But because the opposition were the long-ball neighbours from Wolverhampton, this match was anything but low-key. I wanted that trophy but even more, I wanted evidence that the Baggies were the better team.

We didn't secure the trophy outright but then neither did they. It was shared after a tremendous 4-4 draw and once again Ronnie Allen demonstrated with his hat trick there was no sensible reason for his omission from the England team. As reporter Clifford Webb opined, *"he is without a doubt the best centre forward in the business."*

I still have to remind myself these days that during the 1950's, there was no segregation for supporters. Over 45,000 travelled to Molineux and mingled freely. The game was floodlit which was a novelty and definitely boosted the gate.

Wolverhampton's lights felt new and exciting and by common consent, considered the best in the country. After the game, everybody celebrated as if they'd won. For me there was nothing to debate with Wolves fans on the packed train, Ronnie Allen's hat trick deserved to win the Charity Shield - LUCKY-LUCKY-LUCKY-WOLVES! Albion were invited to play a friendly at the Heysel stadium in Brussels against the magical Magyars from Hungary - Honved. Their side included six of the national team who had already run England ragged twice. To me, this seemed a mismatch. If the national team had been outclassed, what chance did a club side have? The encounter did capture the public imagination with the national press, who never ventured too far out of London, flocking to Brussels. Interestingly the clash of the Titans was billed as "The Best Team in England versus the World Champions." There was never any chance of me travelling to Belgium for this fixture so I had to be content with press reports. Albion gave a great display and with goals from Nicholls (2) and Allen led 3-1. But then injuries intervened and they eventually capitulated 5-3. The legendary Puskas was fulsome in his praise. *"This Albion side are like no other English team I have known - they are better than England and that man Nicholls is a great player".* Most generous of him but I would have preferred such a performance in a League match rather than a glamorous friendly.

Despite these less than positive observations, I was just as keen as Albion on a return fixture but sadly it never materialised. Denied the chance of seeing these fabulous players, I then heard the unappetising news that Honved had accepted an invitation to play Wolverhampton Wanderers at Molineux. The "lure of the lights" and the opposition combined to make this a 'not to be missed' game. I had to be there and judging by the dozens of familiar faces, an awful lot of Hawthorns regulars felt the same way. Home advantage eventually paid dividends. Honved lost 3-2 after holding a two goal half-time lead.

One of the few standout League games was a trip to Arsenal at their imposing Highbury stadium. On the terraces, supporters of the Gunners kept up a discordant barrage of moans and groans as they claimed every decision was given against their team. We Black Country folk remained placid, confident that our team could maintain their early lead, courtesy Ronnie Allen.

In the 40th minute, referee McAbe blew for half time. Cue jaws dropping. It was laughable, bizarre or nonsensical – choose your own label. Within seconds, the Arsenal critics all around me were using their new ammunition.

*"What're yer doing ref, you idiot, there's still five minutes to go!"* Other similar taunts were less complimentary.

*"You're a prat ref didn't yer ever learn to tell the time?"*

*"Bloody hell ref, what's up with yer watch?"* Or pithy words to that effect

Ignoring thousands of fingers pointing at the enormous clock, the referee knew best and took the players off. Painfully quickly, he realised he didn't know best at all. The players were urged back onto the pitch amid much ribald humour, accompanied by a now red-faced official. Later, he admitted to his mistake saying that one hand on his watch had stuck and he misunderstood a linesman's signal that tried to indicate that there were still five minutes to go.

Understandably, Albion's rhythm was disrupted. The London side recovered to take the lead themselves though fortunately Johnny Nicholls hit back to level the scores and share the points.

At least one player wasn't taking the mickey out of the referee. As if to prove that anyone can make a mistake with his timepiece, Johnny "On the Spot" Nicholls was late for the train carrying the team to London that morning and had to travel solo on the next train. With Albion's League form continuing to be indifferent, the FA Cup draw on a December Monday lunchtime somehow became even more significant. I craved more victories, more glory and another visit to Wembley. All round the country; football supporters were doing the same as me, huddled around a wireless eager to hear the BBC broadcast the 3rd Round draw.

The pairings were broadcast in seemingly slow motion but at last I heard *"Bournemouth and Boscombe Athletic versus West Bromwich Albion"*. Bournemouth- more renowned for its reputation of encouraging those of a certain age to retire there, as opposed to spawning a professional football club.

In many ways, this was an ideal fixture offering a new ground and a new town at the seaside. Ok, January wasn't exactly the best time but there are many worse places to visit. I wanted to make the most of the day so endured an early start on a lumbering coach which gave the chance to explore before the game.

In company with other supporters, I took a bus into Bournemouth whereupon a reporter and a photographer approached me from the Bournemouth Echo. My "Up for the Cup" Albion hat was rather a giveaway. In the highly respectful manner of the time, I was asked a range of predictable questions such as *"is this your first visit to Bournemouth, sir?"* and "May I ask *-do you think you'll win?"*

Once the PR duties were sorted out, I had time to stroll through the town and along the beach, holding my hat in place. I quickly discovered that it wasn't only Skegness that was *"bracing."* As did several Albion fans, who when attempting to show off their football skills, found themselves more occupied trying to keep the ball out of the sea! Wind and sand negotiated, it was back to the ground to buy a copy of the Echo .Who could possibly resist reading the flattering (but so true!) headline of 'Famous Throstles visiting Dean Court.' with its front page picture of yours truly and other Albion supporters wielding rattles and proclaiming that we had little to fear. I was quoted as saying *"No problem. The 'Cherries have no chance, we'll be in the hat for the 4th round draw."*

As we waited for the teams to emerge, there was a simple announcement. *"We welcome the Cup holders, WEST BROMWICH ALBION"* Just a basic factual statement but somehow it made me feel so proud. I did wonder whether the announcer once lived in the Black Country and had retired to the South Coast. Fanciful I know, but whatever, it was a tribute I thoroughly enjoyed. Judging by the cheers of the travelling hordes, I wasn't alone.

Fast forward 60 years and fans enter a ground 30 minutes or so before kick-off. Already, there are two full squads on the pitch undergoing fitness checks. Limbering up, jogging, passing balls, shooting and the goalkeepers indulging in shot stopping.
Not then. Five minutes or so before kick off the players filed out together followed by match officials with just a single ball between them. No time to practice skills. They simply stood around chatting, giving the impression they were either killing time or discussing differences between idyllic Bournemouth and the heart of the industrial Midlands! As for the game, this was another illustration that the smooth Baggies machine of the previous season was misfiring. The Sports Argus headline of *"No glory in Albion win"* was apt. Indeed, the game was wide open for an hour until Stuart Williams darted on to a dream pass from Ronnie Allen to put Albion in front. Still we won and the dream could continue for a while longer.

The trip had two long-term consequences. Firstly, even in bleak mid-winter, Bournemouth impressed me as an attractive, clean resort. In later decades, I would spend many happy enjoyable holidays in Alum Chine - one of the four Chine beaches. Also, when I made a FA Cup return visit to Dean Court in the late

1990's, I managed to amass many brownie points just by saying *"last time I was here, Albion were the Cup holders."*

The Fourth Round draw was reasonably kind with a home tie against fellow top tier side Charlton. But Charlton hadn't read the script and it was Albion who became the victims, following an incident packed match and a 4-2 defeat. When deadeye Ronnie Allen had a penalty saved in the first half, I feared the worst. He hardly ever missed from the spot. Defeat hurt.

There was only feeble consolation to be taken from doing a League double over Charlton. However, in a 3-1 win at the Valley, there was the major plus of seeing the debut of a fresh-faced 17 year-old by the name of Alec Jackson. Whether Alec modelled his talents on anyone, I didn't know but he immediately reminded me of Sunderland's Len Shackleton. There was a little bit of the best and the worst of Alec in his first game. At times, the ball appeared glued to his boot and he could leave defenders looking terribly embarrassed. Other times, he'd overdo possession and lose the ball. Young Alec from Tipton scored in the third minute of his debut, which was a great way to become noticed. He was also on the receiving end of some rough tackling, being carried off five minutes from half time. Fortunately, he returned apparently unscathed for the second half when, according to one reporter *"he played like Ronnie Allen"*.

The day was bitter under a miserable, steel-grey sky. We needed a white ball to follow the play and the freezing wind meant I didn't appreciate standing on open terraces. At the time, the Valley was a massive stadium with a 75,000 capacity so our hardy band had a large end all to ourselves. One travelling fan found a solution. He gathered rubbish, newspapers and anything else to hand, screwed them into a tight ball and started a terrace bonfire. To even top that, he pulled out a pair of gloves from his pocket, declared them surplus and chucked them on the fire. This is probably hard for a modern audience to believe, but nobody interfered. No stewards or Police came rushing over to put out what in fairness, was a very modest flame. There was not much warmth to go round but we were all grateful for what little there was.

The last game of the season was at Hillsborough and as always, a group of supporters hung around the Players entrance in the hope of picking up complimentary tickets. Our 'gang' had never bothered but purely on the basis that it was the last game of the season; I asked one of the players if he had any spare tickets. Amazingly, he had and promptly handed over enough tickets to enable us all to get in free. Albion lost 5-0. Ouch! Being a superstitious bunch, we decided the freebies were to blame. No more 'scrounging' of tickets for us.

Who was in our gang? I'm struggling to remember all the names. I can recall Mickey Day, Johnny Charlton, Alan Brettell and the Wakeman family. I remember the latter best of all – Gordon and his sister Audrey plus their very quietly spoken Dad. Wakeman Senior was a keen listener but always seemed reluctant to offer criticism, however badly we'd played. But post-Hillsborough, he was bawling and shouting his frustration just like the rest of us.
It was around this time that fate decreed I'd meet my eventual wife Dot in Birmingham's New Street Odeon Cinema. I am probably the only living soul who can rhapsodise about the merits of 'Woman's Prison' and rattle off its stars - Ida Lupino, Sterling Hayden and Howard Duff - purely because I link everything about

that film to a rather special person who was sitting next to me that night.

In one particular moving scene, out of the corner of an eye, I noticed a few tears slowly trickling down her cheek. Well what else could I do but offer my handkerchief .In the 50's, nearly everyone carried one!  Even though the lights were low, I felt attracted to this petite 5ft 2inch girl. She was pretty, and had a nice smile.

At the end of the film, I made sure we talked and I instantly recognised her accent as being pure Scouse. She accepted my offer to walk her to a Number 5 bus stop where she told me that her family had recently moved to Brum because there were far more job opportunities available in the Midlands than on Merseyside.

She had four brothers, two of which were firm Liverpool supporters. Dot worked in the office of a button-producing firm and many of her non-working hours were spent caring for her blind mother. We agreed to meet same time, same place next week. From then on, it was Dot, Terry, the Odeon cinema, plus a couple of ice creams and a block of Cadbury's fruit and nut chocolate!

When Dot revealed that family lived a mere ten-minute stroll from Villa Park, I immediately saw this girl was in urgent need of salvation before the dark side took her. Could I possibly persuade Dot to become a football loving Baggies fan?  I guess the cover picture tells you everything.

What Dot couldn't have envisaged was being obliged to enjoy a summer accompanying me to public parks and private cricket club grounds.  My dormant cricket bug had resurfaced. I joined a local club J.H Lambourne where I either opened the bowling or came on as the first change off-spinner. As for batting, let's just say that the top nine were never in danger of losing their position.

As the weeks jogged by, bringing the big kick-off ever nearer, I was relatively successful. My best figures, which I still remember with fond clarity, had me bowling eight overs in which six of them were maidens and I took four wickets for just ten runs. Had the Aussies been spared torment from this new resurgent confident competitor? The alarm clock's ringing - time to wake up Terry!

## 1955/56

As the '54 squad were no longer producing the goods on the pitch, there was a whole series of significant transfers and elevations from the reserves to revitalise the club. Jimmy Dugdale was transferred to Aston Villa, of all teams, I considered this was excellent business but for Villa not us. I thought Dugdale excellently fulfilled the key criteria of the time for a defender, being both physically strong and able to tackle forcibly. Jimmy's problem was that he was always behind Joe Kennedy for selection. Although "Spring Heeled Joe" was often in the wars, it was understood by everyone that if he was fit, he played. Dugdale thought he was worth a first team place and Villa agreed.

An equally tough tackling character was Maurice Setters, a new arrival from Exeter City after making just 10 appearances for the Grecians. Newspapers told me that he was a '*competitive' player who never shirked a 50-50 tackle*" but this industry standard phrase of the time added nothing. Frankly, what happened in the rest of the country, football-wise, was just a mystery unless they were in the top Division. On the limited evidence available, Maurice didn't appear to be a classy, emphasis-on-cohesive-attacking Vic Buckingham player. But 96 goals conceded in the previous term meant something had to be done. In his first few games, I noted that Maurice could make excellent passes but never mind winning 50-50 balls, 40-60 balls were mostly his too. That, added to his crew cut hairstyle and a look of fierce determination, made him popular with Baggies die-hards but equally unpopular with referees and opposition supporters.

There were two significant debutants in the Everton home match. Derek Kevan had arrived cheaply from

Bradford PA. He was clearly raw and lacked finesse. Occasionally, he'd chase a ball that he hadn't an earthly chance of winning, and then once defeated, would promptly look for another opposition player to chase.

Yet big Derek had that priceless gift of being a natural goal-scorer. His two goals clinched a 2-0 win and was the start of a fabulous career. It is very difficult to think of a current day striker who bears comparison. Andy Carroll might be the nearest but it would be a stretch for anyone to imagine Carroll with far less hair and teeth, never mind being considerably stronger and scoring far more consistently.

Also lining up for the first time was a 20-year-old Don Howe, definitely the finest right back I have ever seen. Even as a debutant, he had class written all over him. Calm, studious, cool under pressure, and unlike so many other fullbacks, preferred passing the ball, rather than hacking it upfield.

The marquee signing was Bobby Robson, surprisingly prised away from Fulham for £25,000, a remarkably large sum for an Albion board to sanction. I remember my excitement before Robson made his midfield debut against Manchester City. But in a shocking anti-climax, City strolled to a 4-0 win and Robson was just as ineffective as the rest of his teammates. *"How much did he cost?"* was a repeated lament around the terraces. There was no booing or jeering, just looks of disappointment. Bobby was to need a lot of time to show his best form.

With so many new, young players joining our ranks, it was perhaps unsurprising that Albion finished in lower mid-table, 3 wins clear of the relegated sides. At that time, this was a cause for much disappointment. Albion finishing only in mid-table?

We expected more! Allen, Lee and Nicholls amassed 35 goals between them but there was limited support from the rest, which had me wondering whether they'd made a joint pledge not to score many so as to avoid embarrassing the forwards!

As ever, there were some incidents that stand out for me such as during another marathon trip to Roker Park, Sunderland. For me (and judging by the volume of cursing from my terrace neighbours, I wasn't alone), the game was ruined by the referee who decided that a linesman's flag was nothing to do with him.

For most of the afternoon, the Mackem forwards didn't need to worry about offside. Time and again, up went the linesman's flag but the referee allowed play to continue. With this advantage, it was unsurprising that Sunderland won 2-1.

As we took our seats on the Football Excursion for a not very happy long journey home, everyone wanted to moan about the referee.

*"What the hell was he playing at?"* bellowed one still frustrated supporter.

*"Why didn't the linesman keep his flag up?"* retorted another.

Others pitched in and then surprisingly a stranger sitting quietly in the corner joined in. *"I've been listening to your criticisms lads, you can't blame the linesman if the ref ignores him, can you?"*

Renewed arguments! *"Why not? He should have kept his flag up 'til he stopped play." "Not doing his job properly"* etc, etc

Now fully in tune with the debate the stranger admitted. *"Well I know it wasn't their fault because I was one of the linesmen. I waved for offside a few times but he just ignored me so what else could I have done?"*

A momentary silence broken by a fan determined to have the last word. *"Well next time, you get landed with the same ref, put a bloody bell on the end of your flag and ring it until he DOES notice. If he doesn't, it'll prove he's deaf as well as blind!"* Linesman and supporters fell about laughing and with the ice broken; any animosity between 'warring factions' was replaced with a healthy dose of football banter.

In the Cup, the old excitement was building again. We'd put the Wolves in their place in the Third Round and Pompey went the same way in Round 4, I was mentally planning better ways to make an all-night ticket queue more comfortable. Birmingham City visited the Hawthorns in Round 5. Traditionally, never a side to take too seriously, but sadly this was one of the best-ever Blues teams. The Albion pitch was icy with snow on top, which effectively replaced skill with chance. Were you standing on ice or not? City's Peter Murphy found a less slippery patch from which to score the only goal of the game and Albion were out of the Cup. Ironically, this provided me with another visit to Wembley

I'd managed to get a ticket thanks to my Dad, who although being an Albion supporter, was a very minor shareholder at Birmingham City. He successfully applied for a ticket on my behalf, so there I was, standing behind the goal where the Manchester City goalkeeper, Bert Trautman carried on playing despite suffering a broken neck! (Not that anyone realised until several days later).

I didn't join in the frantic, almost desperate support during the game. As the minutes ticked by, the realisation that it would be Manchester City and not Birmingham City going home with the Cup completely punctured the optimism of the Blues fans who firmly believed the Cup was as good as won.

Albion had a chance to win the near equivalent of the Cup Final. On the last day of the season, they had the opportunity to relegate Villa. A prospect, which was almost as exciting (I did say "almost") as Albion winning the Cup themselves. The press had been on Villa's backs for months, surely the end was nigh? It wasn't.

To my intense fury, Albion lost 3-0 and Villa stayed up on goal average. They'd survived for another season but their time would come. But fair play to Villa, if I'd have been one of their supporters, I wouldn't worry how or why they'd avoided the drop.

The big story of the season broke in the Sunday People. In a series of articles, Stan Rickaby, whom the club had released, claimed that he and the rest of his fellow professionals were nothing more than "Soccer Slaves". His prime concern was the maximum wage, a limitation unique to football. Under-the-counter payments offered commonplace recompense but why should this be necessary in a footballing time of plenty? Even more limiting was the infamous "retain or transfer" contract whereby players could only leave if their club permitted them to do so. It was a shocking anachronism in the post-war era. As a D-Day survivor, Rickaby considered his generation deserved more respect. "Retain or Transfer" didn't apply in Non-League, so Rickaby, as player-manager of Poole, took full advantage by signing several disillusioned professionals.

Rickaby also listed petty restrictions imposed by Albion on their players. These included no dancing for players less than four nights before a match. In addition, players were not permitted to own a motorcycle (frustrating as few could afford a car), no weekends away without authority, no joking or laughing on a train after a defeat and many others.

In vain, Albion tried to defend the indefensible, setting out their viewpoint across four pages of the Albion News. Both the maximum wage and "retain and transfer" were to fall within a few years, under a legal challenge

Nearly 50 years later, I had the chance to chat to Stan Rickaby, who was signing copies of his autobiography. He revealed that his admiration for his teammates was boundless. I didn't feel comfortable questioning him about his less savoury experiences but I did suspect from his affectionate tones that the passing of time had healed much of his bitterness.

On a lighter note, I've frequently alluded just how different the relationship was between fans and players in this era as opposed to the 'customers' of today. There is probably no better example of this than at windy Blackpool. As usual, players and supporters travelled on the same train and alighted at South Shore station to walk to Bloomfield Road. Naturally, our group, being loud and proud Baggies, swung our rattles and bellowed "ALBION- ALBION." Suddenly my rattle was snatched by Ronnie Allen who wielded it himself, grinning wildly and joining in with our chants.  It was a wonderful bonding moment and a simple act which meant so much. At that moment, I felt we could take on the world.  I'll draw a veil over the subsequent 5-1 defeat but at least Ronnie did score the one.

The most head-turning sporting performance of the year was not from a footballer, but rather from bowler Jim Laker. Surrey's off breaker amazingly took 19 wickets for 90 runs against Australia at Old Trafford. In a Walter Mitty mood, it bought back memories of the time I was invited to Edgbaston for a trial with Warwickshire back in the early 50's. At the time, I was a fair player whether as an off-spinner or fast medium bowler in club cricket. I loved the game and couldn't get enough of it. Anyway the trial would take place at Edgbaston around 2.00pm. Great news or so I thought! Came the magical day and with time to spare, I immediately said yes, when a couple of pals asked if I'd join them in a morning game. What a clanger! I enjoyed bowling and running around for a couple of hours but after making the short bus journey to Edgbaston, I quickly realised my mistake.

It was a warm sunny day, I was sweating profusely and no amount of towel rubbing would stop it. Taken to the nets, handed the ball and scrutinised by the scouting staff I simply couldn't impart any sense of direction or spin on the ball. It was like gripping wet soap. Yes, there were some 'useful' balls but they were few and far between. No line or length, just an abundance of full tosses or long hops. For me, this was truly a crash course in how to waste a golden (if unlikely) opportunity to carve out a possible career as a professional cricketer. It didn't come as a surprise to receive a letter from Warwickshire, thanking me for attending but confirming I hadn't impressed them sufficiently. Ah well, my chance to emulate Jim Laker had gone. But perhaps it was for the best - for England - and not Australia! I somehow think that they'd have enjoyed facing Laker and Wills in preference to Jim Laker and Tony Lock!

## 1956/57

There were no major transfers, either in or out, as the season kicked off with a 4-2 defeat at Hillsborough. However, this was quickly followed by a comfortable 2-0 home win over Villa (how they keep cropping up) and a goalless draw in the return at Villa Park a week later meant three points out of four and smiles all round. With Robson, Allen and Derek Kevan all finding the net and Frank Griffin working his own brand of magic down the wing, I genuinely thought we could challenge the outstanding team of the time – Manchester United. The League was a big ask but in the one-off nature of the Cup? Maybe.

However this was to be a season laden with frustrations both major and minor. Take the Yuletide fixtures which made no sense at all. The planners, in their infinite wisdom, decided that both Albion and Newcastle United would like nothing better than travelling the length of the country on consecutive days, simply because they said so. The players certainly weren't happy. Supporters were even less so, with diehards like myself dreaming of a non-white Christmas, which wouldn't impact on a torturous coach journey to Tyneside. But it did.

Round One was on Christmas Day morning at the Hawthorns. With snow covering the pitch, Albion slipped and slithered to a 1-0 victory over the Geordies. And then even heavier snow came down. Fans planning on travelling for the return match were in a quandary. Should they start out at midnight on Christmas Day hoping the game would be played or give it a miss?

I had no doubt. So what if it was Christmas night with snow drifting down to add a few more inches to the Christmas card image? There was a match to be played and I had to be there. I caught a tram into the city centre, and then climbed on another passing the home of 'Good Honest Beer' (Mitchells and Butlers) to reach the coach terminal at Cape Hill Smethwick where I joined the other single-minded fanatics. Everyone huddled in shop doorways, waiting for the coach. The conversation was predictable, each trying to out-do the other with the number of people who'd told them not to travel yet at the same time drawing new determination from those around us. We hadn't got a clue what conditions were like 200 miles further North – it was just travel and hope.

At least the coach was a couple of degrees warmer and dry. As we passed the illuminated Council House clock, I pondered how many hours would elapse before we arrived at St James Park? It turned out be eight, punctuated by many calls of 'nature.' I tried to sleep but the bump thump of tyres on packed snow and the regular lurching as traction was lost really didn't help. Eventually we reached our destination- 'Newcastle on Arctic Circle' Bleak? You'd better believe it! Eight hours travelling and we were still none the wiser whether we had a game. We marched on St James' Park, found an open gate and in we went. The pitch was buried under deep snow. There was no need for a pitch inspection but we made one anyway ploughing our way through the snow and digging heels into the pitch in best refereeing traditions.

There was an angry roar behind us. In the absence of a translator, most of the Geordie words were lost but we picked up from the gestures and the red face that we weren't welcome. All we could do was endure several hours in the deserted town centre before returning around midday for the formality of the game being postponed.

Amazingly it wasn't. The ground staff had somehow managed the impossible, shovelling and clearing away sufficient snow for the match to go ahead. With the aid of an official who surely had his eyes closed during the inspection, the match was given the thumbs-up. I was elated if astonished. Truthfully, the fixture should never have been played. The Geordies proved they were better at skating and won 5-2. As our indefatigable drivers (they deserved every penny of our generous whip-round) set out on the Marathon part 2 to get us home, I consoled myself with classic fanatic logic that had the game been postponed, I'd have needed two days off work to travel there and back in midweek. I'd have still gone but it was not an endearing prospect. There were, as I was to find out, several more tribulations this season. I'll never forget how bothered I became at Burnden Park. Frank Griffin had opened the scoring and with 18 minutes left, I was hopeful we could hang on for both points. That was until Bolton were handed an equaliser. The ref had whistled for a foul on Lofthouse near the halfway line. Players from both sides stopped and strolled to take their positions for a free kick. All bar one, the Bolton player with the ball at his feet. He simply carried on running, slipped it to an unmarked colleague who gratefully side-footed the ball home. All hell broke loose as Albion players angrily demanded to know why it had been allowed. They descended en-masse to push, shove, and maul the ref but it was futile

Now, I'm not one to 'lose my cool' but on this occasion I did. I moaned, groaned and cursed at a decision that cost us a deserved point. Naturally, the Bolton fans argued to the contrary outside the ground which only raised my ire further. I had as much steam up as the engine that took us all home. Only much,

much later did referee Chandler claim he'd given advantage because a Bolton player had the ball. As you'll have already gathered, travelling in the 1950's was far less predictable than today, a triumph of hope over certainty. None more so than when travelling to Old Trafford to play Manchester United. Our train was only moving at walking pace due to thick fog. It was patently obvious that we'd miss kick-off.   By the time we reached Crewe, already three hours behind schedule, fatigue and apathy had already overcome our frustrations. A brave soul announced over the train tannoy that the football special would not travel any further North as the game would be over long before we could get to Old Trafford. It was only common sense but was greeted with a torrent of anger and complaints about British Rail incompetence. But the negative cries suddenly turned to cheers as my cracking Bakelite radio announced that the match had been postponed due to the pea-souper currently enveloping Manchester. We'd actually been worrying unnecessarily as the Albion team were on the train BEHIND us! The game was eventually played a week after the season had officially ended. Travel was smooth and on time and thanks to a penalty from Len Millard (his last ever Albion goal), we managed a 1-1 draw, a decent bonus at a ground where we rarely left without suffering a defeat.

The New Year brought with it the magic of the FA Cup.  The Rovers from Doncaster were beaten in a Third Round replay, Sunderland overcome in Round Four and Blackpool in a Fifth Round replay. Each victory was savoured to the maximum. I'd be grinning manically for 2 or 3 days each time and I dreamt of Wembley. *"This could be our year"* I'd tell anyone willing to listen.  Then we drew the mighty Arsenal at home in the Quarter-Final and suddenly I wasn't so confident.

This was a full-on Cup-tie, with tension gripping everyone. I felt as drained as the players at the end if only through frantic use of my rattle. The match was drawn 2-2.

Once again I had to 'beg' time off from work to make the trip to London. But with our midfield kingpin Joe Kennedy injured. I feared the worst.

I was wrong. With stand-in Ray Barlow reigning supreme, Arsenal's attack was muzzled. Brian Whitehouse put Albion ahead in the second half and the Gunners began to look distinctly rattled.

Then Arsenal won a penalty. An Arsenal fan next to me snarled in pure Cockney, *"Clapton's never missed a penalty."* I could feel a heavy weight sinking inside me.

But Clapton missed this one as Jimmy Sanders palmed it away. I bellowed, almost incoherently, something like *"Great save Jimmy"*. Suddenly, I knew we would win. As a supporter, sometimes you just know. Derek Kevan scored a second and despite a late frantic onslaught from the Gunners that had me clamouring to hear the final whistle, we triumphed 2-1. The London Underground never carried a more 'floating on air' standing passenger alongside the lamenting Arsenal contingent. We'd made it and wasn't life great!

There was an unlikely West Midlands bias among the Semi-Finalists, which comprised Albion, Villa and Blues, plus Manchester United. Who might we get? The subject was debated at great length but I had one of my premonitions. I knew it had to be Villa and so it proved. At Molineux.

Naturally, the local press were very excited about three of "their" clubs being so close to the Twin

Towers. Knowing this feat was unlikely to be replicated, the Mail produced a joint team picture, resplendent in their club colours. On the day itself, they aimed to corner the market in pictures of manically grinning supporters, ideally both female and attractive. Dot was featured, in her Baggies hat and scarf and naturally her admission that she was from Aston was seized upon for the caption

Over 55,000 packed into Molineux. With both sets of supporters using the same railway line, a massive operation was mounted to transport everybody to Wolverhampton. Despite the extra trains, ending up being very cosy with our neighbours was impossible to avoid.

I was confident. I was a veteran of Semi-Finals now and the League table proved Albion were the better side. When Brian Whitehouse had put the Baggies in front after only two minutes, I was convinced Albion were Wembley bound, capering around in the limited space available. Albion had Villa just where they wanted them, 2-1 ahead with minutes to go …then disaster. Villa's McParland nipped between two dozing defenders to equalise. What the hell! Wembley was ours … and suddenly it wasn't. I was as sick as a shipload of exotic parrots. Almost worse than the celebrating Villa supporters were the neutral Wolves contingent who also wanted to gloat. It was a short but miserable journey back to New Street.

So another mid-week FA Cup replay was required, sensibly staged at St Andrews. I was pushing my luck to get more time off work. All over the conurbation, other fans were doing the same thing, begging borrowing, scrounging or mysteriously feeling too ill to go to their workplace.

What do history books, Wikipedia and research analysts all have in common? Simply they all report bare facts. They'll give the score in the FA Cup Semi Final and not much else. What they won't feature is the emotion from those matches – the anticipation, tension, anguish, frustration, anger and finally the despair. Rarely have I endured so much in such a short time of space. All were present in abundance for the pair of Semis and as I reeled out of the ground clutched by gloom, I felt the end of the world was nigh. All sense of perspective was numbed. History tells us that Villa won 1-0. What it doesn't say is how the Villains' used up five years fortune in one game. Following an injury to Ronnie Allen (did I mention my foreboding?), the Baggies effectively had ten men and were caught out by Myerscough in the first half. Even though the Baggies performed as if they had a dozen players, they just couldn't score. In my nervous state, I felt like tearing my hair out in frustration.

Such frustration... Villa defending as if their lives depended on it and, to their credit, they somehow survived. They were so, so lucky. Ray Barlow hit the bar. A shot from Kevan amazingly hit a defender on the line as he ran across the goalmouth in the opposite direction with the goalkeeper stranded. Villain McParland later admitted *"we had a bit of luck .I remembered the ball bouncing and rolling along the goal-line and big Nigel jumping up to whack it over the bar. If the ball had dropped, there would have been maybe ten players in the back of the net with it. Whenever players see things like that, they think that the luck of the cup is with them"* A bit of luck? Ye Gods! Pressure, scrambles and missed chances continued right to the death when a header from Joe Kennedy came back off the bar. And then anguish as the game was over.

Leaving St Andrews feeling shattered and angry, I walked back to the city centre in a daze, made far worse by smug Villa fans celebrating with non- stop chanting that the cup was as good as theirs. We were robbed of another Cup Final appearance in the cruellest of circumstances. Even now, half a century on, I still feel a deep sense of frustration, pain and bitterness when recalling those dramatic happenings. I wanted revenge so badly.

Despite everything, I was still unable to resist torturing myself even further by reading all the match reports I could find. I was just looking for crumbs of comfort. Ultimately, the thoughts of the professionals were not much different to my own. Eric Woodward in the Birmingham Mail covered the obvious ground "*Lucky Villa", "credit to the Villa defence*" etc. There was particular sympathy for Ray Barlow, who easily won Man of the Match and deserved a trip to the Twin Towers.

I did find the crumb that I sought in a quote from Villa Chairman Doug Ellis *"In all my football experience I have never known a losing team take a defeat so well. Albion were a credit to football, adding immense respect to the club and those who belong to it."*

In the Final, the 'lucky' Villa tag refused to abandon them when they beat a depleted Manchester United. McParland had clattered into their keeper Harry Gregg who unable to carry on and spent the remainder of the game hobbling down a wing. Jackie Blanchflower took his place between the sticks. A 2-1 win bought the Cup back to the Midlands. I wish I'd put a bet on the outcome because I was absolutely certain after the Semi-Final farce; it was to be Villa's year.

A lighter memory of the Final was that my oldest sister, Pat, had chosen that day to get married. This took place in Birmingham city centre hours before kick-off. Not wanting to miss the game on television, and seeing it advertised as being shown on a 'Big Screen' in the 'Tatler News Theatre', Dot and I paid to see the 'Big Screen' filming only to discover the screen was equivalent to a modern day 50-inch HD television set. Robbery?  More like 'Grand Larceny' but in my eyes not even that could compare with our semi-final disaster. A thousand curses on the Villa flagship and all who sail in her!

The league campaign eventually finished with a 'perfect' set of match results:  42 points from 42 games with 14 wins, 14 draws and 14 defeats.  It was also the end for Johnny Nicholls. I was sad to see him leave for Cardiff. 'The Poacher' hadn't had a good season and it was painful to see him missing so many chances that previously he'd put away instinctively. With so many other goal scorers in the ranks, Albion made a pragmatic decision that Nicholls' contract would not be renewed.  I'd miss him.

## 1957-58

Put simply, this was the most dramatic season I'd ever experienced. I was so proud to be a long-term supporter of one of the most dynamic, almost unstoppable teams in the country. We were a big name and having the Baggies in town would guarantee a big gate. You want to see the mighty West Bromwich? You just had to be there. I swear I grew an inch each Friday anticipating another proud afternoon the following day.

Albion were good Box Office because they scored so many (92) and sadly conceded rather too many (70). The latter figure meant that we didn't give eventual League Champions Wolverhampton too many sleepless nights. An ultimate fourth place finish for me didn't do justice to a magnificent season of entertaining football. With Robson, Allen and Kevan amassing 65 goals between them, somebody was going to suffer. Nine went into Man City's net in a single game. Leicester were beaten 6-2, Burnley 5-1, Birmingham City 5-3 at St Andrews, Luton 4-2, Preston 4-1, Everton 4-0 not to mention 3 extraordinary games against Manchester United. More of those games later.

At the time, Manchester City were famed for their Marsden Plan. Essentially, this meant City played with an extra central defender and one less forward. This was cutting edge stuff at a time when all teams used the same rigid format. Wingers stayed on the wing and big, strong centre forwards always stayed up front. Their plan went awry at the Hawthorns to the embarrassing tune of 9-2 to the Baggies. City abandoned their double centre half plan after realising there was nobody to mark Jimmy Dudley in midfield who'd made the most of his isolation.

This was the biggest win I'd ever seen and I wasn't alone in roaring, "*we want 10, we want 10. Come on, we want 10*" after scoring a miserly nine goals! Had the injured Ronnie Allen been fit to play, a one-man Marsden plan himself, I'd have expected at least twelve goals. Immediately after the game, I was halted by a smiling fellow Baggie outside the ground who informed me gravely "*I think they need a new Plan.*"

Albion had finally wised up and installed floodlights. Arguments for and against their use had raged for a couple of years with the Chairman once saying "*when would we use them? It would cost us £20,000 and we can't afford that sort of money.*"

This seemed backward thinking to me. Opinion was overwhelmingly in favour from other Albion supporters that I'd chatted with. Both Wolves and Blues had lights and they had no trouble finding both a use and an enthusiastic audience. Floodlights still felt new and exciting, even though elsewhere in the country, this was old news. Southampton for instance installed theirs way back in 1950. I couldn't help visiting local floodlit grounds for night matches.

Thus on September 18th 1957, 36,835 were present to see Hawthorns history being made. Albion shared the points with Chelsea after Ronnie Allen scored from the penalty spot. There was much predictable terrace wit along the lines of urging the club to "*put a shillin' in the meter.*" The light cast by the floodlights was a curious yellow, rather than the blue tinge of more modern systems and didn't banish shadows from corners of the pitch but that night the Hawthorns was an stimulating place to be.

A month later, there was an intriguing floodlit friendly against the Russian Red Army team at the Hawthorns. This was a return match following

Albion's earlier Iron Curtain tour. At the time, Russia was seen as a nation not to be trusted, almost "the enemy" so to see their near-international team playing football against the Baggies felt exciting.

The game had everything including the 11 goals and it should have been more as Derek Kevan endured some brutal treatment, inside and outside the penalty box (in a friendly?). The 6-5 score sounds very close but in truth, Albion were always on top and two of the five Russian goals came very late. As the visitors walked off after the game, the home team gave them a guard of honour. The 48,000 crowd also cheered them off. Yet, not one Russian player could manage anything more than a scowl. Proof that "From Russia with Love" was several decades away.

Presumably, they were not amused either by the half-time entertainment. Young Albion player David Burnside, a brilliant ball "juggler", entertained millions watching on live television with a half time display. What can be said about David Burnside? At the time, little was known of his capabilities although one day the Albion coach, chatting to Ray Barlow, jokingly said, *"I can't stop. I've got to go and throw some fish at our young performing seal!"* That unknown 'seal' was David Burnside. At times he was capable of winning games almost single-handedly, yet he failed to make the progress his undoubted talents suggested. He could have made more money as a TV ball-juggler but what a solitary, uninspiring job compared to playing top-level football.

Luton was a low point of the season. Kenilworth Road is grim now and it was just as grim then, the sort of place you'd prefer to leave even before kick-off. Back then, the ground was virtually all terraced, apart from the Main Stand, which was built in 1922, and looked it. When they were promoted two years earlier, the Luton Chairman said he was looking to move the club elsewhere.  Over 50 years later, they're still looking.  Deja vu, anyone?

Grim or not, I had to be there. Albion lay second in the table and unbeaten in 17 games. For me, the run would only continue if I were there to support the team (run was to become the key word)

The British Railways cheap day excursion, costing the equivalent of 60p, puffed out of New Street five hours before kick-off. If I'd have known what was ahead, I might have gone back to bed (as if I could!) We set off on time only to stop again.  Then start; quickly pick up speed only to stop once more.

*"What the hell's going on?"*

*'God Almighty! Put some more coal in the boiler, we've a match to see!"*

Stop. Start. Stop. Start.  Our staccato progress continued almost as if traffic lights had been installed. Complaints rose to a crescendo and then faded away as we all became resigned to our fate. Moaning at each other didn't change anything although after I'd pulled the carriage window open, poked my head out, and bellowed in the direction of the driver "*Get a bloody move on",* I did feel slightly less tense.

There is not much stimulation to be gained from close-up views of grass and weeds yet BR seemed most anxious that we should have maximum exposure. Were we travelling on a Field Appreciation Special by mistake?

The train chugged on and on and on before finally arriving at Midland Road station- 55 minutes late. Compartment doors were flung open (before the train had stopped) and the run was underway. All 500 travellers were being involuntarily entered into the *Luton Half Mile Sprint.*

I played sport and thus had no trouble staying with the leading group as we pounded through the streets, keeping close to those who knew the way. One or two of the group resembled amateur runners, however dodging shoppers, barking dogs and the occasional uneven surface was a challenge to us all.

On the odd occasion that I looked around, there was a sad trail of less fit Baggies lurching and swearing pitifully behind us.  Those who'd "indulged" on the train were regretting it. Contrary to the slogan, Double Diamond doesn't always work wonders. Let's be kind, everyone was running as quickly as his or her personal fitness allowed. The prize for the winners was to be inside the ground for kick-off. Or so we thought. When I, and the rest of the fittest supporters, finally reached the turnstiles, we were greeted by the usual gaggle of latecomers and pub goers, who had frustrations of their own. The turnstile operators were moving as quickly as our train.

*"Gerra move on for Christ's sake. Gerra move on."* was the general frustrated chorus. The queue grew longer as the slower contestants in the Half Mile Sprint joined the end of our ragged line. Their red faces and heaving lungs prevented them adding to the discordant cries of irritation and abuse.

Agonisingly Slowly (with a capital S) and with increasingly fruitier comments being offered, at last we faced our tormentor. *"I don't know why you're hurrying,"* offered the unflappable turnstile operator. *"You've no chance against the Town."* There was no time to argue with the ramblings of an obviously demented person. We crowded onto the terrace; having missed the first few minutes play and (as a reward for our athletic prowess) had to suffer a 5-1 defeat. The turnstile operators' prediction was spot on.  I think the last of the participants in the Non-Fun

Run got in about 30 minutes into the game when our team were already on their uppers.

*"Damn him, damn Kenilworth Road."* I was ranting barely coherently. *"Damn Kenilworth Road"*.

What happened and where was our swashbuckling form? Just over a week away, thankfully. Eureka! After another defeat, this time at Newcastle, ten goals, yes, 10 were scored in the next two games. I could ease up taking the headache pills as the status quo was restored. First up was a 5-3 win at St Andrews. Oh, how I revelled in local derby victories, even though it was only the Blues. Albion's final goal was an overhead kick by Ronnie Allen. It wasn't simply a standard overhead kick, if there is such an animal. Ronnie literally stood on his head as he crashed the ball past the England keeper Gill Merrick. He gaped in astonishment and so did I. Ronnie defied the laws of physics. *"Thank you Father Christmas. Have a drink on me!"*

Two days later and this time it was Burnley suffering a hangover as four goals from Robson and one by 'The Tank' sent them back to Turf Moor, as the topical song goes, *'Bewitched, bothered and bewildered'*. I felt good again.

The FA Cup was our highlight of the season. Man City, despite being the League's top scorers with 104 goals, were routed 5-1 in the Third Round. One Round later, Nottingham Forest were exceedingly lucky to escape with a 3-3 draw at the Hawthorns in front of a huge 58,000 crowd.

Although I complained loudly at the time about Forest's good fortune, the replay was very close to the finest ever performance in all my years of watching Albion. Forest didn't have floodlights so once more I endured the ritual of asking for time off. By now, I had a rugby-loving manager who needed a lot of persuasion before I was finally free to join the madding hordes on the 10.30 Football Special to Nottingham. Arriving in 'Sherwood Forest 'country two hours later, we found Forest supporters in buoyant mood. As we all tramped towards the City Ground, we were regaled in East Midland tones phrases to the effect of "*You missed your chance on Saturday mate, now it's our turn.*"

Forest grabbed an early lead. This was followed by Maurice Setters being stretchered off after 20 minutes with a broken leg, I remembered those gloating pre-match predictions. Game Over. Or was it? The remaining 70 minutes were a sheer joy to watch. Five superbly crafted goals. With Bobby Robson playing in two positions at once, the Baggies were simply irresistible and the fondly remembered Eric Woodward eloquently summed up the display in the Evening Mail "THEY WILL ALWAYS REMEMBER". I certainly will. Chanting was virtually unheard of then but the mood of exuberance among the travelling supporters was such that a cry from a single throat of *"We want four"* was soon echoed in concert. After the Tank, had duly obliged, the chant was amended to *"We Want Five."* and we got that too. No wonder there was an invasion of hundreds of Black Country men onto the pitch, all seemingly wearing identical raincoats.

Into Round Five and after a battling display at Bramall Lane had ended 1-1, Sheffield United were back to the Hawthorns for the replay. Thank heavens for floodlights to avoid more time off work. Again we finished with ten men but again we won in style, 4-1. I could smell Wembley. Three top Division sides defeated, eighteen goals scored. I told everyone this was our year.

But WBA, the FA Cup and indeed everything else in football was being subsumed by the tragedy in Munich. Just a few days earlier, Manchester United, the team of all the talents, were returning from Zagreb after playing a European Cup match against Red Star Belgrade. They touched down in Munich to refuel. The weather was perfectly dreadful and the sensible decision would be to wait until conditions improved. But United felt under pressure as the League had refused to postpone their Saturday League game so the pilot tried to take off. The first two attempts were aborted and the third ended in tragedy as the plane overshot the runaway and crashed. Many people perished immediately, including seven of the finest players in the game. Still more, including the incredibly talented Duncan Edwards, died later from their injuries.

News of the crash dominated the headlines for days. The story ran on every media outlet - television, radio and in the press. Gaumont British and Pathe News at the cinema featured the plane wreckage and Matt Busby and the remainder of his team in hospital. Every aspect was given maximum consideration.

I first heard of the tragedy via a crackling signal on a small Bakelite radio at work, and simply couldn't take it in. I hastily grabbed some paper and a large pen to scrawl the news in big letters for everyone to see. This was mainly for the benefit of the delivery drivers and, if I'm honest, also for myself. Somehow the grim tidings seemed more believable in this format. Everyone was appalled, whether they were football lovers or not

On the Saturday following the disaster, every League game staged a minutes silence, then a very rare gesture. The fate of Manchester United was a dark cloud over the whole country. Amid the waves of sympathy, the normal restrictions about Cup-tied players were relaxed for United to enable them to put together a competitive FA Cup side. Their patched up team of reserves and new boys were set to ride the wave of the most sympathetic support and euphoria the game has ever known. They beat Sheffield Wednesday 3-0 at Old Trafford to reach the Quarter Finals and then out of the hat came the pairing of West Bromwich Albion and Manchester United. These Cup games, plus a League fixture, all in the space of eight days, were to prove unique.

The Cup game at the Hawthorns finished 2-2. Albion supporters in the 57,000 crowd felt inhibited, feeling that shouting for their side would somehow be disrespectful to the dead. The visiting Mancunians were passionate to the point of hysteria. Trying desperately to meet expectations, their scratch side regularly lunged wildly but the referee seemed loath to penalise the Reds for anything. Without their usual noisy backing, Albion couldn't establish anything resembling a genuine grip on the game and needed a late Horobin leveller just to remain in the competition. Another replay meant more time off work for me. Thank you Mr Manager.

I will never go to another game comparable to that Quarter-Final replay. I read that queues at the turnstiles started over five hours before kick-off. (Only the seated areas were all-ticket) with turnstiles opening at an unlikely 5pm. An endless sea of faces continued to queue, increasingly impatiently. Fellow veteran supporter Charles Reynolds remembered *"I travelled early and alone to Old Trafford, allowing myself what I thought would be a ridiculous amount of time to get to the ground, well before the gates would normally open. The crowd was already pushing and shoving to get in. I found myself literally having to fight with my elbows to get through the turnstiles well over an hour before kick-off. "*

His experiences mirrored my own. Only the fittest and most determined were getting through the turnstiles in this free-for-all. Fortunately, I was both and was among the 60,000 inside, rather than the estimated 30,000 howling outside. There was even a doubt that the Albion team could reach Old Trafford. Their coach could not get within a mile of the ground. The players had to walk and shove their way on foot, awkwardly pushing a skip between them.

Old Trafford was a frothing cauldron. As far as the eye could see, United fans were sporting specially made scarves featuring all the Babes with a black cross next to those who had died. Every United move was greeted by a torrent of often incoherent, raw emotion that was near impossible to deal with for both sides. The United rookies were overawed; repeatedly making basic mistakes and their forward line of near-strangers misfired. Albion's defence was resolute but not only were they taking on United, they were also up against a seemingly terrified, biased referee and frankly the whole world. The best comparison that I can make is with an amphitheatre with two criminals unsure as to which would be reprieved. Swap the referee for a Roman Emperor with the power to decide who lived or died. To gain favour, he'd deliberate for a few seconds before giving the thumbs down. For Albion, the thumb was always down.

Both sets of fans were transfixed by the intensity of what can only be described as a manic game. Possession ebbed and flowed, as did my nerves. The quicker the clock ticked down, the more I felt the team scoring first would win. I genuinely feared that Albion would not be allowed to score.

There were just minutes left to play. Five minutes became four, then three, and then two. With just 60 seconds remaining, Roy Horobin was clattered and Albion should have been awarded a free kick. As expected, it wasn't given. Bobby Charlton gathered the ball. I looked up and I sensed danger. I was right. He crossed, the ball eluding three defenders and there was Colin Webster with the simple task of nudging the ball home from close range.

The Albion players raced to the referee to point out the linesman had flagged. But referee Hawley said he'd seen the signal, acknowledged it but gave Charlton the advantage. It summed up the referee's performance. An Albion player had been fouled and United received the advantage?

The moment of Webster's strike was brilliantly summed up by journalist John Camkin "*it produced a roar which will always be in the memory of the 60,560 people lucky to have seen this match tonight. I can find no words to describe the explosion of voices inside Old Trafford. But I will hazard that neither Hampden Park nor Wembley-nor any other ground has ever heard the like*" Sounds strange but I didn't hear any noise. I simply stood dumbfounded. I knew the odds against Albion equalising were astronomical. We were out.

Around 55 years later, I asked Bobby Charlton for his recollection. "*Anyone that was there, players and fans, will never forget the circumstances and a game that meant so much-it's impossible to forget*"

All that was left was to get home as soon as possible but even that was difficult. The United supporters refused to leave. They stood immobile, applauding every Red shirted player, blocking every exit in these pre-segregation days. Far worse were the numbers of locked-out supporters who forced their way in as soon as the gates opened. Their enthusiasm was understandable but the potential for a repeat of the Bolton disaster was simply frightening. Far from leaving the ground, I was looking around for the safest place to go.

Somehow, Old Trafford escaped without any reported injuries that night. With a return League visit scheduled four days later, this was food for thought. I wanted to be there but taking on the whole world again plus a genuine concern about being involved in a similar situation didn't inspire me.

Like all seasoned supporters, I did what I could to minimise risk. I was at Old Trafford ridiculously early and carefully chose my spot. 63,000 others later followed my example. Again, there was a full house and again a tsunami of vocal support. It was hard to imagine how the Reds could add to the raw emotion but they managed it. All the medical staff who battled so hard to keep the Babes alive were invited to the game and introduced before kick-off. The emotion was truly overwhelming, even for stiff upper-lip 1950's Britain... but there was more in the shape of a recorded message from Matt Busby from his hospital bed. How much emotion can one crowd take? Again, I felt as if we'd blundered into a private funeral and I wondered how much this atmosphere would affect Albion. But this time there would be no fairy tale ending for United or their fans.

The Reds were disorganised, appeared dog-tired and drained of all adrenalin. They couldn't cope with their organised, experienced visitors. Stroking the ball around, Albion left United chasing shadows for most of the game and the 4-0 win (Allen (2), Kevan and an OG) underlined the difference in quality between the teams. A difference that I'm still convinced that without Munich would have got Albion to Wembley.

Sadly, the Baggies season more or less ended at that point but I've never forgotten that trio of matches. Shortly after, Dot and I queued to see a new film *'Look Back in Anger'* with Richard Burton and Claire Bloom.  Although there was no obvious connections with Munich or the FA Cup, I somehow mentally linked the two and the odd pairing stayed with me ever since. The film is a black and white classic and still pops up regularly (mainly on satellite channels) and should I lose focus on Burton's brilliant acting talents, a futuristic 'Time Machine' immediately transports me back. Back to a night when I stood squeezed shoulder to squeezed shoulder alongside both Baggies and United supporters watching a game won on emotion rather than ability. In fact, every time I visit Old Trafford and look up at the plaque commemorating the Munich disaster, I recall two dates. February 6th and March 5th 1958. The days of the crash and the never to be forgotten FA Cup replay.

Extremes of mood are part of the supporters' lot and at times it's possible to move from one end of the spectrum to the other. The Old Trafford trips were an example and another followed during a week that started with another trek to St James' Park (funny how Newcastle features so often in my memories) and finished with a near-walkable stroll to St Andrews.

First up was the visit to the Geordies and a mighty long way to witness a 3-0 defeat.  Albion just weren't at the (Blaydon) Races and the three goals could easily have been more. The highlight was a canine intruder as the Birmingham Mail reported: "*The brightest feature of the game from Albion's point of view was the performance of a small terrier dog who kept everyone amused for four minutes just before* the interval.  He romped on to the pitch, evaded a rugby tackle by referee Powell, of Rotherham, playfully forced the 22 players to run around in circles all over the pitch and then happily disappeared back into the crowd" Yes, it was amusing but if I had wanted to see a performing dog act, I would have much rather paid to see it back home at Billy Smarts Circus, rather than a long, expensive trip to the North-East!  Yes, you've guessed, I was not in a good mood.

In those days players, officials, and supporters normally travelled on the same train to certain away games. In the pre-motorway era, going by train was the most sensible way to travel.  Albion tended to reserve either the first or the last carriage in an attempt to reserve a modicum of privacy.

Our not-so-merry band was in moaning overdrive. *"What's the matter with 'em... useless... we've come all this way ... Oh!"* The "Oh" was prompted by the connecting door sliding open and Ronnie Allen, our No. 9 Ronnie Allen, entering our compartment.  It was enough to make the smokers cough on their Woodbines (5p a packet then). Careful to avoid smiling to avoid the wrath of the directors, Ronnie was keen to talk and in particular to apologise. *"We know we let you down. You deserved better than that. We'll try to do better in the next game."* Suddenly the day didn't seem so bad after all. A few simple words but they meant so much to all of us.

If my supporting passion needed another boost, the next game provided it. We were visiting our down-at-heel neighbours Birmingham in the Second City's riposte to Kenilworth Road. As if every player had taken Ronnie's sentiments to heart, the Albion side tore in the hapless Blues from the kick-off.  The boys were definitely back in town! Robson, Kevan and

Allen racked up five goals between them, none better than recent apologist Ronnie's overhead kick. City managed 3 goals of their own but they were well beaten. Ah, the delights of being a Baggies fan. One week a gloomy 7-hour steam train marathon from the frozen North and the next 60 minutes on a local bus quietly revelling in the noisy misery of your neighbours.

Another you might say "less than illuminating" away trip was a lengthy midweeker – this time to Portsmouth. After devouring my 'compulsory' bag of chips and buying a programme, we found a decent spot on the terracing. To me, the lighting appeared dim so turning to a Pompey fan I asked *"How long before the lights are fully turned on?"*

Looking puzzled, he simply replied, *"That's as good as they get."*

What? I've seen brighter coach headlights. Perhaps they were coach headlights? At the time, some clubs had what can only be described as varying floodlight power. Presumably clubs had to conform to a minimum standard of lighting so how did the Hampshire club get away with such poor illuminations?

Both Roy Horobin and Ronnie Allen obligingly scored from the better-lit areas in a  2-2 draw. Floodlighting! A better description would have been candlepower!

One sad feature of this season was Len Millard playing his last game, ending a 21-year career with the same club. Len's retirement wasn't entirely unexpected. His first team appearances were very few due to Stuart Williams' emergence as a top rated full back. His last game was back in October 1957. Even in retirement, and not in the best of health, he still proved his affinity to the club, regularly attending supporters club functions. He was always willing to chat, and I still have a photograph taken with him, Ray Barlow and Johnny NIcholls as a keepsake.

After the dramatic events in the previous World Cup, the 1958 tournament was relatively uneventful though there was much excitement among Albion supporters that two of our team were selected – Don Howe and Derek Kevan.  Don's selection wasn't surprising but Kevan's name wasn't greeted with overwhelming enthusiasm by some London newspaper hatchet men. They bemoaned his lack of skill while conveniently ignored his goal scoring.  This familiar, tedious theme persisted for years.

England, in the same pool as Brazil, the Soviet Union and Austria were handicapped by the tragic losses in the Munich Air Disaster. In the circumstances, they performed with commendable distinction by picking up draws in their three matches. "The Tank" more than earned his selection, popping in two of the four goals.  As England and the Russians finished with identical records, they had a play off to decide who would advance to the Quarter Final. It wasn't to be England's day. They hit the post twice, went close on several occasions but sadly a defensive error led to the only goal of the game in the 68th minute.

What of those Magical Hungarians who should have won four years earlier? Sadly the Soviet Union's invasion of their country in 1956 had devastated their squad. Many of their top players had defected to the West and things would never be the same for them again. Not surprisingly, they too missed the knockout stage.

With home advantage, hosts Sweden reached the Final after defeating reigning champions West Germany. Their opponents were Brazil who included in their line up an unknown 17-year-old. His name was Edison Arantes de Nascimento. Or - as he later became known - Pele. Displaying superb skills he destroyed, almost single- handily, Sweden's hopes. Two magnificent goals in a crushing 5-2 win took the trophy back to Rio. The quality from both sides easily surpassed those of England. It was another reality check.

## 1958/59

If England weren't serious World Cup contenders, I still considered Albion could mount a serious bid to lift the Championship. We signed additional talent such as new goalkeeper Ray Potter who arrived on a free transfer and was to be an immediate hit. Derek Hogg was always a thorough nuisance on the left wing for Leicester with his pace and jinking runs so for me his arrival at the Hawthorns was a great bonus.

The first three matches were all drawn but then the Championship chase began in earnest at a rain soaked St Andrews that again saw Birmingham City suffer the Blues. Younger generations imagine Coventry to be our permanent patsies who only turn up to make up the numbers. Birmingham City was the 1950's answer to Sky Blues. We came and we conquered on an afternoon which made me feel as though I've won the £75,000 jackpot on the Littlewoods pools. The desperate opposition, pitch and weather weren't problems for the superb Baggies. Honestly without any exaggeration, City was lucky to get away with a mere 6-0 thrashing. The Birmingham Evening Mail drew on adjectives from the film industry such as "Stupendous, fantastic and colossal" with the reporter adding, *"I'm still tingling at the thought of the game, still as bewildered as Blues that a team can turn on such a wonderful show."* Even the nationals were lavish in their praise such as Alan Williams from the Daily Express: *"what a magnificent response Albion made. The Wonderful Blended Artistry, that so often disappoints merged into glorious teamwork that ripped Birmingham to pieces that didn't have the skill, speed, or method of these red shirted wonder men. There was a touch of the old Manchester United in West Brom's arrogant attacking play."* Such exuberant reports deserve to be kept for half a lifetime, which is exactly what I've done.

Unfortunately, we couldn't play Blues every week. There were many other good days but not quite enough. Not for the first time, the Baggies just weren't consistent enough and had rather too many off-days to really threaten for the title. Such as a 5-0 setback at White Hart Lane which was bad enough but the 5-2 defeat at Molineux was even more galling, bearing in mind Wolves went on to win the title for the second year in succession.

There were many positives. Albion scored 88 goals including six against Portsmouth to add to that Blues drubbing and fours against Spurs, Chelsea and Preston. Derek Kevan scored 29 of the total. Maurice Setters was now nationally recognised for his ferocious tackling while Bobby Robson was, at long last, beginning to win over his critics with a series of head-turning displays. Our full backs Don Howe and Stuart Williams were both current Internationals, which was an unusually classy pairing in the period. There was much to admire but some of my fellow supporters considered that five years without a trophy was unacceptable and took every opportunity to moan and groan as the mood took them.

One game and experience that stood out for me, and a coach load of Supporters Club members came just after Christmas. We'd enjoyed a 1-0 win at Leeds thanks to a Derek Kevan goal that had left us in high spirits.

The weather was cold, wet and windy with the possibility of snow on the horizon. Supporters Club Chairman Harold Whitehouse rarely missed a game and for him one tradition was sacred. He always sat in the front left-hand seat on every coach. There he could drink in the scenery and chat to the driver on a variety of subjects.

On the return journey with the weather noticeably deteriorating somehow a gust of wind blew out the left-hand side of the windscreen with a loud crash.

The driver pulled up to determine the extent of the damage. Today a replacement coach would be whistled up within the hour but this simply wasn't possible during this era. Either we found a way to carry on or there was a very long night ahead. Snow was already falling heavily. Both the driver and Harold were keen to press on, even without half the windscreen.

Everyone moved as far back as space allowed. Apart from Harold. There was no shifting him. He continued puffing away on his beloved pipe, as snow swept through the side of the coach, hat pulled down and coat buttoned up to the neck. Gradually, he turned into a snowman but didn't flinch and didn't complain. There was something very British and heroic about Harold that night.

Finally, we got back to the Hawthorns. As we filed off the coach shivering, Harold nonchalantly brushed off the snow. To the driver, he said "thank you, well done mate". To his fellow fans, there was the usual *"All the best, lads see you at our next game."* For Harold this was just another away day experience. What a character!

That triggered another away trip memory. Maddening at the time but looking back it's one for my 'Black Humour folder. On this Northern-bound trip, there was an unwanted hitch. The coach slowed down before the driver bought it to a grinding unexpected halt explaining *"engine failure. I'll have to phone for a replacement"*. Damn it.

No Harold to consult. So all we could do to kill time was to get off for a look around. There we were, sporting Baggies rosettes and scarves much to the amusement of the locals. Their sarcastic barbed comments on our plight? *"You support a crap team and travel in a crap coach."* Cleaned up version! Eventually a replacement ended our anguish. Why did the residents of this particular town think it was a great laff? For the simple reason we'd broken down in the centre of Wolverhampton. Supremely ironic or what?

There was no joy in the Cup either despite a promising start. We beat Sheffield Wednesday and Brentford before pulling the short straw with a trip to Blackpool in Round Five. We lost 3-1 – not totally unexpectedly against a team with an outstanding home record but defeat was painful nevertheless. We were out of the Cup again.  As usual, I needed that crumb of comfort.  The best I could find was from Harry Ditton writing in the News of the World who described *"an epic between two magnificent teams who provided 90 minutes of brilliant non-stop football played at breathtaking speed"*. I didn't take as much solace as I'd hoped. We were still out of the Cup.

The season's highlights came against those spoilers from Aston. Revenge! Villa had endured a wretched season.  At Villa Park, our 'keeper Clive Jackman made a neighbourly gesture by dropping a simple cross over the line.  I could hear a warning klaxon in my head *"Semi-Final again, Semi-Final again."*  But it wasn't. To quote the local reporter *"Albion cantered home easily"*. We scored 4 times without any further reply.  I was grinning for several days afterwards reliving every one of those goals.

That comprehensive thrashing of the old enemy was highly satisfying yet there was so much better to come. I believe that April 29th ought to be remembered each year with a minute's laughter from Baggies supporters and conversely a minute's silence from Villa fans!

That night saw the season's finale when either Villa or Manchester City would be relegated. The only way that the former Cup winners could be sure of retaining their top division status was to win at the Hawthorns. There were various hints planted in the local press that Albion would be good neighbours by not giving Villa a hard time in their hour of need. What! Steal our Cup Final place and we're going to take it easy on them? If anything, such an ill-considered suggestion made me even more determined to do my little bit to exact vengeance. I wasn't alone. On trains, trams or buses, inside and outside the ground, every Albion supporter seemed to feel the same way. *"They'm gotta goo down an' our lads ar gonna put 'em there"* was a common, albeit cleaned up, expression.

One might have hoped for decent weather in mid-spring but this was a miserable night. Teeming rain was made worse by driving wind, no fun at all for those on the open terracing.

With nerves soggily jangling, Albion were on top but fell behind to a shock Derek Pace goal. Such was the state of my emotions; I may have shouted a rude word. If I did, it was lost among all the others! How much more luck could the Villa enjoy? Were they lifetime members of the incredible Harry Houdini Appreciation Society? Was their dressing room awash with black cats and horseshoes? After this point, the match was basically played in the Villa half as the Baggies poured forward. It felt like St Andrews all over again though the circumstances were somewhat different. Few were aware that at Maine Road, Manchester City were racking up so many goals against Leicester that Villa were in real danger of losing their miniscule goal difference advantage, all that was keeping them out of the relegation places.

To be sure, Villa really needed to score again but there was little or no chance of that. Roared on by the massed Albion choirs on a "mission", the Baggies were threatening down the middle and on both flanks. Surely the goal had to come soon?

The desperately needed equaliser continued to elude; and then it happened. Ronnie Allen gathered the ball just inside the Villa penalty area with his back to goal. A typical swivel to lose his marker, a thunderbolt strike and the ball was in the Villa net. There was hysteria and pandemonium on the terraces from both sets of fans, for very different reasons. The 'old enemy' were heading towards Division Two, and how we rejoiced at their demise, albeit in the understated way of the period.

Both sets of supporters left the ground apparently chatting to each other as if the defeat was no more significant than any other game. But who was kidding whom? The words used reflected the occasion. *"Not good enough for the top Division any longer. What a shame."* Revenge! Revenge! Yet somehow it wasn't quite enough to bury my personal Semi-Final agony.

Later Ronnie confessed to a few of his closest friends that he hadn't wanted to score as the Villa manager was a good friend and he was sad to relegate a fellow Midlands club. Although we'd had numerous chats, I wasn't within his inner circle which is perhaps fortunate because I would have vehemently tried to change his opinion. But then that's the difference between players and supporters. For players, it's a job but for a fan, it's a way of life.

## 1959/60

After another nine months of often-brilliant football, the Baggies finished fourth again, this time behind the powerhouses of Burnley, Wolves and Spurs. Ultimately, a total of 12 defeats and only collecting one win in October prevented a higher finish. Many regulars were distinctly unimpressed at a mere fourth place. Picking out the common theme from their grumbles, it essentially boiled down to *"We're West Bromwich Albion and fourth isn't good enough".* The highlights were savoured to the full but, not for the first time, there weren't quite enough to satisfy everyone.

A change of manager meant a fond farewell to Vic Buckingham, apparently leaving for personal reasons. Perhaps that was true but rumours were circulating that he'd got into a major disagreement with someone 'high up' at the club and from which neither of them could see a way out. Buckingham hadn't been successful in bringing a full range of honours to the club but for that Wembley 1954 Cup Final win against Preston alone, he would never be forgotten. He'd also been responsible for introducing a brand of football that was universally admired. His assistant Gordon Clarke was promoted to the top job. Being Albion manager opened doors for Vic and he went to manage Ajax, Barcelona and Seville.

There was significant activity in the transfer market, as our defence sometimes resembled a colander. Out of the blue, Scotsman Jock Wallace was signed from Airdrie to replace Ray Potter. Jock was quite a personality but rather like a box of chocolates without a selection list, it was impossible to be sure which Jock Wallace we'd get each week. Sometimes, Jock played in such a determined manner I was convinced that the opposition wouldn't score even if all ten

Albion outfield players were sent off. *They shall not pass!* Then, there was the other Jock Wallace who resembled a 1950's Paul Crichton. The basics became difficult while the difficult was now impossible. It was only much later when I read that Jock had poor eyesight and became possibly the first goalkeeper obliged to wear contact lenses.

Around this time, I was part of a small group of supporters, mainly home and away fanatics, who formed our own Sunday League team. We called ourselves the *'Albion Nomads'* and naturally we would play in blue and white stripes. Home matches to be played on Selly Park Rec or Sennellys Park at Weoley Castle, whichever was less muddy at the time. If it was Sennellys Park (notorious for its muddy pitches) a spade would have been a very useful addition to a pair of well worn, traditional boots

The chosen few included, in goal Micky Wortley who was not only brave and fearless but also so versatile if needed, he could play outfield. Other regulars included Geoff May, Johnny Charlton, Barry Broome, Alan Brettell, Bobby Gee, Geoff May, Geoff Evans and one Tony Matthews. Tony played up front, and for me, was our best player by far. My position, for some unknown reason, was left half (midfield) despite the fact that my left foot was purely for standing on.

Feeling we needed specialist coaching, I wrote to the Sports Argus, asking if someone with qualifications would help us on a weekly basis. An immediate response came from none other than Jock Wallace who volunteered to supervise our weekly training sessions in our hired gymnasium at Handsworth Technical College. What had we let ourselves in for?

Jock was a true taskmaster. In a broad Scottish brogue, he roared out instructions and woe betides anyone who stepped out of line. We practised ball skills in five a side games, and if anyone was foolish enough to kick the ball above knee height, they soon regretted it. The penalty was immediate, as Jock would bark out *"Five press-ups and if you do it again, I'll double them"*. Well, as none of us were that good, we seemed to be regularly doing more press-ups than training!

Jock was such a character. He lived in Handsworth at the time and used to travel everywhere by bus as he hated driving. He wasn't really keen on buses either and had cast envious looks at Tony Matthews' Lambretta.

Tony Matthews remembers the time he almost missed his bus after one coaching session. Jock was already on the bus when he saw Tony running full tilt in his attempt to board the bus before it pulled away. Spotting him, Jock hung on to the passenger rail, grabbed his hand and lifted him on to the platform. It was an impressive display of his upper body strength.

Jock was a man of few words, so despite my weekly personal access, I knew little about him. Oh, he'd talk to us occasionally at the Players entrance, when his first words were always "*I hope you remember what I told you. Pass the ball above knee height, and you'll know what to expect next week.*" I often wondered whether his experiences serving his country in the bitter conflict in Malaya left him less able to express himself openly. It wasn't a question I felt comfortable asking.

His managerial style was *"do it my way or you'll suffer for it"* but that was common at the time. All of the Nomads had endured National Service so we grinned and bore it. We learnt a bit through 'fear' and the need to follow orders and therefore became a better side.

What I didn't know at the time was Jock was a genuine fitness fanatic. The players were regularly required to run up and down the terraces from top to bottom, normally at the Smethwick End. The goalkeeper pounded up and down all the terrace steps while the rest of the squad had only reached halfway up. This didn't always endear him to his team mates as the coach would invariably use Wallace's fitness for leverage. *"That's a goalkeeper beating you, lads and he doesn't need to do any running during games. You're not fit enough, do it again and faster."* Or similar words to that effect.

After a morning's training, Jock was one of only a few players who returned for another session in the afternoon. He generally roped in fellow enthusiasts like Derek Kevan who was always keen to improve and Alec Jackson. Jock loved showing off, diving and saving shots, collecting crosses…. he just loved his football.

Loving football, being a fitness fanatic and already working at Handsworth Technical College collectively explained why Jock was willing to help the Nomads improve. His links with the Technical College started after the Scot had enquired about taking a PE course. The registrar, quickly deciding there was little a college could teach a professional athlete, nimbly asked Jock if he would run PE sessions for them. Hence Jock was already on site for the Nomad training sessions.

The first big win of the season came against Leicester, thrashed 5-0 at the Hawthorns. Luton, Arsenal and Preston all conceded four while Everton found 'The Tank' in unstoppable form as he became the first Baggie I'd seen score five goals in a 6-2 single-handed demolition job. Other highlights included a 4-1victory at Elland Road but best of all was the now regular St Andrews massacre. After we've won 6-0 and 5-3 in the previous two seasons, I was most confident of another away win.

*"It's going to be different this time. We won't concede five or six"* I was assured by one Blues optimist in the city centre prior to kick-off. He was right. It was different -Blues conceded even more than usual. Ronnie Allen and Derek Kevan scored a hat-trick *each* as WBA won 7-1. Among much merriment among the travelling hordes, Birmingham City had to kick-off 8 times. Blues 'keeper, Johnny Schofield, found Baggies fans were definitely enjoying the occasion.

*"Have you been practicing kick offs all week?"*

*"Hey Schofield, you'll need treatment for backache. Bending to pick the ball out of the net so often must be painful"* plus others I can't repeat.

Although Schofield had been the butt of Baggies fans jibes, Jock Wallace found himself on the receiving end of angry taunts when, with Albion 5-1 ahead, he rushed out of his area at the Railway End, whacked the ball into the crowd and sent a young Blues supporter flying. The crowd predictably booed but at the final whistle, he went over to the lad, apologised, picked him up and handed him his gloves. It was hard to imagine what more he could do to make amends but he was still manhandled by a number of Birmingham City supporters.

The difference in quality between the sides was clear. Albion had the finishing power and the determination. City lacked the first two qualities and their morale cracked after 'The Tank' scored his first. In three visits to Small Heath, we'd scored 18 times. It is hard to imagine such a sequence ever being repeated.

There was some relief for City in the return match the following day as they held on for a 1-1 draw. Not that they deserved the point, it was only the brilliance of their keeper Johnny Schofield, fully recovered from his backache that prevented yet another rout. With the games taking place at Easter, certain newspapers couldn't resist slightly tasteless references to City being crucified then rising from the dead.

Twelve years later, Jock Wallace was coaching Rangers (Willie Johnston and all) towards winning the European Cup Winners Cup. Three years later, now as manager, he led Rangers to a treble. His punitive style and pre-Ferguson hairdryer treatment remained his prime motivational tactics. Interesting to ponder whether his comparative success with the Nomads convinced Jock that "old school" was the only way to go. Had I and my team-mates resisted his methods strongly, might Jock have had a re-think? I'll never know but I wouldn't put money on it.

Seeking a replacement coach, I took a chance and wrote to another Albion player. We felt that in some way we already knew him personally. He was always happy to stop and chat when we met up outside grounds all over the country. Before one game, I tentatively asked *"Is there any chance you could help us out with a spot of coaching?* He not only agreed, he even bought his young son with him and joined us when Robin Cairns, another dedicated Baggie, invited everyone back to his house for afternoon tea after a match.

Our new coach – one Bobby Robson - made an immediate impact. He watched in astonishment as we followed our usual routine of charging out of our wobbly, freezing changing room at warp speed before launching into a full-on warm-up, even though the opposition hadn't arrived. He called us together and asked, *"What do you think you're doing? Why wear yourself out long before the kick-off? Take it easy - limber up and no more. Even professionals wouldn't run around like you're doing. The way you're going, you'll be playing the equivalent of three halves rather than just two".* Simple common sense yet this had passed us by.

This was the first step in what was a whole series of exercises, hints and tips, which our diligent new coach shared with us. Our timing was quite fortunate as Bobby had attended a coaching course at Lilleshall and it suited him to have an opportunity to practise his newly acquired skills. Training became almost exciting as we were genuinely learning all the time. We 'Nomads' went on to win a Cup Final, delighting both him and us in the process. Bobby's gentle, thoughtful training style was a shock at first. We were used to being told what to do but now we were asked to think for ourselves and question our own performance. This was radical stuff for the professionals, never mind rank amateurs.

I remember once asking why after receiving the ball and attempting to pass it, I was regularly dispossessed? Bobby had the answer *"Because you invariably turn left and the opposition know what you're likely to do. Try to drop your shoulders one way but move the ball in the opposite direction."* Now why didn't I think of that?

Not everyone could adapt, notably any new arrivals who invariably would ask a variant of *"When is he going to tell us what to do?"* before the first training session was done

England's eventual World Cup manager was generous with his time and knowledge. He enjoyed our League and cup success so much so that he agreed to become President of Albion Nomads until 1962 (though I'd retired long before then). For Bobby, it was football without pressure. Yes, he wanted the Nomads to win but nobody's livelihood depended on the outcome. However that wasn't entirely the end of his time and application with local football. Inspired by his enthusiasm, the West Bromwich based-players continued under the name of Tantany Rovers who in true Albion supporters' tradition, later persuaded Clive Clark to become their trainer/coach. Eventually, as is the fate of so many amateur teams, we disbanded, but in the process not forgetting to thank Bobby for his help in giving us a footballing experience to remember.

There was a sequel. Forty-four years later, my ever demanding publisher Simon Wright nominated me for the Sunday Mercury' Football Fan of the Season Award, throwing in as evidence some of the anecdotes I've already mentioned. Reader, I won that award. I suspect it was as much to do with the newsworthy story about Bobby Robson rather than my own supporting credentials. Robson launching his career with the modest "Nomads" also made the pages of the Newcastle United programme. Even now, I felt so privileged to have known him in his younger days. Bobby wasn't always old with grey or white hair but he was always a gentleman. He was inevitably smart and elegant and wouldn't have looked out of place on a male model catwalk, especially in his official Albion club blazer and tie

When Bobby first started his first ever-coaching job, the reaction of the opposition teams was both fascinating yet predictable, before word got around. There would be the pointing, the nodding, the head-scratching and finally the questions - always the same ones. Firstly, they'd want to know how we got Bobby as our coach, then *"What's he like?"* followed by *"Is he any good?"* Sometimes, I'd pre-empt the questions. *"Can I introduce you to Bobby? He's our coach. He's making something of a name for himself these days. He does a bit for England when he's not looking after us."* All said with a straight face. It was fascinating to see the looks on the opposition faces and I fancied I could see their jaws dropping. Bobby Robson played along with his quiet smile.

Bobby had no airs or graces. He was simply one of the lads. If Baggies fans spotted him, he'd happily chat about football in general or Albion in particular. I remember once at Dudley Port station when a small know of supporters were joined by the Albion team after they arrived in two mini buses.

Bobby Robson sported a bright red waistcoat leading to one bolder supporter piping up" *Sunset over Dudley Port, aye Bobby".* The Nomads coach loved the comment and was quickly posing for photographs, signing autographs and chatting merrily until the train chugged its way into the station.

Bobby played a minor role in one other well-remembered fixture that season at Highbury. Bobby scored one of the four goals in an impressive 4-2 win. There's something always pleasing about securing victory at one of the big London grounds. Partly as it keeps raucous Londoners quiet and also, being the capital, there are so many ways to celebrate. This time, my little band decided to take in our first ever ice Hockey match between Haringey Racers and Wembley Lions. At the time, ice hockey in London was booming. It was certainly fast-paced and with the rules similar enough to the Beautiful Game, the match gave me great entertainment. There was literally a price to pay. We got the tube to Euston and then the last mail train out of London. It arrived in Snow Hill; just minutes after our 2.00am buses had departed. Wait another hour or walk? Buying a drink and chatting with the mobile café owner won.

Albion making another visit to Wembley seemed further away than ever as we went out in the Fifth Round. Leicester City shattered our dream even though. Joe Kennedy scored his one and only FA Cup goal for us. The referee, Jack Husband, suffered a heart attack in the dressing room at half time to be replaced by a linesman, with a club official taking over the flag. It was only after the game that news broke that Husband had died on his way to hospital. This certainly put my feelings into perspective.

But I still went to the Twin Towers in May, this time courtesy of Wolverhampton Wanderers! This was due to Wolves' decision that anyone who'd attended any of their high-profile friendlies could apply for a ticket via a ballot. You simply forwarded your stub and hoped to be lucky in the draw. I was lucky, though 80% of the applicants were not. For all the obvious injustice of the system, I wasn't about to pass up the chance to see another Final so while Molineux obsessives seethed at home, I was off to Wembley. I did enjoy the very hot day as the Wanderers easily beat Blackburn Rovers 3-0, their chances helped immensely by Rovers' Dave Whelan being carried off the pitch.

As prime exponents of the long ball, physically dominating teams was Wolverhampton's forte (though thankfully not breaking legs). But royal entertainment was expected at Wembley. Not that we saw much. Both Wolves and the referee were being booed long before the end. When the victors headed for the tunnel, both they and the referee were pelted with orange peel, apple cores and any other rubbish to hand. The official was the main target because of his perceived leniency but any target would do. According to the national press, this was the "Dustbin Final." It was just another game to me.

With not much at stake for Albion's final League game v Arsenal, two youngsters had a chance to show off their skill, 17 year old Geoff Carter and the even younger Bobby Hope. Neither of them looked out of place and I was so pleased to see the club trying to develop their own talent. Even though Carter only went on to play 20 or so WBA games, the Birmingham Post reporter was otherwise sagacious with his words *"On Saturday's showing, both will make the grade, and it will be surprising if Hope, a natural with a sound knowledge of the games basic principles, does not reach international standard early in his career. On what to them was a great day, the lads performed easily and with commendable modesty".*

**The remarkable "Swinging Sixties"**

If ever time travel becomes realistic for Albion followers, I'd commend the 1960's to them. Apart from events on the field, there are so many other experiences and sights to admire such as flower power, the Stones, the Beatles, Minis and mini-skirts, Cassius Clay, Henry Cooper and Coronation Street.

Not so positive were the Berlin Wall, the Cold War, the Vietnam War, the Great Train Robbery and match fixing. The opening of the decade saw the ending of football's ridiculous maximum wage. From that point onwards, riches became increasingly concentrated at the top end of the game.

My own contribution to Sixties culture was actually fairly minimal. Granted, I bought a ridiculous number of 78rpm records, those heavyweight predecessors to the later 33rpm lpees, which broke all too easily. I also had tastes in shirts that, shall I say, matched the fashion of the time. I even remember buying a bright red dazzler that Bobby Robson would have been proud to call his own!

I also became a serious Animal Welfare campaigner, protesting against cruelty and ill treatment worldwide. Not just domestic animals, but also seals and whales and indeed all endangered species. I took the opportunity to become the Honorary Secretary of two organisations (primarily in the absence of anyone else volunteering) for years of hard work, albeit rewarding work. One of the organisations later presented Dot and I with a beautiful Old English sheepdog puppy that became the official mascot of the 'The Birmingham Branch of the Animal Welfare Trust'. We named her 'Holly', and what a treat laid in store for her a few years down the line.

## 1960/61

The start of the never- to-be-forgotten decade and how! The new season would kick off on August 20th with Albion at Hillsborough. . However for me, the start of the season took second place to another date a fortnight earlier. Dot and I tied the knot. As she lived just down the road from Villa Park, no prizes for guessing our wedding was staged in close proximity to the home of the Claret and Blues

The sun shone and after enjoying the ceremony and the reception complete with good wishes and telegrams at the now long demolished West End cinema, we were off on honeymoon. We were not heading anywhere exotic- simply to tiny, leafy Wootton Wawen, which is a short distance from Stratford upon Avon.

Here we'd live in a caravan for 4 years. Why Wootton Wawen and why set up home in a modest 28-foot long caravan? Pure economics! We hadn't sufficient income to afford a house. However, we both worked at Shirley, which is a relatively short distance from Wootton, and it was easy to travel from one to the other even with a limited public transport service,

Let me describe our caravan. There was a through lounge which incorporated a pull down bed, a kitchen, a bathroom (in name only) and an end bedroom that wouldn't have looked out of place in a large Dolls house! But the main consideration was that it was affordable and a realistic distance from the Hawthorns.

Marriage was the start of a new adventure that was far more enjoyable than Albion's season. The first five matches were lost including two morale-sapping defeats by, of all teams, the 'Blues' from St Andrews. That certainly wasn't in the script - was the world about to end? Our new home bought my cricketing career to an end because of travel difficulties but maybe that was no bad thing as my infamous lack of skill with the bat led to an embarrassing moment.

My team were set just over 100 to win which looked a modest figure with our Captain in such fine form. Unfortunately, no one could stick with him for long. I was last man to the crease with our Captain on 49 and just two runs needed to win. He gave me words of wisdom *"I'm facing the bowling, don't do anything stupid and I'll get the runs"* He didn't, because as he played the ball into the covers for what he felt was at least one run, a fielder swooped on the ball and hurled it to the wicketkeeper.

Confidently he bawled at me, *"come on, come on"* and started running. I didn't and consequently managed to run him out! He finished on 49 and we'd lost by two runs. No prizes for guessing what he 'politely' said to me as we left the field! After such a mishap, I needed something positive to focus on at the Hawthorns.

The season rapidly went downhill with only occasional bursts of excitement such as a 6-0 demolition of Newcastle and a 6-3 defeat of Manchester City. The expected Cup run failed to materialise due to an appalling defensive display at Lincoln. Second Division City cruised to a comfortable 3-1 win, even though they'd not won a Cup match for several years. It was hard to say which teams' supporters were more shocked. Albion results had to improve and mercifully they did. A blistering sequence of nine wins from the final eleven matches enabled the revitalised Baggies to finish tenth.

The last game was away to the recently crowned League Champions Tottenham Hotspur, described as being 'the team of all the talents' and 'the finest Spurs team ever'. A fruitless journey on paper but matches aren't played on paper and in a truly enthralling display, the Baggies spoilt the party by winning 2-1. Goals from Derek Kevan and Nomads Bobby Robson left even the Spurs hierarchy admitting Albion had been by far the better team. Their Spurs side was so clearly fatigued by a heavy fixture list; it looked as though they'd strolled through recent away games. Clive Clark in particular had left a succession of bewildered defenders trailing in his wake. With his socks rolled down and his confidence high, he terrorised whoever had the unenviable job of marking him. Signing 'Chippy' from Queens Park Rangers had been a masterstroke though it was only with hindsight and later Cup runs that I could fully understand how vital his signing really was. Oh yes, hindsight. The Baggies had a chance to sign Denis Law from Huddersfield that season but Gordon Clark wasn't sure. Now there's a classic "What If" to ponder on!

After 20 years of support, I finally bought my first season ticket. I'd not previously joined the ranks of "official supporters" before partly due to cost but mainly because I really didn't need one. I continued to arrive early before the rush and virtually no away matches were all-ticket. £3 bought me what was then called a Ground Season Ticket (essentially a terrace season ticket). I took simple pleasure in no longer having to pay at the Hawthorns turnstiles each time.

For me, even the best part of the season was meagre compensation against seeing the last appearances in Albion colours of two truly outstanding players. Joe Kennedy was almost the last survivor of the 1949 promotion team and in a bizarre way; I felt I'd grown up alongside "Spring Heeled Joe". Kennedy was in his mid-thirties and had lost his place so his release wasn't a shock but the news still stopped me in my tracks.

The departure of Ronnie Allen hurt even more. Joe Kennedy was an outstanding defender though notoriously was a man of few words so I didn't get to know him. Ronnie, by contrast, was always content to pass the time of day with supporters. I so admired that dapper man who had 276 League goals to his name. His last appearance, thankfully at the Hawthorns, saw Bolton trooping back home on the back of a 3-2 defeat and fittingly he poached the winning goal. Ronnie "walked on water" for me and I doubt I'll ever see his like again. .

Remember Stan Rickaby's newspaper claims about being a Soccer Slave? Ever since then, the PFA had battled with the Football League over pay and contracts for their members. No other profession endured such restrictions. The PFA realised they needed a legal test case to query the League's position and so backed George Eastham who wanted to move from Newcastle to Arsenal. The League lost. Out went the restrictive contracts and so too the maximum wage, which was officially £20. The Eastham saga made headlines for weeks. There were accusations that other clubs were willing to pay Eastham above the maximum wage. This was hardly a shock as discreet additional payments in cash or left in players' boots were notorious throughout the game. I did wonder whether WBA were one of those clubs pursuing Eastham and so during one away trip, I asked Chairman Wilson Keys

"Have *Albion made an approach to Newcastle or George Eastham?"*

Keys response was predictable. *"West Bromwich Albion isn't a club willing to breach laid down regulations even though others may be prepared to do so."*

Everyone waited to see how the court decisions would affect the game. They didn't have long to wait as Fulham announced that their English international Johnny Haynes was now the first £100 per week player. The football world was shocked and astounded. Yes, they were entitled to a living wage. But £100 a week! The press made many comparisons between his earnings and those of other workers (the average wage was about £15 per week). Elsewhere, the change was far less significant initially but of course the richer clubs could afford to pay more and the best talent could now follow the money.

## 1961/62

Another season, another poor start. We lost five of the first seven games so after that sad sequence; we were firefighting just for respectability. Back to back wins against Arsenal 4-0, and another win (a mere 2-1 but beggars can't be choosers) at St Andrews, steadied the ship but a disappointing ninth position was as much as could have been expected.

My personal highlights came late in the season during Easter visits to Spurs on Saturday and Fulham on Easter Monday. It made sense not to make two separate journeys so together with Tony, Alan and two others, we all booked into a Bed and Breakfast establishment. Before heading to North London and our first game, we savoured the pageantry of the trooping of the colour. Privately, I felt this was the calm before the storm. Playing the Double winners Tottenham "the team of the century" on their own turf felt a terribly uphill task. But West Bromwich Albion dominated from start to finish. Derek Kevan scored both in our well-merited 2-1 victory. I was high on adrenalin all night after that.

On Sunday, we overdosed on the famous sights of London – Piccadilly Circus, the Mall, Petticoat Lane and so on, never missing a chance to point out that we supported a pretty famous football club ourselves.

One day later, we travelled to Craven Cottage to savour another away win. Who can ask for more? I did. Rather greedily, I hoped for another win over the Cottagers in the return match on Easter Tuesday. And I got it.

Having previously beaten relegated Chelsea 4-0 prior to our Easter tour; the Baggies had completed four consecutive victories against capital opposition. 1962 was a full decade ahead of James Alexander Gordon on the radio but just imagine his intonation.

(Solemn) *"London Clubs 0 (pause/ raise tone) West Bromwich Albion 4."*

Just to round off the season perfectly, mid-table Blackpool were hammered 7-1 at the Hawthorns. Derek Kevan scored four but it was so satisfying to see the Nomads coach also find the net. But a season is more than one glorious month and overall there were a number of dramas.

Just days after a club statement in August that manager Gordon Clark was definitely not leaving the club to join Vic Buckingham at Sheffield Wednesday, off he went to Hillsborough. Some aspects of football don't change.

His replacement, Archie Macaulay came to us from Norwich, where he'd made his name taking the Third Division Canaries to a FA Cup Semi-Final. His first job was to fend off a string of transfer requests from unhappy players, now able to exercise their right to take their labour elsewhere. Macaulay gave the initial appearance of being a dour man of few words. Hardly inspiring and as time and events were to prove, I think my first impressions were correct.

The season jogged on in unspectacular fashion but another cup run did look on the cards after Blackpool had been despatched after a replay. It's always satisfying to beat the Wolves, any time, any place, but in the cup and at Molineux? Sheer Magic!

Initially, when the draw was made the press made great play that as it bought together 'the old enemies' anything could, and probably would happen. A Birmingham Post headline suggested that Wolves could spring a surprise. They didn't thanks to two splendidly taken goals from Clive Clark, and Jock Wallace's return to something like his best form. This was a big relief as his recent displays had left him open to criticism from many supporters and more than a few "jokes". Knowing him as I did and realising he'd given everything for the Baggies, this felt personally quite painful.

At the final whistle, skipper Bobby Robson sprinted 20 yards to pump the keepers hand and thump him on the back in a well-done gesture. Yes, a very satisfying victory and a headline to store away in the memory box. *"West Bromwich triumph in a glorious battle"*. A photograph of the delighted team celebrating in the team bath featured prominently in newspapers. I wish I could have joined them.

The luck of the draw is vital in the FA Cup and ours was right out in the Fifth Round. We were paired with the mighty Spurs, at the Hawthorns admittedly, but Tottenham were the current Cup holders and League Champions, then an awe-inspiring achievement. When I heard the draw, my reaction was subdued..."Was my dream of a Wembley Final over before we'd kicked off? Yes, we'd beaten them the previous season in a League game but this was the Cup.

Nevertheless, I had to be optimistic and along with the rest of the 54,000 crowd I savoured the sense of occasion. It was reminiscent of "the old days" but sadly the outcome was predictable. Spurs ran out 4-2 winners and went on to retain the FA Cup themselves.

For me, the highlight of the season was 'The Tank'. His 33 goals made him joint top goal scorer in the First Division, alongside Ray Crawford of title-winning Ipswich, and featured ten goals in the Baggies' last five games. We won all five which was a satisfying way of finishing albeit in mid-table. Among those 33, my personal favourite came at Molineux in a 5-1 slaughter of the not so innocent. He stormed in to meet a left wing cross at full tilt and hit the ball with such power; it was hard to believe it was a header and not a shot. Instinctively, I was trying to both celebrate and rub my eyes. *"Did I really see that right?"* To this day, it remains the fiercest header I have ever seen. To propel a heavy leather ball with such velocity could easily have injured mere mortals. I still wonder what such mighty crashing headers cost the Big Man later in his life.

Has anyone ever been promised a lift to an away game, only for the arrangements to go awry? This happened to me and half a dozen other Baggies diehards as we stood waiting outside Birmingham's Hall of Memory. Our midweek destination was Cardiff's Ninian Park.

Normally, we'd have no hesitation in travelling by rail but on this occasion we were initially let down by a minibus driver who'd agreed to provide the transport on behalf of a friend, Peter Kay from Wednesbury. He was due to arrive at 4pm. At that time, he was nowhere to be seen. Where was he? Several increasingly concerned phone calls were made and he eventually arrived around 5 o'clock. Scrambling inside, we belted down crowded 'A' roads at frankly foolish speeds. I have no idea how he got us there with ten minutes to spare but guilt was surely a factor. Was it worth it? A point from a 2-2 draw enabled us to return home at a more leisurely pace while I celebrated lavishly with two of my favourite cheese and onion sandwiches.

The 1962 World Cup was staged in Chile. This was a curious choice as the country had no football tradition and no suitable stadia. Having just endured an earthquake, Chile played the emotion card to hang onto their big event even though logic suggested that another country should step in. In the end, Chile made a decent fist of the event, building two new stadiums (two were ample in those days!) and managed to reach the Semi-Final themselves before being beaten the eventual winners Brazil, who'd already defeated England in the Quarter-Final.

## 1962/63

This was a season of bitter, no very bitter, disappointment. For once, the headlines were not about the team but instead focussed on decisions made by the manager and the board. The discontent, and eventual calamities, started even before a ball had been kicked. David Burnside was in dispute over personal terms and relations between Macaulay and his players were rumoured to be on a knife-edge

Bobby Robson, who'd just become a Dad for the second time asked for a wage increase to bring him in line with fellow international players at other clubs. Fulham, his former club, had tabled a £20,000 bid. Bobby was absolutely clear he wanted to stay. He told the press, the football magazines, the Nomad regulars, indeed, anyone who would listen. *"I don't want to leave the Albion. I have had six happy years here and made a lot of friends. I want to stay at the club."* But equally he felt he deserved more money.

Macaulay and/or the board called his bluff by refusing a pay rise so Robson left for Fulham. To add insult to injury, Fulham got their star man back for £5,000 less than the figure they sold him for six years earlier. During that time, Robson had grown into one of the best players in the country. The London club didn't argue about wages, offering Robson double his Albion income. The Cottagers couldn't believe their luck while I couldn't believe my ears! There was universal dismay among supporters leading to a barrage of criticism in the local press. For the period, this was as strong as protests ever became. Football supporters as passive consumers remained the norm although probably coming to an end. Boards were generally still trusted to "do the right thing" and after all, with the exception of Accrington, no club had gone out of business. Rallying supporters was very difficult as even a home telephone was still a luxury (indeed, direct dialling, as opposed to asking an operator to connect a call for you, had only just arrived). Concerted terrace singing was still a novelty.

Next to leave the stage was Stuart Williams, Albion's most capped international, off to Southampton. Again, there were loud complaints and another volley of letters to the Sports Argus and more stay-aways. Gates were dropping sharply. The dreadful winter contributed but even so, average gates had dropped by 10% every year for 4 years to 18,500, the lowest since the war. With turnstile revenue making up the lion's share of club income, the Board were under pressure.

The season that would always be linked to the "Big Freeze" started inconspicuously. This was hardly surprising considering the background turmoil. We did the double over rookies Leyton Orient (though many others did the same) but otherwise were not that impressive. 1962-63 only came alive after Kevan had slammed four goals in a 6-1 battering of Fulham. A fortnight later, another hat trick in a seesaw match against Bolton finished 5-4 in Albion's favour. The `Tank' at his rampaging best continued to bang in the goals thankfully as there was little else to enthuse about.

The weather played a major part in prolonging the season until mid-May. Several weeks passed in continual sub-zero temperatures and every aspect of life came second behind trying to keep warm. Dot and I learnt the hard way that there was another side to caravan living.

We didn't have the luxury of running water. We had to queue at the nearest standpipe to get water to manually fill our water tank. Apart from that horror, we also had the joy of relying on Calor gas for heating and cooking. I'm convinced those wretched blue bottles were somehow pre-programmed to run out at the most inconvenient time possible. If that wasn't enough, we regularly got home from work to discover that our water tank had frozen. Let's say caravan living was "character building". I didn't find it impossible. I'd endured the War, National Service and years of rationing so hard living wasn't exactly a new experience.

Against this grim background came the draw for the Third Round of the FA Cup. I desperately wanted a home tie, for obvious reasons, but to hear Albion would have to travel to Second Division Plymouth was a major blow. This was a tedious trip at any time but during the winter of '63?

My little gang would travel by train, along with 90% of all the Albion support. Or rather that was the plan until Friday night. With Dot and I huddled together for warmth almost on top of our modest heating came the radio news that British Rail had cancelled all the scheduled excursion trains. Instant panic! What could I do? Then I remembered that the Oldbury Branch of the Albion Supporters Club had booked two coaches for the long, long, ride to the 'end of the world'. Was there a chance even now, there might be a spare seat? I hastened out to the nearest telephone box. I optimistically made my 'pleading' call to find that there was a single seat available. Using best football logic, I considered it was definitely my lucky night.

A midnight departure from West Bromwich High Street just added to the drama or so I told myself. A quick cheerio to Dot before I headed out for the first stage of what turned out as an unforgettable journey. I was fortunate to catch a bus out of Wootton into Birmingham as they only ran every two hours. Then I took another bus over to West Bromwich to board the "midnight special".

This was Newcastle all over again. The appalling weather wasn't in the mood to ease off as we uneasily trundled South in the dark. Twice we slid off the road and it was up to us gallant 40, wielding a few shovels and heaving against savagely cold metal in the night time blackness to ensure the coach carried on to Devon

. It is perhaps only with hindsight that I can fully appreciate the determination of our drivers to battle on when everything was against them. No driver safety aids, no motorways, no knowing what was around the corner, but still they persisted just to get people to a football match. Many car drivers quickly gave up and turned for home.

Ten hours later, our vehicle finally lumbered into Plymouth though everyone was too weary to cheer. Once slid into the Home Park car park, we quickly learnt to our consternation that our efforts could be in vain. The referee was concerned about the patches of ice on Home Park even though volunteers had been working on the surface throughout the night. The referee gave Argyle three hours to make the pitch playable after which he'd inspect again. The Devon club didn't need any more extra labour so we weary coach travellers entertained ourselves as best we could. I mooched miserably up and down Plymouth Hoe. The snow and ice on the coast made for extraordinary photographs but in my extreme weariness, I couldn't appreciate the natural beauty. All I wanted was to hear the game could go ahead so that our journey hadn't been in vain.

Mercifully, the ref gave the pitch the thumbs up. This was such a massive relief for me and also for the largely volunteer workforce who'd literally spent days and nights battling the elements on the pitch. Argyle desperately wanted their big game on.

Somebody was going to be disappointed at the final whistle and thankfully it was the Baggies who would be in the Fourth Round draw. Plymouth hung on grimly but once their main striker was carried off with a broken leg, they collapsed to a 1-5 defeat thanks to goals from Derek Kevan (2), Keith Smith, Bobby Cram and an own goal. I was almost as relieved as I was pleased and shivering. The route home was long, dark and tortuous so I badly wanted that small, warning beacon of success inside me.

In the Fourth Round, mercifully we pulled out a home tie against Nottingham Forest. But there was no chance of playing on the original January date. Or any date in February either. The snow and ice held the country firmly in its grip for 6 football-less weeks and everybody was weary of tramping everywhere in such miserable, unrelenting conditions. With delicious irony, Cliff Richard was top of the charts with *"We're all going on a summer holiday..."* Well he might have been but the rest of us had to battle on in our personal Siberia. For months, the only goals that the Baggies had scored in 1963 were in Devon and I'd seen them all, as I regularly reminded my football-starved pals.

Our Cup opponents Nottingham Forest had ample time to devise a strategy to stop Albion playing and that's exactly what they did on a cold March night. Albion's attack was suffocated in what turned out to a very dull (and drawn) Cup match. One reporter summed up the evening: *"Nottingham Forest bored the soccer starved fans of the Hawthorns with a successful but depressing show to hold earnest but so muddled Albion last night."* That was depressing but as if to prove we could still score goals, Ipswich

Town were the next visitors and returned home on the back of 6-1 hammering thanks in the main to a hat-trick from 'The Tank'

Onto the Cup replay in Nottingham and a miserable display, in a 2-1 extra time knockout that left fans who'd endured the nightmare of our Plymouth adventure, pondering whether the time and the effort was worthwhile Of course it was. You live for the moment in the Cup. Anyway, there was now a far bigger concern for the Hawthorns regulars.

Derek Kevan made his last appearance in an Albion shirt. Even now, after all these years, I still find it impossible to believe Albion decided to sell Derek Kevan, one of their greatest goal scorers. For weeks, there had been rumours that he was wanted by several clubs, and despite the player being happy at the Hawthorns, the board announced they'd received a £45,000 offer from Chelsea. Surely the board and manager couldn't go for the money again as with Bobby Robson? They could, and they did.

Within days, Archie Macaulay released a verbose statement. *"Both of us feel most concerned about the situation that has been created by press reports about Kevan associating his name with other clubs. I have given Derek every assurance that not one of these reports emanated from Albion. These have all come from outside sources and I feel most concerned. Such things are doing Albion and other clubs irreparable harm. All they are doing is upsetting players and team spirit. Derek is most concerned. He knows he hasn't played well this year and he feels his colleagues have lost a wee bit of confidence in him. He is concerned in case they feel he is disloyal to them and the club, because of the reports. I have had a good friendly talk with Derek. He has been open with me. I feel very unhappy about the situation but we have agreed that in the circumstances if someone came along and enabled him to make a move which would be satisfactory to him."*

Now read these words again. Who said spin Doctors are a modern invention? Let me rephrase these words. *"All this terrible speculation is nothing to do with Albion but our star player still feels guilty. Rather than reassure him, we have decided that his only scoring one goal every two matches this season isn't good enough and we're going to sell him anyway."* I wonder why they didn't use this version.

`The Tank' was one of the top goal scorers in the country, an England international and was an ever-present. He was always willing to meet and chat with supporters either at the training ground, on trains or at a player's entrance. One day at Spring Road, I took along one of my many Albion scrapbooks. In a flash he asked, *"Can I borrow them to read at home?"* Naturally I agreed, never realising it would be many months before I could collect them back from the Hawthorns! I didn't have the chance at the time to ask Derek for his thoughts but I did 40 years later when I interviewed him for the 'Grorty Dick' fanzine.

*"I had to get away because of Macaulay's attitude"* Kevan explained to me in his Castle Vale flat.*" He felt I was one of the oldest players (although several others were even older). When I went in to see the directors, they said: "We've had a bid come in for you." I was struck rigid and I didn't know what to say or what to think. They said, "Would you like to talk to Chelsea?" It came out of the blue as there hadn't been any rumours but as I obviously wasn't wanted, I went, and that was the biggest mistake of my life"*

Supporters were up in arms and Archie Macaulay faced even more embarrassment the day after the transfer. A demoralised Albion and their equally demoralised supporters were hammered 7-0 at Molineux with Kevan looking on bemused in the stand. This fixture was rearranged as the original match was abandoned after 20 minutes with Wolves two goals ahead. As the referee put it *"things were becoming farcical and dangerous for the players- the falling snow made it very difficult to follow the ball and see the pitch markings."* I thought we'd got away with it. How wrong could I be?

Archie Macaulay's 'popularity' then sank even lower, if possible, after he recruited two players supposedly to replace Derek Kevan. Enter Ronnie Fenton, a reserve player from Burnley, followed by the `capture' of Max Murray from Glasgow Rangers. Fenton turned out to be a 'job lot' player, hardworking and a battler, but as a potential replacement for the `Tank', who was kidding who?

I'm convinced that Murray is probably Albion's worst buy of all time. A complete and utter disaster who only played three games for WBA before moving on to Third Lanark. Ironically when Macaulay clinched his transfer, he offered a classic comment that *"Murray can be another Ronnie Allen. I am confident he will do the job for us".* On paper, Maxwell Murray, to give him his full name, had pedigree with 80 goals in just over 100 games for Rangers. How he managed this, I couldn't begin to imagine, but he had obviously convinced Mr Macaulay. He turned out to be more chum than pedigree at the Hawthorns.

Archie Macaulay's reign came to an inevitable end just two weeks after the Molineux debacle. He resigned claiming he couldn't settle at the Hawthorns. For me and the vast majority of fans, resignation was no more than a face-saving exercise. He later became a traffic warden, which probably suited his skills rather more. The press had a field day, accusing the club of refusing to pay decent wages to attract top players, in essence blaming them for Macaulay's lack of success.

Shortly afterwards, Chairman Major H. Wilson Keys also stood down so it was the new Chairman Jim Gaunt who appointed Macaulay's replacement in Jimmy Hagan. The incomer had made his name as an outstanding player at Sheffield United. As a manager, he'd led Peterborough into the Football League followed by an immediate promotion into the Third Division. Following his heated bust-up with his entire playing squad, the Posh sacked their most successful manager. This was an ominous sign but the Board preferred to concentrate on his successes. Former Major Hagan was unashamedly old school and perhaps deep down, the revamped Board wanted just that outlook to deal with any uppity footballers. But there's a world of difference between lower Division journeymen and the best players in the country. The board boldly declared *"we will not quibble over spending money for new players."* I think I laughed when I read that one. Other reactions from the rest of Albion's dwindling band of supporters were downright earthy. We were becoming increasingly cynical and militant.

A final position of 14th summed up a season bubbling with simmering discontent. There were some redeeming features such as the blossoming skills of Alec Jackson and consistent displays by Keith Smith.

The European Cup Final was held at Wembley involving two of the biggest names in world football, Inter Milan and Benfica. At the end of a pulsating 90 minutes, Milan won 2-1. This occasion was too interesting to miss so I was among the frankly pathetic crowd of 45,000 savouring the action. With so much room, many chose to watch sitting down on the Upper tier terrace. What a pity that so many could not see beyond the "Only English football matters" viewpoint. How many chances do you get to see Eusebio live in England? Their loss! We'll never know but Dundee were one of the losing Semi-Finalists so if they had replaced Milan in the Final, would the old place have been sold out?

During this season, though curiously not on April 1, a group of shareholders led by Robert Gifford suggested that the club should change its name to 'The Albion' or simply 'Albion'. Gifford explained, *"I hate the present title being abbreviated. The Albion part so often gets left out. We are called West Brom, W.B.A, West Bromwich A, and a variety of other names. The accent is always on West Bromwich rather than the most important factor, Albion."* He added, *"It should be remembered that the Hawthorns ground is in three districts, part in West Bromwich, part in Smethwick and the remainder in Birmingham. Our support comes from all three areas and indeed if the club had to rely solely on West Bromwich support, I don't think we could even run a Fourth Division side."* Not surprisingly, the idea was 'quietly' put to bed and forgotten. The beleaguered Board had received enough negative comment for one season

Maybe we should give thanks for just being alive. In October, we all endured the Cuban Missile crisis. Russia, under Nikita Khrushchev's leadership, had placed nuclear missiles on Cuban soil, just 90 miles from Florida. America's President John F. Kennedy threatened to invade Cuba if the missiles were not removed, effectively starting a nuclear war. Kennedy conveniently overlooked the US nuclear missile base in Turkey, just 150 miles from Russian soil. As the two leaders negotiated or threatened in a series of letters to each other, the rest of the world became very frightened indeed. Had not Khrushchev put world peace before his career, my younger readers may never have been born. I discussed the subject endlessly with friends, family and workmates but it was talking for the sake of it. We were all helpless. The official advice to build a shelter in your house (curiously caravans weren't mentioned) to protect against a nuclear blast was comic if the situation weren't so serious. All we could do was to watch and listen to news bulletins, hoping and praying that common sense would supersede delusions of world supremacy. I was reminded of the war huddling in air raid shelters. Had the world learnt nothing?

On a much lighter note, the football season coincided with the introduction of the American sport of 10-pin bowling to our shores. The new sport was plugged heavily on TV. Even though TVs were small, with flickering black and white pictures, they still managed to convey the excitement of the game.

New bowling alleys were opening all over the country, including the 'Fairlines' Hawthorns Alley in Birmingham Road. This was an exciting novelty for everyone. Both Dot and I were intrigued so we regularly joined the madding crowd pre-match. A "Strike" - knocking down all ten pins with one ball – was celebrated noisily as was the jeering and mickey taking when the ball ended up in the gutter, rather than on the alley. By coincidence, the only other bowling alley to open in the area was close to Villa Park. As Dot wanted to visit her blind mother as often as possible, at times we'd stay overnight on Saturday after a home game at her parents' house, particularly when the weather made returning to 'leafy' Wootton Wawen difficult. It seemed an ideal opportunity to show off my newly acquired bowling skills but so popular had become the sport, if an alley hadn't been booked in advance, you could forget it!

In fact it was so popular that 'Midnight Leagues' were set up enabling the fanatics and insomniacs to show their skills into the early hours of Sunday morning. Much as I enjoyed the game, that wasn't for me.

## 1963/64

Fearing the winter of '63 could be the first of many; we decided to sell the caravan, bid a fond farewell to the countryside and move back to dear old Brum. We would be nearer our families (and the Hawthorns), enjoy more public transport and savour the delights of water taps, natural gas and a convenient Doctors surgery (Previously, we'd had to trek to Henley in Arden for medical help). So lots of significant advantages but even so it was with a certain amount of sadness that we caught a number 150 bus for a final time that took us to the first of our two homes. Initially, there was a spell at my parents' house which was followed by a rented flat on Pershore Road, close to Edgbaston; I could walk to watch Test and County cricket in just three minutes so I did just that at every opportunity.

Dot had a new job. She was now working in the Birmingham Incorporated Building Society (which much later became part of the Halifax). As for me, I invested in a bicycle so that I could make my own way to and from Shirley each day. The exercise was welcome but the rain was not!

Back in 'Baggie Land, there was no improvement on or off the pitch. And again, before the season started, more of our remaining best players wanted away. This time, it was full back Don Howe and Alec Jackson. Howe, another England defender whose classy thoughtful style was widely acknowledged, asked for an increase of £10 a week or £520 per year, but apparently even this modest amount was beyond the finances of a side competing against the top clubs in the First Division. Again fans were outraged and inevitably the local press was swamped with letters of protest. Others joined the ever-growing stay-away brigade. This of course perpetuated the vicious circle of smaller gates - smaller income - smaller wages - players wanting to leave - smaller gates. The lifting of the maximum wage was not Albion's friend.

In this uneasy climate, the season kicked off with several newcomers in the squad including Doug Fraser, who became one of the Albion enforcers, from Aberdeen. There was also left sided Terry Simpson from Peterborough plus John Kaye, a big centre forward from Scunthorpe, who had cost £45,000. Kaye was yet another attempt to replace Derek Kevan.

Surprisingly, the Baggies enjoyed a terrific start with four early wins but our spirits were quickly lowered again when Don Howe made a second transfer request because the club wouldn't meet his terms. Feeling helpless and powerless once again, some supporters asked the Supporters Club, more in hope than expectation, whether they could mediate in the dispute. The Supporters Club committee felt they couldn't get involved in club politics.

Somebody had to do something so I did. I couldn't accept that Albion could argue over a miserly tenner a week. Working with another Baggie 'nut', Alan Brettell, I drew up a petition listing five points why *"Don Howe must stay at the Hawthorns"* and sought support. For the early sixties, this felt quite revolutionary. The two of us worked the Hawthorns terraces for the Fulham match and as all petitioners know, repeating your message over and over again is hard work but naturally easier when people agree with the sentiments. There were just two refusals and at times there were queues patiently waiting to sign. For many, it was just a relief that so many others felt the same. Albion had already lost too much talent and it was time to draw a line in the sand. Local journalists were quick to report this embryonic example of "supporter power" which boosted interest enormously. Alan and I had an ambitious target to gather at least 5,000 signatures and then present the petition personally to the board before the dispute went to arbitration. This was doubly ambitious, firstly 5,000 was a quarter of the average attendance and hugely time-intensive for just two collectors and secondly how would the Board react to such a challenge. They were the club directors so clearly they must know best. Or so they thought.

The next game was at Old Trafford with a slim 17 year old making his debut. He wasn't an Albion player but I feel privileged to have been at the match. Football publications were clear that this lad could be something special and Matt Busby, the United manager, claimed he was a superstar in the making. How often had we heard that only to see them eventually disappear without trace? Would this be another to add to the list? Only time would tell.

But on this occasion the claims were justified seeing as he went by the name of George Best. Not many players make their debut in a battle between the two top teams in the country. I remember thinking that while Best had all the skill he might struggle against a hard tackling defender. And we had Graham Williams. Graham showed Best little respect and as the tackles went in, and the crowd voiced their displeasure, (you know what I mean!) he antagonised them even further by blowing kisses in their direction. This gesture hardly improved his popularity. Best eventually became the greatest but not that day.

Not every supporter who travelled saw the whole match. One of our football specials eased into Manchester station but didn't stop! The driver thought he was taking Birmingham City supporters to Burnley and clearly had no time or need to stop in Manchester. Dozens of furious Baggies fans besieged the guard. Eventually, he managed to contact the driver and subsequently stopped allowing the fans to get off at Bury! More chaos as the only way to get back to Old Trafford was by catching a local train back to Manchester.

Moans, groans and curses all round with the luckless 600 not arriving until half-time. A subsequent inquest led only to a standard-sounding apology, which was neither use nor ornament.

United took the points without playing particularly well but the Man of the Match, by common consent, was Baggies skipper Don Howe. This had to help the petition and when we worked, carriage-by-carriage, through the Football Special train back to the Midlands virtually everyone was happy to sign. We barely had to say anything as the protest took on its own momentum *"Is that the petition, pass it over."* The strength of feeling was so powerful. We were repeatedly congratulated for our initiative, which was flattering, almost embarrassing at times.

Arriving back at New Street station, I ritually bought a copy of the Sports Argus to read Howe's weekly column. Under the heading "Albion Fans - Forget Petition" was a carefully worded plea not to continue with the petition because he believed agreement was not far away. That was a surprising turnaround in less than a week! Could there have been a Board re-think that "the fans are right and we wrong?"

A few days later I met Don after a training session. He thanked me for our support, adding, *"It is not the sort of thing I feel should be done in a dispute of this kind but I appreciate the support and encouragement from the supporters."* This was very much a toe-the-party-line line. I suspected Don was "encouraged" to share this line with me but it was hard to object as we apparently had the outcome everyone wanted. Still, the full back was both convincing and eloquent, normally far from the party-line type.

Howe did sign what was described as a satisfactory new contract a few days later.  Ironically, as events transpired, Don said that he and Mr Hagan had reached an understanding and recognised each other's point of view. This recognition was however to have a very limited shelf life

September 28th was significant for the debut of Albion's greatest ever goal-scorer, Tony Brown. The slim 17 year -old Manchester- born youngster scored what was reported to be 'a dream goal' in a 2-1 win at Ipswich. Albion made the most of a wretched start by Town, League Champions two seasons earlier. The Suffolk club were ultimately relegated. As I was campaigning at an Animal Welfare rally in London, I missed the game but that didn't stop me cheering when the news came through!

Club fortunes deteriorated in December. The Baggies internal strife was now national news. Many players couldn't get on with Hagan, complaining that he didn't treat them as adults. Hagan held old-style virtues, perhaps learnt during his wartime service in the Army's Physical Training Corps.  Major Hagan (his Army rank), wanted his men to be disciplined and accept his word without question.  However top 1960's footballers had just thrown off their perceived yoke of oppression and considered themselves above such regimented training regimes.

Once again, some hasty smoothing quietened the mood – briefly. Then all hell let loose when nine of our top names asked for transfers because they simply couldn't accept his ethos. There were more hasty diplomatic interventions but just eleven days later came the notorious tracksuit revolt. Nineteen players refused to train without tracksuit bottoms during a spell of icy weather. "Sergeant Major" (note the less flattering rank) Hagan bluntly refused and he turned up every day in shorts, while the players, inevitably led by the ever-eloquent Don Howe staged meetings to put their case to the media.

The dispute rumbled on and on with neither side determined not to back down. Eventually the players returned to training with the board issuing a predictable *"the situation had been resolved amicably".* A compromise was agreed whereby the players warmed up in tracksuit bottoms before taking them off. This simple common sense could have been agreed in a few minutes, rather than the loggerheaded fortnight. Nobody, particularly the manager and the Board, emerged with much credit after this embarrassing episode.

Just a month later, there was another twist in the story. On the eve of the Arsenal FA Cup match, Jimmy Hagan reversed his car off the road after a training session and plunged 200 feet down a steep bank into the Grand Union canal that boarded the Spring Road training ground.

The players rushed to help and were astounded to find their manager was not seriously injured. Graham Williams risked his own limbs by half-sliding, half running down the same bank. By the time he'd scrambled down to canal level, his manager had crawled out of his car and was barking team selections at Williams. Several team mates also survived slipping and sliding down "the bonk" and with the aid of a stretcher were able to get their manager into an ambulance, further along the towpath. Famously, Hagan told his panting players they weren't fit enough.

Despite this barb, seeing the managers Vauxhall disappearing was such a shock that everybody tried to pull together for the big game. Albion did everything they could to beat Arsenal but despite all their efforts could only manage a 3-3 draw.

Prior to setting off to Highbury for the replay, I posed alongside Chris, another Albion nut, our heads thrust through the open train door, for the local press. Our big grins were combined with the now traditional hat, scarves, and rosettes. Defeat was not imaginable. Good job the same photographer wasn't on hand when we returned. Arsenal basically strong-armed their way to a 2-0 victory.

The unrest completely overshadowed events on the pitch, which did have some memorable moments. There were derby wins over Villa, Blues, and Wolves, a cracking 4-4 draw against Spurs to savour, while in a 4-2 win against Everton, I was convinced I'd seen another talented youngster with a very promising future. This was striker Mickey Fudge, who at 18 had just turned professional. Mickey, at only five foot four, was very small for a professional footballer in the boot-swinging sixties. Everton, League Champions and League leaders were completely knocked out of their stride by the newcomer. Fudge scored a hat-trick amid excitement and delight around much of the Hawthorns. The youngster's exploits proved a great bonus to sub-editors who had fun composing headlines such as "Fudge chewing up Toffees" and other sweets-related puns. I was cynical that George Best would become a star but I believed straight away that Fudge would "make it". If only!

With the season petering tamely out, the final bombshell exploded when Don Howe made his third transfer request. This time it was granted.by a Board pleased to see the back of the "barrack-room" lawyer.

Everyone wanted the full back including Wolves, Spurs and the Arsenal but it was the Gunners who won the race when their record bid of £45,000 was accepted. A great WBA career had been ended, not through choice, but through a style of man management and club policy that was a throwback to the previous decade. I felt sad and to this day, I'll always mentally link Howe's departure with three songs of the moment *"Can't buy me Love"*, *"A World without Love"* and *"Don't throw your love away"* Somehow they fitted together. Well, they did for me.

The Baggies finished the season in 10th spot with some encouraging signs. Top scorers were wingers' Chippy' Clark with 16 and Ken Foggo 11; two players capable of getting behind the full backs and causing problems for defences. John Kaye also enjoyed a good season, he too netting 11, while the promising "Boy" Brown finished with five from his thirteen matches. With the promise of Bobby Hope, Mickey Fudge and Tony Brown to come, and the hope that the off pitch squabbles had been put behind them, I so hoped for a future of stability and common sense. In April, the Sunday People gleefully broke the story of fixed football matches. Ex-footballer Jimmy Gauld gave them the story, in return for a large fee. Gauld had lots of compelling evidence, mainly because he was the ringleader. Over 30 footballers were charged and a dozen served time. Gauld received the longest sentence of four years which was something of an own goal for him. The biggest names involved – indeed the only names ever remembered - were three Sheffield Wednesday players, now alarmingly managed by ex-Albion man Vic Buckingham. "Bronco" Layne, Tony Kay and Peter Swan were then household names; indeed two of them were England internationals. All 3 bet on their own team to lose at

Ipswich in 1962. The trio served short jail sentences and were given life bans, though the bans were later lifted. Unsurprisingly, some mud was directed at Buckingham himself but nothing was ever proven. In court, the players claimed to be guilty of no more than insider trading, seeking to profit from their knowledge that Ipswich were a far stronger side who would beat them anyway. The whole miserable process numbed me. Various friends suggested that football was now no better than the rigged bouts in wrestling matches but I wasn't prepared to go that far. I told myself sternly such wrongdoings were very much the exception rather than the rule and once a supporter, always a supporter.

Away from the great game would see a Birmingham visit from the World's most popular pop group - the Beatles. For those who only know of them by name believe me, they were phenomenal. They were visiting the ATV television studio to record a nunber for a 'Thank Your Lucky Stars' programme. They needed a Police escort just to get through the doors. Wearing Police helmets, they posed for photographs and autographs for Police and fans alike.

Another concert visit to the Odeon Cinema resulted, and can you believe this, fans queued for 10 hours to be certain of getting a seat. Personally, I was never an admirer of their musical talents. Now I confess to having a CD of their greatest hits. How time and tastes move on.

Was it worth it? Asked by the press boys how much they enjoyed the concert,
most admitted they couldn't hear a word due to the non-stop shrieking and wailing from the 'Fab Four' crying devotees. Shades of an Albion game, where supporters shriek and wail if things weren't going in

our favour but with the advantage of at least being able to see the action.

## 1964/65

The "Handsworth side" is always the warmest part of the Hawthorns and a hugely popular meeting place but the terrace was showing its age. The concrete was crumbling and the club decided to replace it with more profitable seats. Officially, *"the Hawthorns will be a new look ground, geared to the modern age, with 4,000 extra seats and cover for everyone enabling the Hawthorns club to start the new soccer season as second to none in spectator comfort"*

I was among the many regulars who couldn't imagine watching home games from any other position. So I splashed out on a seat season ticket, twice the cost of the terrace, at the equivalent of £8.40p. I was going upmarket in my support, resident in the smartest structure in the ground with its banks of multi-hued seats and a licensed bar. From then on, it was a prime tip-up seat with an unrestricted view for me (I chose carefully to avoid the supporting pillars), and my days of standing were nearly behind me. Thankfully, Mrs Wills understood my logic.

On the field, it wasn't a bad start. After a 2-2 draw at Old Trafford, Sunderland were defeated 4-1-thanks to a 'Bomber' Brown hat trick. The next win saw another hat trick, this time from full back Bobby Cram in a 5-3 defeat of Stoke. Admittedly two of his goals were from the penalty spot, but a full back scoring three? Almost unique, surely? Sadly, this fine form didn't last.

Realising his team needed strengthening Jimmy Hagan went window shopping in Nottingham and returned with a King. Jeff Astle made his debut at Leicester in a 2-4 defeat and then just two games later, he took his first steps on a road on what turned out to be an unforgettable Baggies career Little did I realise then how fortunate I'd be to enjoy it with him.

Just a week earlier, the 'Daily Express' detailed how he'd turned down a move to Albion because the wages offered were not good enough. Thankfully Jimmy Hagan and his chairman Jim Gaunt travelled to Meadow Lane and after another long session of negotiation persuaded him to put pen to paper. Jeff was honest enough to admit he'd asked Albion for various sweeteners. This was a common practice at the time but Gaunt played a straight bat and eventually persuaded the striker to sign without any 'incentives'.

Wolves came to the Hawthorns for Jeff's home debut. Our new striker looked tall and gangly and made copious use of Brylcreem. Far from uncommon in those days of course yet somehow Jeff's usage stood out. Perhaps he just used more than the rest and wow how he could head a ball. As the first of his two goals hit the net, I sensed there would be many more to come. Amid my celebrations for Jeff's first-ever Albion goal, I did catch a glimpse of Wolves defenders gesturing at each other. Those gestures were even more frantic after his second and to this day, I'm convinced I saw one defender shrugging his shoulders. Many others were to follow suit over the years. The Staffordshire visitors were routed 5-1. Cue happy silly grins all round and not just for those goals. Jimmy Hagan's prize legacy was to score 8 more goals that season.

In December, there was a new TV channel to admire in the Midlands. Up to then, there were just two channels – BBC and the commercial ITV. But now, 6 months behind London, the middle of the country could enjoy a third channel offering new programmes including Match of the Day. The new football show was ground breaking stuff offering a chance to watch extended highlights of a top game.

All the key moments were there to admire without having to pay for the privilege. We had a TV (many didn't) so I savoured every moment of this new experience. I was interested to watch Liverpool. Scouse Dot's home town of course and they were League Champions but more importantly, the Kop was the most vibrant supporters end in the country. Even on a small black and white screen, it was possible to partly savour their exuberance with so much singing, so many songs. This reflected the success of their team and the Beatles too. Liverpool was just an exciting place to be. I particularly remembered a Panorama programme which dedicated five minutes to the "novelty" of singing supporters. The commentator breathlessly exclaiming *"they are all singing together and nobody seems to be conducting them..."*

The exuberance of the Kop was a reflection of the success of both their team and the Beatles. With older teenagers free from national service and having their own money to spend, the sales of recorded music shot up. The clean-cut Beatles, with their charm and simple but effective lyrics, were the right band at the right time. Sales of their music were phenomenal both in Britain and the UK but there was a price to pay for the Fab Four. They were greeted by thousands of screaming admirers wherever they went. When they flew out to America, 4,000 young people were there to wave them off. Can you believe that before a concert in Plymouth, Police had to disperse the crowd by the use of high powered water jets! Astonishing to say the least.

I particularly remember when the Beatles visited Alpha Television Studios in Aston (which later became BRMB) in January 1963 to record a song for a TV programme. Word had got around and a massive crowd besieged the studio and refused to leave. There was no escape without endangering lives so the four Scousers reluctantly spent the night at the studio.

I was amazed by their popularity. Bought up on the music of Frank Sinatra and Doris Day, etc, I was bewildered why any group, or singer could generate such passion. But then I remembered I was a teenager myself once. After Frankie Laine performed brilliantly at the Birmingham Hippodrome one night, I frantically peddled my bike, following a taxi taking him to New Street Station, hoping to get a glimpse of the singer before he disappeared into the station. I wasn't screaming but it was pretty obsessive behaviour. Pah - stupid kids. They should know better! But as the years and football seasons passed it bought home to me, and other cynics, why the 'Fab Four' had generated such enormous pleasure and sold God knows how many records!

With no regard for the travelling fan, Albion's Good Friday game at Upton Park was scheduled for an 11.00am kick-off. I travelled to London on Thursday morning with two other fanatics – Alan Brettell and Tony Matthews, determined to enjoy the sights and sounds of the big city. Just like the Beatles, I had "a ticket to ride." We stayed overnight and pointed our cameras in all directions. To this day, I've got a picture of Tony looking most bemused with a loaned parrot on his shoulder.

Was the time, effort and cash outlay worth it? In a word NO - a 6-1 hammering without a single redeeming feature apart from the consolation of a Jeff Astle goal. But determined to extract some value from our trip, we immediately decided to travel to White Hart Lane to see Spurs play Blackburn Rovers. Although the embryonic Match of the Day had just taken its first tentative steps, the rule remained that if you wanted to see any club play, then you had to be there.

We received some funny looks from the Londoners as we stood alongside them in our Albion colours as we watched them romp to a 5-2 victory. I wonder if any other supporters who've been at two top-flight games in the same day, have seen fourteen goals?

Overall, this was far from the best season for Albion memories. The League position was a safe but unspectacular 14th with no joy in the Cup.  The headlines were elsewhere including the retirement of Stanley Matthews. He'd played his last first team game for Stoke in February when aged 50 years and 15 days. At his peak, the "Wizard of the Dribble" was a must-see with his extraordinary ability to control the ball.  Yet today he'd probably be considered a luxury player, great on the ball but unable to track back.

I've had the privilege of meeting Sir Stan twice, most recently at a 'Match of the Day' exhibition at the NEC.  Perhaps because we are both in the veteran stage of life, the great man seemed most content to chat with me at considerable length. Apparently he *"always enjoyed playing against the Baggies, they had some great players."* I couldn't resist asking the obvious question. Did he resent missing out on big wages?  Sir Stan's response was clearly much rehearsed. *" I was happy playing the greatest game in the world, and a footballer's wage in those days was much more than the average working man earned. No I'm not envious, but today's players don't realise just how lucky they are to be playing the game they love with so much reward."*

To round off my season, I travelled to Wembley for the FA Cup final between Liverpool and Leeds United.  For once, I hadn't got a ticket so took a chance on a tout. Never again!  There was much demand and very limited supply so prices were eye watering. I'd almost resolved to walk away and enjoy some sightseeing instead when I was offered a ticket at a mere four times face value. I pondered for a moment and then bought it. The match brought together the two new powerhouses in the game, neither of whom had ever lifted the trophy. The game was dour until extra time when Liverpool scored two of the three goals to win the Cup. But what stood out for me were the variety of songs from the Liverpool supporters which added an exciting new dimension to the game. Obviously, I'd previously heard them in action at Anfield and on Match of the Day but this was the annual live TV game.  The whole country was picking up on *"You'll never walk alone", "Ee ay addio ..."*, *"Liv-er-pool* and *"We Love you Liverpool."*  Within months, every ground was following suit.

**1965/66**

*"The times they are a changin'..."* was a popular Bob Dylan tune of the era and with sound reason. New TV's, new cars, space rockets, mini-skirts, the Beatles, the Stones, although being truthful I was never a Mick Jagger admirer. Like most of my generation, I found it difficult to adjust from the smooth music of Frank Sinatra and the 'Rat Pack' to what I felt was merely orchestrated 'noise'.

Car ownership was increasingly common though not for Mr and Mrs Wills. I've never owned or driven a car in my life and only regret it during cold weather.

Our skies became gradually less clogged with pollution thanks to a new Act of Parliament and I felt more able to wear my blue and white scarf around my neck rather than over my mouth in any industrial area. Strange how quickly we forget the downsides of each era. Pea-soupers, extremes of fog caused by pollutions were regular events in the winter. They led to accidents, often fatal ones. I hated them.

Even the Football League embraced the 60's mood of change with two new ideas. Firstly, a single substitution was allowed to replace an injured player. For me, this was most welcome. Several Cup Finals had been spoilt as a spectacle through injury. On a more personal level, I'd witnessed Albion players hobbling along the wing as a passenger, and I was so horribly aware they were risking further injury or even their livelihood. Later on, the definition of what was or was not an injury became quite impossible to clarify but in the short term the move was just common sense.

Five years earlier, Football League Secretary Alan Hardaker, announced the introduction of a new competition - the League Cup. In general, fans welcomed this venture to make better use of floodlights but at the time the additional knock-out tournament didn't receive 100% support. Entry was optional and several top clubs, including Albion, declined the invitation. But for the new season, the League dangled a carrot. Future winners would be guaranteed a place in Europe. Now almost everybody, including the Baggies, wanted to play in the League Cup.

This decision ultimately led to one of the most exciting campaigns for many, many, years. Add this to the fervour around staging the World Cup in England and you might just begin to appreciate the "feel good factor" that swept the country for the next ten months.

Just as in the previous season, the Baggies started well with 6 wins in the first nine matches. Encouragingly, "Yorky" Kaye, Jeff Astle and Tony Brown were all scoring regularly. The signing of yet another forward in Ray Crawford added to the pressure. Ultimately, Albion went on to find the net in all bar three of their League games. Stoke's goalkeeper was in danger of backache after conceding six and there were also wins over West Ham (3-0), Sheffield Wednesday (4-2) and 4-3 against Northampton. Yes, Northampton in a League game – the times were indeed a changin'.

Famously, the Cobblers had swept through all the Divisions in a matter of seasons. The First Division was a shock for them... and a shock for visiting supporters. The County Ground was an unfortunate compromise between a cricket ground and a football stadium. When the Cobblers were playing, one side of the pitch had nothing more than duckboards for spectator comfort. Behind one goal, was a temporary stand hastily erected while the other end – known as the Hotel End – with its very low roof, looked anything but top Division terracing.

With Northants CC taking priority in September, the Baggies' game was switched to Friday night, hardly ideal for visiting supporters interested in a novelty fixture. Northampton were bottom and ripe for another defeat against the rampant Baggies. Indeed, they were beaten again but pushed new League leaders Albion all the way.

The Cobblers continued to endure a thoroughly miserable start in Division One, being without a win until late October. Form did pick up but not quite enough to avoid relegation after which they carried on being relegated until they returned to the basement division. *"It was the best football trip of the decade"* observed one trendy hack.

Building on their impetus, Albion took the extra games of the League Cup in their stride and it was mainly fellow Midland teams who couldn't cope with the rejuvenated Baggies. Walsall predictably went down fighting 3-1 before an extraordinarily large crowd of over 40,000. No Mickey Mouse Cup apathy here! Next was Elland Road and Leeds but Don Revie had no time for the competition and his deliberately weakened team were comfortably seen off 4-2. The reward was the Baggies' first competitive match at Highfield Road for two decades. City, pushing for promotion to the top flight, imagined they could win. It was a comparatively short midweek journey for many Albion supporters making their first ever visit to Highfield Road. I wasn't one of them as I'd seen Albion play League matches there just after the war. During my first time, I saw another of my personal heroes, Dave Walsh, scoring twice in a 3-2 defeat. I really was feeling an old stager! The game was drawn 1-1 but in the replay, Jeff Astle reigned supreme with a hat trick. Coventry were hammered 6-1 in the first of what were many similar demolition jobs in the decades to follow.

Then in the Quarter-Final, fans were on the proverbial cloud nine against Aston Villa as goals from John Kaye (2) and another for 'the Bomber' saw the Villa deposited on the League Cup side lines. I remember best the tension in the closing stages. Yes, we had a comfortable lead but everyone so badly wanted the game over for full-on bragging rights. I still hadn't forgiven them for that FA Cup St Andrews robbery!

Our whole team inspired me and I was more excited about forthcoming games than at any time since the late 1950's.Stan Jones was uncompromising in central defence. Bobby Cram was consistent, in addition to knocking in his fair share of goals from spot kicks. Doug Fraser, a teak-hard constructive midfielder, and then there was young Graham Lovett.  Graham was sheer class.  Brilliant in the tackle, a first rate distributor of the ball, he was a genuine midfield dynamo. If anyone looked like a future international, it was Graham.

The League form continued to be impressive with two wins and ten goals scored before the Semi-Final First Leg.  On paper, Third Division Peterborough United should have been overrun by a top Division powerhouse. But they weren't. Ex Albion man Gordon Clark set up his team to defend en masse. They were horribly effective and the Baggies could only manage an unconvincing 2-1 victory. The situation could easily have been worse as Posh hit the post in the very last minute.  I was not alone in feeling rather uneasy. Leaving the country under my own free will (National Service is not free will!) to support the Albion on the continent had greatly appealed ever since we'd defeated the Saddlers back in August. Was that fantasy to be snatched away in some remote Fenland? Questions were also asked about the Albion support or lack of it. The 20,000 gate was only half the numbers that turned out for the Second Round match against Walsall and this was a Semi-Final? There wasn't any easy explanation. But for all that everyone I spoke to was definitely "up for the Cup."

Peterborough was a new ground for everyone. The clubs had never previously met – indeed the Posh had only been a League club for five years. I'm often asked how grounds have changed over the decades and the honest answer for London Road is that it has hardly changed at all. The current main stand and the two brick end terraces, give or take the odd modern addition are as solid today as they were now. The Peterborough local paper were noisily confident that their local club would reach the two-leg Final and being honest after the huffing and puffing of the first leg, I understood their argument.

On a cold December night, the first goal would be vital and it was ours. I can still see it now. 18 minutes gone, John Kaye passed to Tony Brown and the Bomber doing what he does best. "YEESSSS ..."

Our now doubled lead changed the dynamics. The Baggies became dominate and really rubbed in their First Division status as Ray Crawford and Tony Brown added more goals. Roars of support? You'd better believe it!

Fair play to the 'Posh', even though they resembled a 'down and out', they pulled two goals back that theoretically gave them a little hope. Predictably, they charged forward in the late stages and just as predictably, the Baggies caught them on the break. Chipper Clark steamed past three defenders as if they weren't there and set up Tony Brown for his hat-trick. Goodnight, Mr Posh!

We'd done it and our happy band of fans spent the whole of the ride home discussing the appealing prospect of a long overdue Cup Final appearance.

I had a double cause for celebration during this month as Dot and I bought our first-ever house. Our very own property was in Stirchley, just down the road from Edgbaston. No cause for celebration at Elland Road as the Baggies were given a 4-0 run around by the burgeoning Leeds United.

A tame 3-0 FA Cup exit at lower Division Bolton in January raised our interest in the new League Cup competition. It was like having a substitute, a reserve Cup competition to bring on when we needed it. Not a trip to Wembley admittedly but all those local clubs we'd knocked out en-route - Walsall, Coventry, and especially Aston Villa, I daresay that they'd be more than happy to have swapped places!

Our Final opponents were to be West Ham, significantly below us in the table but if you want big names, the Hammers had them in abundance. Their ranks of full English Internationals included the skipper Bobby Moore, Martin Peters, Geoff Hurst and Johnny "Budgie" Byrne. Many sides had crumbled under the pressure of a screaming passionate East End crowd and the London based press were unanimous that Albion was in for a rough ride.

There were nearly three months between the League Cup Semi and the two-legged Final, a period so long that it was easy to forget we had reached a Final. Towards the end of the Long Wait, Albion had a League game at Upton Park. After the 6-1 hammering the previous year and 3-0 the year before that, this match felt somehow significant. Try to imagine my squirming discomfort as once again West

Ham made Albion look like poor country cousins. 4-0 this time and to use a cliché, we were lucky to get nil. I consoled myself that at their best Albion could compete on any stage. We were a Cup team. So were West Ham but I tried to ignore that fact.

The big news for the Cup Final return to Upton Park was that Jeff Astle was back, injured in an era when a cartilage problem meant months in recovery rather than weeks. As Bobby Moore was to discover, King Jeff was simply too big and too strong for him. Forsaking their usual attacking formula, the Baggies sat deep with big Jeff as a counterattacking spearhead. The Londoners were taken by surprise with this cunning, unexpected plan and looked shell shocked when 'Chipper' Clark set up Astle for one of his trademark headed goals.

The strike changed my mood even more than it did the game. I'd convinced myself the first leg was a lost cause and now I was cheering frantically. The Londoners continued to be rattled and unable to subdue Jeff Astle and an unexpected away win was on the cards.

Very much against the run of play, Bobby Moore equalised. That was bad enough but when Byrne scored a last minute, highly unexpected goal to seal a 2-1 win, I could barely believe it. What I'd come to think of as "our trophy" was slipping away.

We'd not heard much from West Ham supporters all night, not even from the notorious Chicken Run wooden terrace, but when they poached that undeserved late winner, we had to endure a lusty chorus of

*"We're forever blowing bubbles,*
*Pretty bubbles in the air,*
*They blow so high,*
*Nearly reach the sky,*

*Then like my dreams*
*They fade and die".*

It's guaranteed to put your teeth on edge. Little did they realise just prophetic those words would turn out to be.  But in the meantime, there was two weeks to wait for the Second Leg. Two weeks of doubt and friends and workmates teasing me. *"I'd put your passport away, if I were you Terry..."* In vain, I explained that the Londoners were most fortunate to win at Upton Park. With no TV highlights to back me up, my arguments were easily dismissed along the lines of *"you would say that, wouldn't you".* Mandy Rice-Davies has much to answer for.

Why did I harbour such doubts? Those Hammers fans dreams of winning the Cup didn't just fade away; they were simply blasted into orbit at the Hawthorns. In the first 30 minutes, the Cup was signed, sealed and delivered by four cracking goals from Clarke, Kaye, Brown and remarkably even Captain Graham. Graham hadn't scored for a year but this was one of those nights, wretched pre-match traffic jams aside, that players and supporters fantasise about.

I felt there was a first leg injustice to be put right and maybe the stars in stripes felt the same way. The Londoners lead lasted just ten minutes and after Graham Williams had rammed in the' icing on the cake' fourth goal, he knew it, I knew it. We'd won the Cup. All the skills of Bobby Moore and his fellow internationals counted for nothing; they were simply outplayed. The European Cup Winners Cup holders managed one goal near the end but it wasn't even a consolation. They didn't celebrate and their supporters were mainly on the train home by then. West Bromwich Albion had won the League Cup 5-3 on aggregate at the first time of asking.

Waves of unrestrained joy swirled around the Hawthorns. Graham Williams accepted the Cup from the Directors Box. The players waved their silver tankards in celebration while I, along with the rest of the deliriously happy supporters, refused to curtail our celebrations, despite the chilly night. Chants of *'Hagan, Hagan'* and *'Albion, Albion'* interspersed with a chorus (unashamedly lifted from the Liverpool v Leeds FA Cup final of the previous year.) *"We won the Cup, We won the Cup, eye-ay addio. We won the Cup'"*

The celebrations continued on the buses, in the dressing room ("the proudest moment of my career" exclaimed Graham Williams) and even in the Board room where Jim Gaunt admitted *"it was the happiest night of my life."* Even Jimmy Hagan picked up the mood of celebration. *"I'm pleased we won by means of attacking football that took us to the Final and provides crowds with such entertainment."* On the bus back to the city centre, Terry Wills said *"Bloody Brilliant!"*

Albion were brilliant that night, a fact later acknowledged by many of the team and the press. As is my wont, I bought every newspaper the following morning just to be sure. I had a permanent fixed grin for three days and jokes that *"Terry's suffering from very bad wind"* just bounced off me.

The Baggies finished the season in style, unbeaten in 9 matches. Conversely, one of the victories at the Hawthorns was a convincing 5-1 demolition of Leicester City aided and abetted by two own goals from the same Leicester defender. He clearly looked unhappy along with the Foxes supporters while along with Baggies fans I was more than happy to wallow in his misery!

Jeff Astle, John Kaye, and Tony Brown managed over 20 goals each in this great campaign. What lay in store next season was the intriguing question? We'd finished  sixth in the League, won the League Cup at the first time of asking and would be lining up against Continental opposition in the Fairs Cup.

But that wasn't quite the end of my domestic season. I was off on my annual visit to Wembley seeing Everton and Sheffield Wednesday do battle. Wednesday included Don Megson in their ranks – Gary's Dad. My ticket had me standing among the blue Scousers who were both excitable and certain of victory. Sometimes, it's a blessing to be neutral. Wednesday took a two goal lead, normally a clinching position in a Cup Final. The mental torment of the blue half of Liverpudlians surrounding me was all too obvious. This was not in their script. Famously, Everton fought back, equalised and then secured victory with their third goal ten minutes from time. Unheard of stuff and I couldn't help but join in the celebrations.  When in Rome...

## 1966 World Cup

The countdown to the first game was perhaps rather similar to the London Olympics with lots of hype but no proper action.  Naturally, souvenir sales did wonders for the country's economy. Best sellers were the World Cup Willie t-shirts and caps (Willie was the official England Lion mascot) while Union Jack flags were rampant in house and car windows. I spotted two wheelchairs owners who decorated their chairs with the national flag.  Sales of black and white TV's also rose markedly – the World Cup would be a rare feast of televised football. But not for me as I'd booked time off work and I was going to take in as many live matches as possible and not just in Birmingham. The best in the world was coming to England and I wanted to be here, there and everywhere to get maximum benefit.

Any hope of seeing the "King" in his country's shirt had long gone. Jeff Astle didn't make the 22 man squad. He didn't even make the provisional 40 man squad announced in early April, although John Kaye did.  His three-month long injury which kept him out of the limelight was fatal. Old hands Charlton and Greaves were the attacking main men with Hurst, Flowers and Hunt also in the squad. It is interesting to note how widely England's perceived top talent was distributed. Leicester, Southampton, Wolves and Blackburn were represented while Blackpool donated more players than Chelsea and Arsenal.

The opening game – England v Uruguay at Wembley – brought with it immense expectation on a home nation already burdened by Alf Ramsay's bold declaration of ultimate success. But England's "wingless" 4-4-2 formation could find no way past Uruguay and so the first game of the tournament finished goalless.

Taking full advantage that one of the four Qualifying groups was based almost within walking distance, I was at Villa Park two days later to see Argentina take on Spain. The Latin American side won 2-1 but this was almost secondary to the terrace carnival. I've never seen flamenco on the Holte End before and consequently my attention often wandered away from the pitch. I wanted more of the same... and quickly.

I've never considered Birmingham as a tourist destination but just for one month, visitors from Europe and South America were everywhere eating, drinking and often queuing to buy Birmingham souvenirs. I took much simple pleasure by being among them at every opportunity.

I missed England's win over Mexico to see West Germany v Argentina, also at Villa Park. This was a wholly more serious affair which was often downright brutal. The light blues had a simple game plan to bring their opponent down every time their goal was threatened. This was a not uncommon tactic during this period of hard men, but it felt plain wrong at this elevated level. The referee finally lost patience and sent off Rafel Albrecht but the Argentines hung on doggedly for a 0-0 draw. FIFA cautioned them for their violent approach which made no difference whatsoever.

Other similar incidents followed elsewhere in what was mainly an ugly, functional tournament of few goals. Pele was literally kicked out of the World Cup by Bulgarian and then Portuguese defenders as the Cup holders could only finish third in their group.

Tickets were easy to obtain for whatever game took my fancy. I travelled to Wembley for the Quarter-Final between England and Argentina. This was my third game involving the Latin American side and in many ways, it was a re-run of the first. It is such a well-known scenario that I hardly need repeat it here. Every type of foul in Argentina's repertoire, and there were many, was pulled out on such a regular basis. .The England players were unceremoniously battered, bruised and frequently left face-down after brutal challenges.

The whole world remembers captain Rattin committing one cynical foul too many and being ordered off. But he wouldn't go and there was an impasse when all his team mates threatened to walk off in protest. Infamously, the long arm of the law was extended a little further to remove him from the playing area. I vividly remember an apoplectic supporter next to me bellowing *"For Christ's sake, get him off or I'll do it for ya"* Geoff Hurst, deputising for the injured Jimmy Greaves, scored the only goal. This according to Argentine sources was "the robbery of the century."

The chance to see a World Cup Semi-Final at Goodison (West Germany v Russia) was too good to miss. I booked a seat on one of the fleet of coaches transporting the Birmingham-based German supporters to Liverpool. Many other neutrals followed suit and on every coach, conversations were attempted. Many Germans spoke decent English fortunately and they shared their absolute belief that their country would win the Cup. .

Everton, concerned about a possible flashpoint, had cut out a huge concrete semi-circle behind the goalmouth to create a new artificial barrier. It just looked so odd (not to mention unnecessary) yet was to remain an oddity at their stadium for many years to come.

Which team were the England fans supporting? Every time the chant *"Deutchsland-Deutchsland"* rang out, the Scouse-led England contingent, drowned it out with non-stop cries of *"England, England."* Unusual, but no way could we let the Germans win the vocal battle.

The German side were a better all-round team and deserved their 2-1 victory. This of course meant their following were even cockier returning to Birmingham. They pointed out that England still had a difficult Semi-Final against Portugal win before they could even contemplate taking on Beckanbauer's men. All true but such barbs got my patriotic blood going, heightening my awareness of England's big match.

The second Semi-Final was the following night so I had no more than a bare few hours at home before I was on a London-bound train, with Wembley on my mind. There's is nothing quite like the key closing stages of an international football tournament to bring a country together. Conversation flowed easily with so many strangers. *"Give them a shout for me"* I was urged, over and over again. My good fortune to get a ticket was repeatedly envied even though there was no great skill involved.

Thank heavens for Bobby Charlton! His two goals took away much of the biting tension. We were as good as in the Final until, with just eight minutes left; Portugal pulled a goal back from the penalty spot. An uncomfortable last few minutes and it was all over, we'd made it. Bring on the Germans.

The Final was just four days away and wearied by regular travelling, Dot and I decided to holiday in London prior to the Big Game. If it all went pear-shaped, at least we'd have enjoyed ourselves beforehand. Perhaps too, the distractions would take my mind off the biggest game I was ever likely to witness live.

In London, everyone had football on their minds. Union Jacks and memorabilia abounded, as did supporters of so many nations around the world who'd bought Final tickets in advance. I quickly realised at such a time, London was the only place to be. Dot and I made the most of our sightseeing days. We had so many meals at the Silver Restaurant in Leicester Square that it became as familiar to us as the local chippie. We visited Hampton Court, took in a show and Harrods but for something really different; experienced the 'Whispering Gallery' inside St. Paul's Cathedral. For anyone who hasn't savoured this unique activity, you climb 259 steps to enter a circular gallery. Here any words spoken quietly will be heard by anyone at the other end of the chamber. Spotting half a dozen German tourists testing it for themselves on the opposite side, I couldn't resist whispering, *"England will win the World Cup!"*

On the day of the Final, I woke early. Sleep was not easy to find. Throughout the morning, I acquired a half-reasonable understanding of the pressures that players were enduring. They were assailed by weighty burden of expectations from the whole country.  There are no second chances to get it right. I felt their strain. With the endless choruses of good wishes and inane, repeated questions, it was a relief to get inside Wembley just to get a clear focus.

Fervour was mounting long before the teams took the field - chants of *"Deutschland, Deutschland"* drowned out by *"England, England"* (Goodison Park revisited but far louder)

The events of the game are simply not allowed to be forgotten by English football supporters, regardless of generation.  The Germans scored first but to near universal relief, Geoff Hurst equalised four minutes later just in front of Dot and I. We hugged each other in relief. The half ebbed and flowed but from my biased perspective England were the better team. Into the second-half and anyone who was there will never again see a more dramatic game leavened with anger, frustration and relief. Martin Peters' goal with 12 minutes remaining felt like the winner. It was a moment to share with young relatives. *"I was there when Martin Peters won the World Cup."* But then horror with just one minute remaining, the Russian referee awarded the Germans a dubious free kick. The kick was blocked but Wolfgang Weber equalised from the melee. It was a criminally shattering blow on both pitch and terraces. England players claimed handball but the referee was not convinced. Numbness descended on most of Wembley before extra time commenced. Everyone needed a lift but unbeknown to everyone except the players, Alf Ramsey was doing just that with his Churchillian moment. *"You've beaten them once, now you've got to do it again. Look at them, they're finished."*

So to 30 minutes that is part of our folklore. Enter Geoff Hurst as he went on to score the most controversial goal in World Cup history. With his back to goal, he controlled the ball instantly, swivelled and smashed a shot against the underside of the bar- from there it bounced onto the line and was cleared. Roger Hunt, following up turned away, arms raised in celebration. But did the ball cross the line? From the far end, we obviously couldn't tell and while England's players appealed that it had crossed the line the Germans were equally convinced it hadn't.

The referee himself was unsure and went over to consult his Swiss linesman while both sets of supporters agonised, waiting to see who would be celebrating or cursing after the consultation. Please, please let it be us. It was! Massive celebrations, back slapping, complete strangers hugging each other (a reprise of the V.E Day celebrations) and tears of joy.

They were all there but the Germans weren't about to throw in the towel. They pushed forward desperately.

As time ran out, Bobby Moore deep in his own half, spotted Geoff Hurst on a run and measured a magnificent long ball to the onrushing striker. Trying to ignore supporters already on the pitch, Hurst scored again. Every England fan leapt high in the air to celebrate as they'd never done before. Geoff Hurst had become the first player to score a hat-trick in a final. You'd better believe it! All accompanied by the classic commentary adjustment by Kenneth Wolstenholme's immortal words *"some people are on the pitch, they think it's all over, IT IS NOW!"* Wembley had no fences at the time and offered no greater barrier physical or human than a low wall.

Decades on, I still find it almost impossible to do justice to the moments that followed. Far greater authors than me have tried to do justice to Bobby Moore's trophy elevation, Nobby Stiles' toothless dance and the later presentation at the Royal Kensington Hotel. Everyone had seen the moments on TV or video but to be there, to be part of the occasion – it is beyond the art of the wordsmith.

1966 was a great year for me. Albion won the League Cup. England the World Cup and I'd been privileged to be present at both. How much did this unrepeatable venture cost? The most expensive part had been the cost of travelling here, there, and everywhere. Match ticket prices? For the World Cup Final, a standing ticket cost 10 shillings (50p) so for Dot and Terry, a grand total of £1.

**1966/67**

Only a tremendous end of season run from the Baggies saved them from clawing frantically for the safety ledge dividing Divisions One and Two. The season contained so much suspense, drama, thrills and spills.

Four defeats in the first five games set the mood and although comprehensive wins against Newcastle and Fulham steadied the ship, it was becoming plain that this wasn't an Albion team that would be challenging for League honours.

The defence leaked regularly. Ray Potter and Rick Sheppard shared the green jersey but neither inspired much confidence. . Despite this, the defence of the League Cup started in great style and again it was Aston Villa were the first to suffer. A rare hat trick from Bobby Hope was instrumental in a 6-1 thrashing. Such a victory deserves remembering in more depth.

Albion set the pace by forcing 8 corners in the first ten minutes. 'Chipper' Clark hit the bar but just two minutes on, Doug Fraser hit the first of his two goals. His second followed six minutes later and when Bobby Hope added a third after 28 minutes, I was cock-a-hoop but wanted more, more and more.

So did the Baggies. Four Villa sightseers were mesmerised by the twisting, gyrating will-of-the-wisp 'Chipper' as he put away number four. Bobby Hope added two more late goals to which Tony Hateley's penalty response was generously described as a "consolation." The shuffling-out-early Villa contingent didn't look at all consoled!

Manchester City and Swindon were also defeated in the early rounds of the League Cup. Things were looking good for another long run. But before the next Cup fixture, Albion were going to Europe in the shape of Dos Utrecht.

Clutching my temporary passport (I didn't own a full one), I boarded a Throstles club coach with many of the other "faces". The coach trip was tediously long but the alternative of a plane trip was ruinously expensive.

According to an interview with "Yorky" Kaye, the players were determined to enjoy Amsterdam culture such as visiting Rembrandt's House, the Opera House and the Queen's Palace. I wonder where they really went. As for us supporters, our time was painfully restricted to trying some delicious cheese and learning more about Anne Frank, though there was no time to visit her attic. Somewhere, I've still got photographs of the trip. There is one with me hoisting a Baggies flag walking down a main street and another with a female supporter sandwiched between two very tall policemen at Schipol airport.

I knew nothing about Utrecht other that they'd been competing in the Inter City Fairs Cup for a number of years. It was only when we rolled up at the modest ground 23 miles from Amsterdam, with their even more modest support that I appreciated that Albion were the big-time visitors. The meagre floodlighting reminded me of Portsmouth's candles from an earlier era and the temperature of minus five took me back to St James' Park.

The Baggies first European match was a strange affair with both Albion and the part-time Dutch side concentrating on not conceding a goal. In the end, both did. Bobby Hope scored our first ever goal in Europe and the equaliser came frustratingly and irritatingly with just four minutes to go. For the tiny Dutch side, a home draw was a major achievement and I had no concerns about our ultimate progress.

In the return match, the Dutch were flattened 5-2 (their manager predicted 7-1). Jeff Astle won everything in the air and the Bomber, with his hat trick, seemingly put away every chance he had. Although the press were quick to highlight all of the obvious shortcomings again, I was happy just to get through the tie to earn another trip to the Continent. There was a huge novelty feel that evening. The Black Country was a parochial place in those days and to see foreign opposition in a competitive fixture felt so new and exciting.

Next in what was becoming an increasingly crowded fixture list with a League Cup Quarter Final away at Northampton Town. The Cobblers were rapidly heading back to the nether regions of the League and it showed. Albion ran out 3-1 winners with relative ease.

One incident stuck in my memory for all the wrong reasons. Disgruntled Town supporters hurled various objects at us. In these pre-hooligan days, I was so disgusted that I wrote to the Town officials who replied that they'd passed on my complaint to Denis Follows at the Football Association. In turn, Fellows wrote to me explaining the FA was preparing a report and as soon as he received some information, he would contact me further. Seven weeks later, I received another letter, this time from the Northampton Secretary who informed me that the Police would not be making a report as they had no knowledge of the incident and the matter would be closed. That was very convenient for everyone bar our pelted supporters but in truth I didn't really expect anything more.

Albion were now just two matches from another Cup Final and this year for the first time, it would be at Wembley. The whole world seemed to have changed since the Baggies were last at the twin towers. There were performers setting fire to their guitars on stage.

There were credit cards, gas coming out of the North Sea and the British Empire was breaking up. But there were still wars abroad so not everything changes.

Without appearing arrogant, I thought we had a brilliant chance to retain the Cup. The other survivors were West Ham, Second Division Birmingham City and ridiculously, a Third Division side in QPR. Naturally, I wanted Rangers but what we got was the toughest of the three in West Ham. We'd already had our customary tattering at Upton Park that season (3-0) so with the first leg at home, securing an advantage was virtually essential.

At Christmas came the incident that I'm convinced cost Albion, and England, the services of a player who could have turned out to have become one of the all-time greats. Graham Lovett was in a car crash on the M1. The first motorways were rather like the Wild West with no speed limits and a subsequent volume of crashes. Graham's car ended up in a ditch with the unfortunate player suffering a broken neck. With the limited medical knowledge in the period, I couldn't ever imagine him playing again but he did. A whole years' recovery period was required together with some risky bone graft operations.

The League form continued along its uneven way, culminating in a last day of the year 5-1 hammering at Burnley. Something simply had to be done to shore up our defensive frailties. The Baggies were only two points above a relegation slot and even Villa had more points.

At last the manager moved into the transfer market. A new keeper was signed, John Osborne from Chesterfield for a fee, a bag of coal and Green Shield stamps (the Tesco Clubcard of the period) if Ossie can be believed. Also new through the door was the rugged-looking John Talbut, a centre-half from Burnley. John never really won over all of Albion's support. Many were never convinced of his value to the team and I have to admit that I took some convincing.

The miserable League performances were endured because of the prospect of seeing Albion reach the League Cup Final again and make progress in Europe. The latter hope came to an inglorious end in the Fourth Round at home to Bologna. They were only mid-table in the Italian League but were packed with international big names. They proved a far superior team and won 3-0.

I was fearful about our League Cup Semi-Final hopes against West Ham after that European mauling but the other Albion turned up. The one that was unstoppable. Once again, Jeff Astle was too powerful for Bobby Moore OBE to block and this miss-match was crucial "The King" scored a hat –trick in a marvellous 4-0 Hawthorns demolition. Oh yes, I enjoyed that. Even with the second leg to follow, everyone knew who was going to Wembley and it wasn't West Ham.

What was it about this Albion? Brilliant at their best but otherwise they resembled a relegation team. The question was repeatedly asked but no sensible answers were forthcoming. Presumably Jimmy Hagan was equally baffled or he would have found a solution.

The return leg felt odd in that it was a big Cup match but one in which the outcome was already almost decided. Note the "almost", I initially refused to accept the match was won but once in Upton Park I relaxed.

I was told that I grinned the whole night. Wrong! I was far more manic than that. I resembled a clown outside Blackpool Pleasure Beach in a fixed state of delight. Nothing the Hammers could do would change that. People who didn't know me very much might suspect I was *"on something."*

There was even the bonus of not losing at Upton Park for once. Thanks to Chipper Clark and Bobby Hope's goals, we enjoyed a comfortable 2-2 draw and a stroll overall. Guess what? There couldn't have been a more 'over the moon' set of supporters on that or any other night. What a trip home that was!

When we heard the news that the Blues had lost their Semi-Final to a Third Division team, we didn't know whether to laugh or cry so we did both. Going to Wembley and up against a third tier team in QPR – hey, the Cup was as good as ours. In our mutual post-match elation, none of us paused to reflect that Rangers had reached Wembley for a reason – they were no ordinary side. They'd put 7 goals past Blues

Any fantasies of a double Wembley triumph came to a grinding halt at Elland Road in the fourth round of the F.A Cup. A 5-0 defeat gifted Leeds a stroll into the fifth round. Albion's inconsistency infuriated me. We had a decent side. Ian Collard was a classy looking full back. Eddie Colquhoun, another new boy from Bury, was a genuine tough nut. We had three regular goal scorers in Astle, Brown and Clark plus the brilliant Bobby Hope.

Despite being uncertain which Albion side would travel, expectancy was high as Wembley drew ever closer. There was no artificially- low ticket restrictions for the participating clubs - marvellous! With all tickets sold, every coach and train in the area booked solid, it was a very confident set of supporters who arrived at Wembley in high spirits.

With plenty of time to spare, our little band meandered along the High Street and came across the greengrocers shop owned by the British Heavyweight Boxing Champion Henry Cooper. Surely he wouldn't be there serving customers himself?

But there was *'Our Enry'*, large as life, chatting to his regulars plus Baggies supporters who promptly offered him their custom, at the same time having photographs taken to commemorate the occasion.

I've always loved fresh fruit so bought a selection of apples, pears and bananas. As I rummaged for coins in my pocket, I explained just why the Baggies could not lose to Queens Park Rangers.

*"Well, best of luck lads but I think Rangers will beat you."*

*"No way, Henry"* I told him. *"OK, you're a Boxing champion but you obviously know nothing about football!"*

This was one match Albion couldn't possibly lose. Obviously, the West London outfit were a decent side as they'd got to the Final. Apparently Rodney Marsh and Mick Lazarus were the stand-out players but I just wasn't worried. The London-based media are always going to talk up one of *"their own."* I'd read in the newspapers that a large number of Rangers supporters were walking to the game. I do recall reading out those lines to various Albion diehards and the response was either *"What does that tell you about London transport?"* Or *"That's a lot of unnecessary effort just to see your team lose."* It was fortunate that I didn't realise at the time they were carrying an Albion coffin with them.

The difference in class at Wembley quickly became apparent. Albion tore the Londoners apart and with Chipper Clark terrorising his old team, goals had to come. It was Clark who drew first blood. Then he added a delightful second. At half-time, with the Baggies 2-0 up and strolling, I was asking my pals where we could meet on Sunday to see Albion bring the cup home. Yes, I was that confident. The Cup was already won. Look out Europe, we won't make the same mistake next time. My caution in the Semi-Final was completely forgotten!

Recalling that second half, even now, is painful. Gron Williams in the Birmingham Post: summed it up more coherently than I could. It's not a match I can ever be coherent about. Wrote Gron: "*This was a defeat that never should have happened. For Albion, holders of the League Cup and a First Division club, to have taken a two goal lead in the competition's Wembley Final against a Third Division side and then lost is a disgrace that cannot be lived down for a long time*

Albion lost this match rather than Rangers won what remains the only trophy in their history. For us to defend for the whole of the second half was folly. We had striker John Kaye playing behind our full backs and this against a lower Division team that we had on the run.

Rangers couldn't believe their luck and surged forward. Chants of "*Rodnee-Rodnee - Rodnee*" inspired Rangers and demoralised Albion. In the final half hour, Marsh struck fear and apprehension into our defence every time he received the ball. To this day, whenever I hear his name mentioned, either as a player or football analyst that cry automatically springs to mind.

The winning goal was just a bad joke. Our goalkeeper Rick Sheppard was clearly flattened. And yet this was the "other" Albion, the side who couldn't do anything right and to strike out the Londoners' third goal was only to delay the inevitable. However much Dot, I and other stressed Albion fans urged the team forward, it made not the slightest difference.

We sat in dumbfounded silence at the final whistle. How could it have happened? All I wanted was to get home as soon as possible and mope in peace but even this was thwarted due to pre-booked tickets to see a West End Show.

We boarded the coach and sat for two hours on the Wembley car park before we set off for central London. I just didn't want to be there and even then there was a final indignity. A party of QPR supporters wearing club colours arrived and sat just three rows in front of me. They were as bouncy as I was miserable.

Years later, I got Tony Brown's view of the game. *"To be fair to the manager he just said carry on playing the playing as you are -you're 2 nil up, there's no need to change anything. I don't really know what happened, we probably got complacent. You know how it is, you're coasting a game, you lose the rhythm and it's difficult to pick it up again. Rodney Marsh had one of those days when everything went for him and he won the cup for Rangers."*

Supporters wanted a scapegoat and naturally it was Jimmy Hagan who took the brunt of the blame. Fans were convinced he was to blame for defensive tactics, although, to be fair, he had always been a firm advocate of attractive attacking play.

This game taught me a painful lesson. Never assume a match is won if you're a 'mere' two goals ahead, a maxim I've stuck by ever since.

Four days later, we had Mission Impossible in Italy to recover a 3-0 deficit. This was immensely difficult at any time but just after losing a Wembley Cup Final in such circumstances? No chance. We scored just one through Ray Fairfax while Bologna added three more to make a 6-1 aggregate score.

I was still determined to travel to Italy for the second leg and did so via my first ever plane flight.

Sadly once again, our time on foreign soil was so limited. We contented ourselves with photographing everything in sight. As it turned out that was all that could be enjoyed. Even though defeat was expected, this was another stick to beat the manager with. We were out of all the Cups and the League position was becoming parlous. After thirty games, we were just four places off bottom spot and relegation felt uncomfortably close.

But now the other Albion came to the rescue. The stylish Albion won 8 and drew 2 of our last eleven games to ensure Aston Villa would be relegated instead of us. I'd like to say that we helped the Villains on their way but in truth we'd taken more points from clubs around them than Villa themselves so if anything we gave them a marginally better chance of staying up. Fortunately, they were too hapless to take advantage. Bye Villa! We signed off with a splendid flourish, demolishing the Geordies 6-1 featuring a hat trick by Tony Brown.

What happened to cause this transformation? Various theories were circulating including one which made sense to me. The players were tipped off that Hagan was on his way soon and their careers would be enhanced if his replacement was coming into a top division club. So it proved. With just two games remaining, Jimmy Hagan left the club. He didn't leave by mutual consent. He didn't resign. He was sacked. In a statement, Chairman Jim Gaunt insisted the season's poor results had nothing to do with the sacking! I didn't believe such nonsense and neither did many Albion supporters though the further detail in the statement made more sense. *"There has been a build-up of incidents. We have been concerned for some time regarding the policy and general management of the club. We've tried hard to sort out our problems, but the problems could not be resolved and we have been concerned for some time now about the rather poor dressing room spirit. This has been discussed with the manager several times this week, it was decided that the future policy the club wished to adopt could not be fulfilled with Mr Hagan. So we relieved him of his duties".*

So it was a `fond' farewell to the Sergeant Major. For me, Hagan had plus points and minus points. Hagan could spot a talented player (Lovett, Brown, Hope and Astle) but simply couldn't interact with them in a way that was appreciated. The world had moved on from the days of Army-like discipline *"Do as I say because I know best."* He certainly didn't know best at Wembley. Yet I did feel some unease. Under Hagan we'd won a trophy, should have retained it the following year, had a European experience and savoured much exciting football.

Probably, in the final analysis, he could feel unjustly treated considering what had gone before. Would we be so critical in today's climate of limited success? I think not. Hindsight is a perfect science. Past criticism can seem an unfair epitaph.

**1967/68**

Sometimes I have to remind myself that 1967 isn't "recent" and resort to recalling key events just to give me the necessary perspective. In 1967, Henry Cooper was winning his third Lonsdale belt while Davina McCall, Paul Gascoigne, Paul Ince and Noel Gallagher were being born. 1967 also included the first airings of "*All you need is Love*", "*Whiter Shade of Pale*" and "*If you're going to San Francisco.*" Aah, such great music but it wasn't from last year.

Meanwhile, Albion had a new manager. After the usual flurry of names being bandied around, it was the Carlisle United manager Alan Ashman who got the nod. Alan had achieved great things with the Scottish border-huggers, earning two promotions and coming very close to a third. No doubt doing a lot with limited resource was of great appeal to the Albion board. Previously, Alan had tried out various jobs including a chicken farmer which was too good a gift for football cartoonists to resist.

I'd assumed that the stars in stripes would resume their fine form from May but I should have known better. We only won once in the first seven games and supporters around me were wondering whether we'd have been better off with Hagan.

Nearly all our early points had been secured from Wolverhampton, the only local opposition left in the top flight, which did temper our discontent somewhat. We'd stolen a 3-3 draw at Molineux in August that famously included Bomber Brown's late "Hand of God" punched equaliser. All-round fury ensued in best Molineux traditions. There are few who can match Wolverhampton folk for incoherent incandescence. Wolves' keeper Phil Parkes decided the most effective way of getting the referee to change his mind was to jump on his back. He was sent off provoking chaos. The Wanderers fans were outraged as I'd have been in their position, but for all that the fault lay with the one man who'd forgotten his glasses – the Man in Black. Travelling back on the train was also quite, shall we say, lively. God knows what it would have been like if the modern more intense rivalry was involved.

Just to rub things in, otherwise struggling Albion comfortably beat Wanderers 4-1 in the return fixture weeks later thanks to goals from Astle, Kaye, Clark and Kenny Stephens. The demolition derby eased tensions all round and thus began a series of steadily improving performances highlighted in a tremendous display against Burnley at the Hawthorns. Six different players got their names on the score sheet as the Clarets made the return journey to Turf Moor on the back of an 8-1 drubbing. For me, the Lancashire club had observed Armistice Day too literally (the match was played on November 11) by lying down on the pitch. The Baggies were 5-0 up by half-time including a Crichton-type howler by the Burnley keeper who literally threw in our third goal.

Graham Lovett's return to the first team on Boxing Day against Manchester City was an emotional moment for me and the other diehards. It was no doubt emotional for him too but professionals were not encouraged to show their feelings on the pitch. As I mentioned earlier, our young starlet had endured a full year of treatment and pain. His return was more important than winning the game 3-2.

Christmas matches at the time were always "emotional" in a different sense due to the wide variety of alcohol on offer. In addition to the regular bars around the ground, all sorts of combinations were brought from home in hip flasks (or just mixed on the spot) and circulated to your neighbours.

Apparently not knowing what the contents were was part of the "fun." I remained determinedly sober that day – part of a small minority in what became a raucous atmosphere.

The League was OK but after two successive Cup Finals, knockout football was clearly our forte and I thirsted (no pun intended) for more. I wasn't getting any more in the League Cup, knocked out in the Second Round following a shocking 3-1 defeat at Third Division Reading. I was fuming for several days. Had nothing been learnt post QPR?  Our players promised they'd do better in the FA Cup, chastened by the wrath of Ashman.  Of course making promises and keeping them are poles apart. Proof would only come with positive results.

Several months later, the team had the chance to make good on their promise. The FA Cup draw had not been kind with yet another fixture against a Third Division club. Was some divine force giving us endless third tier opponents until we finally beat one? This turned out to be a classic Cup match of the type that a modern day audience will rarely see. Colchester's season was miserable (they were relegated four months later) so a Third Round match against the famous West Bromwich Albion was very much their highlight of the season. A gate 400% above their average attendance squeezed into miserable little Layer Road. Here, I could see definite parallels with Kenilworth Road with its narrow entrances; small terraces pressed in between houses and roads, poor view and limited cover.  After the Reading fiasco, the weary travelling few with tickets were concerned that their team couldn't play on what felt like a postage stamp size pitch.

The events on the day are well chronicled. The U's, looking more like a top tier team than the Baggies, took the lead. Albion equalised with a very generously-awarded penalty but Colchester thought they'd won the game in the last minute, as did everyone else bar the referee. Despite mass outrage, the goal was disallowed. This remarkable let-off led to the now famous theory that Albion's name was on the '68 FA Cup.

Colchester weren't getting another chance. Such was the Baggies reputation for "doing the business" under floodlights over the previous two seasons, that nearly 40,000 packed the Hawthorns for what turned out to be a precise 4-0 dissection of the Essex club. The perception of a bigger pitch and room to play in made all the difference.

The next round was literally tough. Doug Fraser and Graham Williams were our enforcers, players who frequently bundled opponents into the terraces but Cup opponents Southampton seem to have a whole team of hard men. Famously, Bill Shankly later described them as *"alehouse footballers".* At the Hawthorns, all our front men suffered grievously at the feet and elbows of the South Coast hard men. The Sinning Saints were determined not to lose and their regular dislocation of the play (and nearly some limbs) secured a 1-1 draw. Omens were not good. Southampton had already won 4-0 at the Dell in the League. A long midweek journey to see potentially another battering deterred the faint-hearted but not me.

With British Rail having all but scrapped steam trains by this point, I travelled South by diesel locomotive. Although there was no longer any danger of being covered in soot, I missed the individuality of steam and of course the service wasn't any more reliable. No complaints this time as trains ran perfectly and I could stroll to the Dell, rather than run.

Those of you who visited the Dell in the 1980's will remember the odd-shaped narrow stands and open terraces. The only real difference from the Dell then and two decades earlier was the absence of ugly security fencing. I'm repeating myself, I know, but segregation just wasn't necessary.

To a football supporter, the most satisfying victories are always the unexpected ones, achieved against the odds. At the Dell, we were matching the home side for aggression and worrying them at the back when John Osborne was concussed. With no reserve goalkeeper to turn to, this appeared to be a fatal blow. Ossie stayed between the sticks for the rest of the half with the Albion trainer giving him directions from behind the goal, in a crazy but brave effort. In front of our stricken keeper, our back four – at times a back five or six – did everything possible to divert the ball away from our goal. Every minute survived was a triumph. At half-time, Ossie was mercifully taken to hospital and Graham Williams reluctantly took the green jersey and the survival battle continued. I was convinced we wouldn't be able to hold out. So did the home support who "*pumped up the volume*" as or backs-to-the-wall efforts staggered on. Our wagons were definitely circled that night.to keep out Mick Channon, Ron Davies and Co. The boots of our defenders and the crossed fingers of supporters seemed inadequate and yet it was just enough.

I was so proud of the teams' battling qualities and pulling off a great win under difficult circumstances. Two from the King (including a late winner) and one from Bomber Brown just saw us home 3-2. The fans were ecstatic and I even spotted Chairman Jim Gaunt joining us in a few celebratory chants outside the ground apart from when we left the home supporters brassed off after our rendition of *"When the Saints go Marching out."*

It was back to the South Coast again at Portsmouth in the Fifth Round. On a very warm day, our team turned on the style in a 2-1 win. Astle and Clark silenced the Pompey chimes in a 40,000 crowd. Prior to kick-off, a sailor walked around the running track, as was Portsmouth's custom at the time. He seemed quite immune to the "wit" from the Black Country hordes. *"You're out, Pompey. Pompey you're out"* was our rather witty refrain this time.

After such a travelling marathon, I felt we deserved a kind Quarter-Final draw. Wishful thinking as we came out of the bag with one of the most feared teams in the country, the mighty Reds from Liverpool. The Reds weren't quite the dominant force they later became in the 1970's but were getting closer season on season, and were well nigh unbeatable at Anfield. Much like Southampton, the Liverpool team were physically imposing. They included the hulking Lawrence in goal plus hard men Ron Yeats and Tommy Smith at the back. They'd have made up a ferocious tag wrestling team.

We were set for a series of three tremendous battles before the winners would move into a Semi-Final. After a dull goalless draw at the Hawthorns, the Merseysiders were installed as firm favourites to win at Anfield. Much to the Scousers horror, the Pride of the Black Country refused to lie down in the replay and after a bruising two hour slog; the tie remained level at 1-1. A third match on a neutral ground was required

Maine Road got the nod and it was to host one of the best battling performances by an Albion side that I've ever witnessed. The 'Pool remained the favourites but this only made WBA even more determined. Around 20,000 Albion supporters travelled to Manchester that night. Just ponder on that figure. More people than attended some Saturday home League matches found a way to get to Maine Road that night. Yet, even with such outstanding support, the red half of Merseyside outnumbered us. Goals from (who else) Astle and Chipper Clark were just enough to nullify a goal from Roger Hunt and the Baggies held on for a deserved 2-1 victory despite the Kop favourites battering our lines

After that night, I was convinced we would win the Cup. The euphoria was overwhelming as we capered along the platform at Piccadilly Station - singing, dancing and the odd bottle of beer being consumed by even those who'd taken the pledge! It must be said that Liverpool supporters, waiting on the opposite platform, took the defeat in tremendous style. Not a hint of aggravation or abusive chants, merely praise for the Baggies as they wished us good luck and hoped we would win the Cup. (The fact that Everton were already in the last four might have had something to with these sentiments?)

Up to then there wasn't much conviction that Albion's name could be on the Cup. But now, increasingly, there was a feeling that luck was going our way. The Semi-Final opponents could be Everton, the all-powerful Leeds United or Second Division Birmingham. We pulled out the plum – the local derby against the weakest opponents and we got to play them just "down the road" at Villa Park. I was thrilled. Truly we had the luck of the draw whereas heavyweights Everton and Leeds had to fight it out between them for one Wembley place.

An electric atmosphere enveloped Villa Park and for 90 minutes both sets of supporters gave everything as they willed their team on with tremendous passionate support. If there was one difference between the teams that difference was undoubtedly John Osborne. Ossie, as he was fondly known, must have wanted that Wembley appearance more than anyone such was his performance between the sticks. The Blues caused Albion unending problems with Fred Pickering, an outstanding centre forward, seemingly permanently engaged in a personal shoot out with Ossie. He fired in shots from all angles but this was to be our day. We hadn't created much all afternoon but lethal strikers such as ours didn't need much. History records that Astle and Brown made the most of their opportunities.

The Blues fans cursed and moaned about the 2-0 score and I suppose if I'd been in their position I would have felt extremely hard done by. But at that time, I could only think of Wembley and rejoice that unlike 1954, obtaining a ticket would be straightforward.

Two days later came the perfect opportunity to show our appreciation of our Wembley-bound team. Title-chasing Manchester United were at the Hawthorns and as if needing to prove their superiority, a wonderful display from Albion sent them home on the back of a 6-3 defeat. Despite the presence of Best, Law, Charlton etc, this was our night. A thundering hat trick from Jeff Astle led the way with Tony Brown, Ronnie Rees and young Asa Hartford scoring one apiece.

United did fight back determinedly.  If both sides had taken all their chances it would have needed the scoreboard from West Bromwich Dartmouth to record all the action. That night, it seemed to be that everyone in the town wanted to be at the Hawthorns and dare I say that cramming more people in was thought more important than safety? There were hundreds of supporters sitting on the perimeter of the pitch. Such was the crush it was quite impossible to get injured people out. I found the official attendance of 46,000 rather hard to believe.

The biggest mystery of all was just what more did Jeff Astle have to do to gain that elusive England cap? He had led the scoring charts for the bulk of the season and yet manager Alf Ramsay was still ignoring him for reasons he locked away in his mind.

Just two days later, Albion were in action again and so was King Jeff. West Ham United had no answer to his aerial power and all round game and with his second hat trick in three days spearheaded a comfortable 3-1 win. No strolling to the Cup Final for the Baggies.

By this time of course the football world knew that the world's most famous Cup Final was to be contested by West Bromwich Albion and those other Merseyside giants Everton. The Albion team were again the underdogs. In the League, Everton had already completed the double including a 6-2 embarrassment at the Hawthorns. Graham Williams professed not to be concerned; claiming that very rarely does one team beat another three times in a season. This rather dubious message was clung to and repeated ad infinitum as the big day approached.

Looking back at Ashman's first season his biggest critics, and there had been many, would be forced to admit he'd done a superb job. He was popular with the players, forged a team playing a brand of attractive football, and he'd introduced the brilliant 17 year-old Asa Hartford into the squad.

May 18th 1968. The FA Cup Final was a brutal, ugly game with boots and bodies flying in all directions. The turning point for me came with the game goalless and Everton on the attack. A cross from the left dropped invitingly onto the head of Jimmy Husband. He could pick his spot. I wanted to turn away.

*"He's missed it - he's missed it,"* I howled in disbelief as did others around me. This turned out to be Everton's last real chance, and the end of their challenge.   Now we believed. We can win the Cup.

The solitary 'King' Astle goal, (scored with a far better strike than his original shot) bought every Albion fan to the edge of delirium. We were nearly there. In fact, it should have been 2-0, as in the dying seconds, Graham Lovett missed a sitter.

Behind that lay a unique confession. Everton, knowing that they had to score pushed players forward en-masse.  But they'd lost the ball and suddenly the break was on.  Bomber Brown and "Shuv" Lovett against just one backpedalling defender.

Terrified at spurning the opportunity 'Shuv' screamed *"don't give it to me, don't give it to me!"* But Tony, about to be tackled by the last defender, had no choice but to roll the ball gently to Lovett.  The midfielder lunged at the ball and missed the goal with embarrassing ease. *"Told you not to give it to me"* he moaned at his bemused team-mate.  This is of course one of Bomber Brown's favourite anecdotes and is always popular with supporters. Mind you if it had subsequently denied us the win, I suspect Bomber would have kept "mum".

Back to the action. We implored, no demanded the final whistle. Eventually it sounded..."*We've won, we've won the Cup*"...Let the celebrations begin

The band struck up the traditional Cup Final anthem... *"When the Saints go marching in",* and Baggie fans immediately changed Saints to Stripes, although we'd played in an all-white kit. Graham Williams proudly took the Cup, passed it around the team and no one wanted that lap of honour to end.

Reluctantly we eventually left the ground only to congregate outside the giant Wembley gates to see the players and the Cup once again. They had their formal celebrations pre-booked. Ours were strictly informal but no less fun. There was non-stop singing on the trains back to New Street and a posse of Evening Mail photographers waiting to capture all those manic expressions.

The magnificent reception at the West Bromwich Town Hall rounded off our season perfectly. Tens of thousands turned out, cheering the cavalcade all the way from Birmingham City centre, accompanied by Cliff Richard's Eurovision Song Contest entry *"Congratulations"* at full decibels. That Cup was so hard-won. Was our name always on it? It's impossible to be certain. We may have been lucky at Colchester, no, we were definitely lucky. Birmingham fans still think they should have won the Semi-Final; but we had Ossie in unbeatable, magnificent form and if anyone deserved a winners' medal, he did. Husband of Everton missed a gloriously simple header in the Final. In contrast, we'd battled so hard throughout.

Alan Ashman's first season had ended with a finishing position of eighth in the League, FA Cup winners and another crack at Europe. Albion, so often, were exciting to watch. Again, Jeff Astle had led the way with a magnificent tally of 35 in all competitions followed by 15 each from Tony Brown and Clive Clark. I still wistfully reflect on the easy rapport between the fans and the team during this period. Everyone was approachable but as ever it's the goal scorers who always get the attention as in *"We all agree*

*Astle is better than Pele*
*The Bomber is better than Eusebio"*
*They're so good they should be on the telly*

There were numerous other versions of the Black Country ditty that on reflection sounds terribly dated. The combination of Black Country humour, and valiant attempts at singing, were regular highlights for Baggie supporters at any game.

While the Wembley win was our highlight of the decade, there was another result that boosted the country's spirit. Ten years after the Munich disaster, Manchester United had reached the European Cup Final.  The whole country was behind United that evening.

I managed to get a ticket for the Final and on that historic night, the Red Devils eventually crushed Benfica at Wembley after a tremendously passionate game. Sat among a ferocious crowd of United followers, I did my best to roar on Best, Charlton etc. as if they were playing in a blue and white Albion shirt. Well almost...

The 4-1 win, naturally dedicated to Matt Busby, was a fair result though I didn't appreciate the occasion properly as I was suffering from a dreadful cold. The worst element was standing up on the train all the way back to New Street on the "sardine-crammers" Express. United would be competing in Europe the following season but so would we and that was a consoling thought to hang onto during those tedious hours and of course I still had some residual FA Cup Final glow about me.

The residual glow then morphed into another happy event. I was a passionate Animal Welfare worker and Secretary of the Birmingham Branch of The Animal Welfare Trust.  As a thank-you for all the fund-raisers and publicity events that Dot and I had helped to organise, we were presented with an Old English sheepdog puppy. We named her Holly and she automatically became the Branch mascot. The presentation was made appropriately during the annual West Bromwich carnival.

As well as the memories of our FA Cup triumphs, I also have the photographs. Lots of lots of them but the ones that mean most to me were taken at the annual cricket match between West Bromwich Dartmouth and who else but West Bromwich Albion.

Skipper Graham Williams paraded the Cup around the ground as everyone took pictures. But I wanted something a little better and I negotiated an arrangement with the professional photographer for my personal collection. I have a picture of Graham and myself shaking hands while holding the Cup. Even better, I have a unique photograph of Dot, myself, and Holly, (she was sitting in the Cup) To this day, they remain on proud display in our hallway. I still live in hope of a more modern picture of another FA Cup triumph.

## 1968/69

The home of the FA Cup winners in 1968 - let me repeat that as it sounds so great- the home of the FA Cup winners in 1968 was actually very plain, arguably drab, for such a cool and trendy 1960's audience. The inside of The Hawthorns, excepting the brightly hued Rainbow stand seats, was mainly grey. Variants of grey, it was true but just grey all over the two mainly covered end terraces, the Rainbow paddock, the Woodman Corner and the bare benches which filled the front section of Halfords Lane. All these structures were modest in their colourings enlivened only by large advertisement hoardings. Many promoted the joys of alcohol such as the large Johnnie Walker whisky board over the Rainbow Stand or the grinning suppers of M&B beers topping the Smethwick End. Cigarette advertising was also prominent.

Just a low white painted wall separated spectators from the running track. During matches, stern-faced Police, often in groups of twos and threes, patrolled this area. They made a point of steering clear of the little knots of photographers who had their own uniform of formal shirts, ties and sports jackets early in the season. No doubt colder weather would see them revert to the universal grey or sludge brown raincoats worn by supporters.

Sad to relate, the outside of The Hawthorns would also receive the thumbs down from Prince Charles with its acres of dull brick, largely unrelieved by any items of architectural interest. But Prince Charles wasn't exactly a regular. The only time he was likely to attend the shrine was during a Royal visit and given his ancestors public dislike of the Black Country; this was about as likely as John Osborne scoring a goal. Hawthorns regulars were largely blind to design subtleties – this was the shrine, their place of dreams and the best escapism in the world.

Football kits were simple in 1968, plain and unchanging, unadorned by advertising or names. Boots were black of course, and if anyone had told me that in decades to come, boots would incorporate all the colours of the rainbow, I'd have laughed at them.

Players were invariably white with the Regis/ Cunningham/ Batson revolution was some ten years in the future. Albion fans were also pale-skinned and almost all male.

The club shop resembled a local corner shop. It didn't provide too much choice. Scarves, rosettes and programmes, plus a limited number of other odds and sods comprised their entire range. I remember thinking the rosettes were far too modest and so I persuaded my wife Dot to make me a proper favour, not as large as a dustbin lid but not far off! This eye-catching work of art was promptly festooned with badges and proudly displayed to universal admiration at Wembley.

Despite the shop being modest, supporters flocked to see what was on offer. Because of the unassertive dimensions, a queue was guaranteed if more than 20 people wanted to get in. Somehow, standing patiently for so long acted as an encouragement to choose something from the meagre range. I invariably ended up emptying my pockets, though never on a titchy rosette. A few replica shirts were on sale, albeit as a novelty. They weren't worn to matches, unable to compete with the fashionable universal raincoat. The clackety wooden rattle, albeit an endangered species, could still be found if you knew where to look, ditto small children standing on wooden boxes or milk crates provided by doting Dads anxious to inculcate their sons into the faith as early as possible.

Chants were simple, usually featuring the name of a favoured player, though songs reflected what was in the Top Ten of the day, their lyrics bent and twisted to a football theme. Sometimes they were downright obscene, but often witty. Even more surprising was the conscription of folk songs to the cause. Many were directed at Wolves – our only remaining local opposition still in the top flight.

*"Jingle Bells, Dougan smells, Parkin's got no hair,*
*Peter Knowles misses goals and Wagstaffe is a*
*square"* were one of the milder examples.

Goal celebrations were low key – a handshake or a brief hug, compared with today's over-the-top antics. But then, as it's a safe bet that some current players have contracts incorporating additional payments for every goal scored, what would you expect?

Some anti-social habits were creeping in to football. Throwing toilet rolls towards the pitch had very much caught on. Every public convenience within miles were relieved of their stock. Sometimes it was a reflection of the poor quality of football but far more often simply because it was fashionable.

As for me, I just wanted to get the new season underway. A warm summer did offer numerous opportunities to show off my latest garish shirt purchases. However, I'd seen the light. My shirts henceforth would be conventional and all the loud purchases were donated to a variety of local charity shops.

Simon & Garfunkel had just released "Mrs Robinson" and the Stones' "Jumpin' Jack Flash". The latter was not really my taste but it was hard to get away from it in the "swinging sixties". The "Beeb" launched a new comedy series called "Dads Army."

The 1968 Olympics was imminent. So there was much to distract me yet my focus remained firmly on anticipating live football at The Hawthorns.

Most of all, I eagerly awaited my Cup winning team demolishing all their non-Cup winning opposition. I'd laughed off any suggestions that the 6-1 demolition by Manchester City in the Charity Shield meant a season of struggle. Albion put out a weakened team that day due to injuries, but I was aware that our leaky defence did need a boost.

Alan Ashman clearly shared my optimism, as there were few personnel changes to his FA Cup winning squad. Ashman's men relied heavily on their first class goal scorers (King Jeff and Bomber Brown) to outscore the opposition. Let's just say our defence was more second class than first class.

My regularly ear-bent friends and workmates were even more relieved than I was when the opening-day fixture (Sheffield Wednesday at home) finally came around.  A goalless draw wasn't what I had in mind. The game had been chosen for the first ever Star Soccer, the new ATV football highlights programme, on the Sunday afternoon. Industrial action meant they were never shown. I wasn't about to complain, enduring such dull fare once was quite ample, thanks.

Still, the next match was home to European Champions Manchester United and a 3-1 victory left me more than content. Oh yes, chest-puffing out time. Three points out of four, United defeated so surely this season was going to be enjoyable? Arguably it probably was but not so for regulars at the Hawthorns.

Four of our first eight League games were lost leaving me crestfallen Losing heavily at Upton Park was normal as snow in January so that was acceptable but enduring -newly-promoted Coventry put four into our net was hard to take. Coventry!

Had I possessed a crystal ball and knew what was coming, I really wouldn't have complained.
Within two years, there was another Wembley defeat to endure and far worse, as Albion's main men aged, a gradual slide towards relegation in 1973 followed by obscurity until Johnny Giles rolled up. Nine months after that, Oldham became the most beautiful place on earth.

But I didn't have a crystal ball so I continued to grumble my way through much of the early season. *"We won the Cup. It's not supposed to be like this."*

The inconsistencies that always seemed to be an Albion forte were highlighted early in September. First tilt at the League Cup saw us away against Nottingham Forest, the tie played at the novelty venue of Meadow Lane. The City ground was unavailable due to a fire in the Main Stand. At the time, I didn't pause to consider the implications of the conflagration. The fire started near the dressing rooms during a full-house game with Leeds United and due to the wooden structure, spread very quickly. Thankfully, everyone got out without serious injury and football life went on without any additional consideration for spectator safety.

With Forest deprived of home advantage, two goals from Astle and one from Ronnie Rees guided us into the next round via a 3-2 win. Four days on, with Forest visiting The Hawthorns for a League match, I anticipated more of the same. Forest turned that cup result on its head, cruising to a 5-2 victory. Ouch, what a debacle! And although an uplifting counterbalance 3-2 away win at Newcastle was next, it was a somewhat perplexed set of supporters who set out for a new European campaign. A different competition too as we were now eligible for the slightly more prestigious European Cup Winners Cup, solely for national Cup winners. We were off to Belgium, to play first time Belgium Cup winners Royal Football Club (RFC) Bruges. (If the name sounds unfamiliar, the club changed its name to Club Bruges KV four years later)

Around 300 supporters made our second venture into Europe via a combination of coach and air travel. Sealander (Des O'Connor's company) took us from West Bromwich to Luton Airport. We clambered aboard a plane to Brussels, where a noisy but well behaved set of supporters including football journalists Bob Blackburn and Denis Shaw, savoured the sights and sounds of Brussels.

What the bemused citizens thought of my large Union Jack Albion flag, I hadn't the faintest idea but I still have a black and white press photograph of it as a permanent keepsake!

Our last lap was a coach trip to Bruges, where I would have liked to have spent more time exploring. I'd heard so much about its delightful little bridges, canals and shops. There isn't much to admire through a steamed-up coach window at night. (I finally had an opportunity to wander around Bruges town centre some 30 years later during a European touring holiday)

Bruges' home, the Albert Dyserynckstadion, was tightly packed with supporters. I remember thinking at the time how small and intimate the place was yet I was astonished to read later that over 28,000 were crammed in.

As for the match itself, it was one of the most unpleasant 90 minutes I've ever endured. Bruges was the 'dirtiest' team it has been my misfortune to see, and ever wish to see. Add a partisan set of fans that literally wanted to see blood from every tackle and it makes it easier to understand why I, along with every Baggies fan, wanted to hear the final whistle.

Today visiting fans would be corralled into a designated area, easy to be 'protected' if circumstances dictated. That wasn't the case for this game. A number were housed opposite the main stand on the halfway line, and others adjacent to the edge of the penalty area. If circumstances dictated! This foreign adventure definitely came into that category as Bruges bullied their way to a 3-1 first leg advantage in a blatant demonstration of unchecked on-field thuggery.

Jeff Astle, with ten goals to his name, was a marked man. Literally. He was kicked, punched, shoved, tripped, and manhandled in brutal fashion. And as we screamed in protest, he was finally stretchered off to hospital with concussion after a kick in the head following a goalmouth flare up. (Later, Laraine Astle confided to me that Jeff had no recollection of the incident at all. Perhaps that was a blessing.)

Consequently, players of both sides engaged in angry confrontations. Fans ran onto the pitch. Coins were thrown. Several Albion players were struck and it took at least thirty armed Police to calm down a situation that could well have led to a riot. The villain of the piece was the most incompetent referee I have ever seen in charge of a prestigious European match. He was Danish, a Mr de Haser, and his non-performance has surely never been equalled.

Were we glad to get away from that stadium! But even then it was a case of looking over the shoulder, as a minority of fuming Bruges fans appeared determined to continue the aggravation. Safely back on board the plane, fans swapped experiences. A few told of scuffles but thankfully nothing of a serious nature.

A welcome return flight, and although still smarting and angry, there was a mutual feeling that the goal scored by young Asa Hartford could be a lifesaver. With the recent innovation that away goals would count double, a 2-0 win would see us through to the next round. But it was a brooding set of supporters who finally arrived home, and already the thoughts were turning to a second leg Hawthorns revenge. Would Bruges be allowed to get away with such thuggish tactics for a second time? Indeed, would they choose the same tactics on foreign soil bearing in mind the eyes of the European press would be focussed on them after what they labelled as *"The Battle of Bruges."*

A week later and our League Cup interest ended in of all places Peterborough. The 'Posh' gained consolation for their Semi-Final defeat two years previously, winning 2-1. Were the events or more particularly the bruises from Bruges, to blame? Fingers were being pointed in all directions. That a full strength West Bromwich Albion side should lose to a struggling Fourth Division outfit was inexcusable. One curiosity – Jeff Astle was marked that night by a very young John Wile.

I hoped for better in a League match at Goodison Park. Put a modern day supporter into Goodison in 1968 and essentially they wouldn't notice much difference. There was more terracing of course and inevitably thousands of those universal grey raincoats. But the shape of the ground and the surrounding streets remains unspoilt by progress as does their theme tune, Johnny Todd (Z Cars).

My hopes were dashed. A totally unconvincing display saw both team and fans 'limp' home on the wrong end of a 4-0 score. Everton supporters were chanting *"4-0, 4-0"*, delighted they'd gained revenge for their Wembley defeat. But as a more discerning fan said to me on the way out: *"If we'd won 10-0, it still wouldn't have made up for losing the Cup Final"*. Very true, but it certainly wasn't a happy omen.

And then nauseating Bruges were in town. Fired up by the physical and mental scars inflicted on our favourites, a very hostile full house at the Hawthorns wanted, no, craved revenge. Yet the visitors ploughed into the Baggies once again, with Jeff Astle singled out. Seconds Out ... Round Two for Bruges defender John Moelaert. Rather than wait for Astle to be in possession before making his move, he simply, and cynically, obstructed Jeff as soon as the Albion number nine attempted to reach any kind of cross.

However much we collectively bellowed at Swedish referee Einar Bostrom, Moelaert was largely allowed to continue his one - man assassination attempts unchecked. The fury from the terraces was generating enough energy to power the match floodlights.

Had the Baggies not been on top, I do wonder what might have happened. I'm not an aggressive person. But many of my fellow supporters clearly were, unable to fully contain their emotions about the assaults upon our striker. I did wonder whether anyone would invade the pitch because if they did, I knew exactly who the target would be. Part of me, perhaps the dark part that everyone has within them, was almost wishing that to happen.

Fortunately an early-ish goal for the Baggies relieved much of the simmering aggression. For once, Astle dodged his hit man, knocking a cross down for Bomber Brown to tap in. One more goal would do it providing Bruges didn't find the net themselves. The visitors rarely looked like scoring, with their players ever mindful of mass abuse or having coins hurled at them whenever they got too close to the touchlines.

Asa Hartford scored the crucial second goal just before half time. Teammates rushed over to celebrate with him while I, together with the rest of Hawthorns faithful, celebrated as if we'd already won. King Jeff demonstrated how he in particular had savoured the moment. Standing over the Bruges keeper he slowly and deliberately clapped his hands and shared his personal unprintable thoughts, which I suspect were in line with my own "*Take that you B...... you're getting your just deserts*" At 3-3, Albion were ahead on aggregate and everybody was reminding Bruges of the score.

Asa himself appeared to be second on the Belgium's hit list after Jeff Astle, but his slight frame stood up to everything the marauders threw at him. Unbelievably it was only in the 88th minute, that the dithering referee entered a name in his little black book and unsurprisingly it just had to be Moelaert for his umpteenth foul on Astle. But by then, unable to exert any pressure on Osborne, the unsavoury Bruges were down and out. Good riddance, hope you enjoyed the flight home-but what a satisfying bus ride home for this ecstatic Baggies fan!

This very satisfying win became the launching pad for a series of improved League results. We were unbeaten in the League through October. First up were the Rangers from West London. Much as I was relieved to beat QPR 3-1, and note grimly that Rodney Marsh wasn't saving them this time, it still didn't make up for losing the League Cup Final. Newly promoted Rangers were all at sea that season and up to then hadn't won a single game. Anything other than victory would have twisted the knife even further. Three more wins followed the defeat of Rangers including a 6-1 revenge inflicted upon Coventry City, which stabilised our position in the table. We then played the really big boys in Leeds and Liverpool and shared the points both times with much pride restored.  United's Jack Charlton was (as ever) regaled with cries of "Rubberneck." Perhaps that was true but I don't recall anyone using that term when he was part of England's unforgettable World Cup victory against West Germany. Based on these encouraging performances, I began to inwardly believe this Albion side was now on the way to more great things.

If the Baggies and their fans thought they'd had their fill of the downside of European football, they could think again because as Al Jolson often famously remarked "*You ain't seen nothing yet.*" The draw was not kind, pairing us with a Rumanian side - Dinamo Bucharest. Around this time, an instrumental by Hugo Montenegro "The Good, the Bad and the Ugly" became Number One. Naturally Hawthorns wags quickly seized on the phrase as an apt description of our European adventures.

Rumania was the great unknown. What was widely understood is that under the oppressive regime of Nicolae Ceauşescu, citizens were cowed into toeing the party line. That didn't sound like my idea of fun. I didn't go, deterred by cost, location and reputation.

This was a largely cheerless experience for determined Albionites, undeterred by crossing the Iron Curtain (essentially a division separating the Soviet Union and their allies from the rest of Europe). If the Hawthorns looked a little downbeat in 1968, it was a positive riot of noise and colour compared to Bucharest.  Here, visitors were regularly eyed suspiciously by hostile armed Police in a mutual atmosphere of distrust. I remember one fanatic recalling to me how one of his chums had become very merry on cheap alcohol and burst into a ribald chant about Ceausescu. The whole group rounded on him immediately lest the Police move into action.

The bare bones? The match at the 15,000 Capacity Stadionul finished 1-1. Asa Hartford again scored a very handy away goal. But this was counterbalanced when Ronnie Rees was sent off and Albion were forced to defend short-handed for the last fifteen minutes. The crowd invaded the pitch at the end, and Albion players had to 'run for their lives', amid a hail of missiles. Dinamo were aptly named the "Red Dogs".

Doug Fraser was unusually vocal in his summary. *"It was a terrifying experience. I've never seen a mob like it at home or abroad before".* Gron Williams in the Birmingham Post made a very telling observation in his summing up." *Albion should enjoy themselves hugely at the Hawthorns against Dinamo's flimsy defence. Had they snapped up their chances more sharply, the equalising goal scored by 18 year old Asa Hartford after 28 minutes could have been only one of three".*

How prophetic. The return was strictly a non-contest. Two goals from the 'Bomber' (one a penalty), one apiece from Astle and Lovett gave Albion a stroll through to the Quarter Final. I was one of the 33,000 who savoured what turned out to be another Hawthorns floodlit glory night.

My hopes were rising, especially with the Baggies paired with the Scottish side Dunfermline. I really was beginning to believe that we could go all the way in the Cup Winners Cup. After all, weren't we West Bromwich Albion, holders of the FA Cup? Dunfermline felt like a dream draw. Another new place to visit but no need for a passport, plane or foreign currency – excellent! I didn't know much about our Scottish opposition, so I just accepted the common wisdom that if they weren't Celtic or Rangers, they wouldn't be too much of a problem. Hadn't their top goal scorer Alex Ferguson (yes, him) just moved to Rangers? Few noted how immersed the Pars already were in the cynical world of European competitions – this was their sixth tournament in 8 years.

But before that, the arrival of 1969 meant my attention switching back to the FA Cup. Having just experienced the thrill of seeing the Baggies run around Wembley with the trophy, I greedily wanted a return visit. Naturally so did the players. Laraine Astle confided in me that following the let-off at Colchester the previous season, Jeff decided to wear the same clothes for every subsequent Cup day. And if that was the official club blazer and tie, a simple compromise, just pack them along with any other items. The Third Round draw was favourable with a home match against Second Division Norwich City. The Canaries surrendered fairly easily, 3-0, and Wembley's first obstacle was overcome.

Back to European action and the first leg at Dunfermline in mid-January. Around 1,000 supporters travelled, mainly on a special train. The travellers had a fierce determination to enjoy themselves, which included drinking the bar dry. Local breweries were pleased as allegedly, the train bar needed restocking by Crewe. Empty bottles were everywhere. They were jammed onto tables, rolling around the floor or in the luggage compartment. While I've never been a drinker myself, serious imbibing was part of Black Country culture at the time. The plethora of heavy industry meant that for many blokes in particular, the imperative was simple fluid replacement rather than wishing to get drunk quickly. Many pubs always had salt cellars available, as salt replacement was also vital

Even making allowances for such necessities, train staff in the small Fife town had a massive and unpleasant clean-up job to deal with. What must they have thought of their Black Country visitors as they weaved their way unsteadily on the 15 minute walk to East End Park, filling up every pub en route?

The match was all-ticket and limited to 25,000, an artificial figure imposed by the Police after frightening crowd scenes earlier against Celtic when 28,000 crammed in. Perhaps fearing a repeat, nearly two thousand ticket holders didn't show up, which prevented the Pars setting a new crowd record for European football.

They missed a fast and furious affair though lacking the evil-edged intensity witnessed against Bruges and Dinamo. John Kaye was outstanding in a defence that effectively shut out the Scottish Cup holders. A platform was thus created for an away win but chances created were all missed. Jeff Astle wasn't at his best so ultimately neither side scored. The Baggies team were disappointed not to have made the most of their dominance.

Fortified by a few more "wee drams" en route, Albion supporters were content enough. Away goals didn't count in the Quarter Finals so with the home leg still to follow, our position looked rosy. The special train headed back to the Midlands via Edinburgh, a long, long trip arriving deep into the early hours. But what an experience!

There were so many Cup matches that month. Our reward for beating Norwich in the FA Cup was a popular trip to the Smoke, this time to play Fulham.

The Cottagers were having a desperate time in the second tier; eventually finishing bottom with only 5 home wins all season. They were "up for the Cup" for sure but were eventually sunk 2-1, courtesy of goals from Asa Hartford, and sub Ronnie Rees who grabbed the winner with his first kick. The smell of Wembley was growing ever stronger as I was convinced that nobody could stop us. Did I mention we're the Cup holders?

League matches were pretty much secondary during this period. Our earlier solid form meant we didn't need to be too concerned about securing only one point from five games. It became almost a way to keep in practice between the Cup matches.

Into the FA Cup Fifth Round and another London side stood in our way. We were paired with Arsenal, thankfully at home. Unlike the Baggies, the North London side were not worthy of European competition but did have similar problems of weariness as they were still competing in the later stages of the League Cup. The Gunners were building slowly towards an all-conquering team and already featured many of the big names – Wilson, McNab, Radford and McLintock though they still needed to offload Bobby Gould before they could possibly win anything.

The interest in the big match was impressive. Albion had been pulling in 30,000+ for their European matches but this was the FA Cup. Over 46,000 passed through the turnstiles though comparatively few were backing the North Londoners. Arsenal returned 4,000 tickets with Secretary Bob Wall making feeble excuses. *"I am afraid that our fans now are being brought up in luxury. Very few of them like to stand on the terraces. If they cannot get a seat, they do not want to go. This seems to be the general trend in football."* Cue head scratching. Who did Bob

Wall imagine was filling up the North Bank and the Clock End at Highbury, two of the most celebrated standing areas in the country? The Highbury terracing was recognised in a sinister-sounding chant heard at the Hawthorns that season

*"Tiptoe through the North Bank*
*With a razor and a twelve-bore shotgun*
*Tiptoe through the North Bank with me"*

(Even Lennon and McCartney at their composing best, couldn't have bettered that witty ditty)!

More realistically, a prolonged period of very cold weather probably deterred many from travelling. Several of the eight FA Cup matches were postponed, including the Hawthorns clash. Four days later despite a frozen pitch, the stars in stripes took the field against Arsenal. Albion, with their massive support, were indeed the stars with a 1-0 victory thanks to Bomber Brown.

All over the Black Country and Birmingham, there was the usual tense huddle around a radio on Monday dinner-time to hear the draw for the 6th Round. Who'd be the next team to find themselves with the thankless task of stemming Albion's second successive trip to Wembley? The presenters were calmer than their audience. *"Chelsea will play West Bromwich Albion"*. I realised that this would be certainly be our sternest test to date.

For weeks, there was only one word to accurately describe the weather- dreadful. One of the many victims was Bobby Hope who caught flu and was confirmed to his bed. His loss, for me, was the key for the return leg of the Dunfermline Quarter-Final. The pitch was still frozen with the temperature registering minus 4. Both the Scottish team and their supporters made very slow progress on a rail network crippled by snow and ice but there was no doubt about the game going ahead. The Hawthorns ground staff had the novel idea that dumping tons of sand on the pitch would make for a more playable surface. Dropping sand on top of ice? I wasn't a groundsman, but clearly to him, and fellow turf experts, it was the only way to counter the conditions. Nowadays, a postponement would be guaranteed.

On the eve of an historic event, the wind was violent, driving the freshly laid sand in all directions. Was this Siberia or West Bromwich? Nearly 33,000 people determinedly battled the elements. It's customary for Scots, when venturing over the 'border, to proudly wear the traditional kilt to prove nothing could deter them. On this occasion, to prove it really was cold, they left them at home, and dressed as normal. Grey overcoat, hat, scarf, gloves, plus, if like me, two pair of socks!

Albion diehards standing up were marginally warmer than those with seats because they could pack together tightly. Teeth chattering and involuntary foot stamping in the Rainbow, I slightly envied the squeezed-together ant colony in the Brummie Road. But of course I had to be there regardless of conditions because I was convinced that the Baggies would create history and reach the Semi-Finals

Dunfermline manager George Farm said pre-match: *"We'll try to score an early goal and defend to the bitter end".* Such an extraordinary understatement! The Pars scored after just 90 seconds from a free kick and from then on adopted a very cynical attitude to protect their advantage. Their defence was led by centre half Roy Barry, who later made his name at Coventry. Any hint of danger and the Pars whacked the ball into touch. If an Albion player found himself in a potentially dangerous situation, they had no hesitation in kicking him as well. Painful memories of Bruges were rekindled.

Astle's close marker Barry easily blocked the Baggies main tactic of humping footballs into the penalty box. The plan wasn't working. Showing all the wisdom of a World War One General, the aerial bombardment continued more frenziedly with the same outcome. It was hard to say whether the players or supporters looked the most panicked. We literally had no Hope. And then a heavy blizzard began and didn't stop. What awful crime had we collectively committed to endure this? But we had to carry on. My hopes were swamped by trepidation. Tony Brown thought he'd equalised but his free kick was struck off for offside. Albion new boy Dennis Martin was clear through only for the keepers trailing leg to prevent an equaliser. If it was possible, I felt colder by the minute as dread overcame me that this was not our night and our European dream was almost certainly over.

Indeed it was and as the cold-immune Scots ran onto the sand to celebrate, I felt so bitterly disappointed. We'd outplayed all 3 teams in Europe but if European football only consists of dirty teams, bent referees and violent fans; we're better off without it.

Yet such is the nature of supporters within a few days I was dreaming of winning the FA Cup again and returning to Europe. Chin up, Terry. We've got another Quarter-Final to go yet!

That game, at glamorous high-flying Chelsea, featuring Osgood, Cooke, Bonetti, Webb, Chopper Harris and their other big names was simply a massive barrier. They certainly didn't play like the world renowned 'Chelsea Pensioners', even though this was their nickname at the time. The Bridge was the place to be for the London glitterati. The club programme featured a different regularly-attending celebrity in every issue.

Yet despite its trendy reputation, Stamford Bridge was actually rather run-down and behind the times. It was essentially a large bowl with the remains of a dog track separating the spectators from the playing area. The big open terrace behind one goal where the noisy Albion contingent gathered was a telescopic distance from the pitch.

Opposite of course was the Shed End, also mainly uncovered and home to numerous aggressive characters. The days of hooliganism were not far away and already rumour had it that supporters of the West London side were best avoided. Not easy when trying to jam on to the same underground carriage after making our usual train journey from Birmingham New Street to Euston Station!

Everyone wanted to be at the Quarter-Final, with 52,000 packing the terraces. Remarkable the lure of the Cup holders! Chelsea took the lead and with them dominating midfield. I was feeling desperately anxious until Bomber Brown equalised from what had to be an impossible angle. The goal gave the team and every Baggies fan an inspirational lift. Graham Lovett was now back to his scintillating best, eclipsing Chelsea's midfield with his speed, quick eye and anticipation.

Then cue mass exhilaration. The King headed home a corner only for the celebrations to be cut short, as the referee had awarded Albion a penalty. How bizarre! Still, as I told myself sternly, with Bomber's Deadeye Dick accuracy, we could live with the idiotic decision. That was before Bonetti saved the penalty low by the post. Apparently, I was ranting incoherently. That's according to my pals who weren't making any sense to me either.

Minutes later, I was raving again. The King had broken clear and only had the onrushing goalkeeper to beat. I was roaring" *come on Jeff, come on, you can do it"*

He did. *"Gooaalll."* The ball was in the net and we were ahead at last.

Understandably, the Baggies fell back on defence to defend their advantage. Ossie made some tremendous saves, highlighted by an astonishing incident when, after a ridiculous goalmouth melee, the ball miraculously stuck under him as he sat on the ball. When I asked Ossie years later to share his recollections, I was hoping for a brief sound bite. What I got back was two pages of beautifully crafted prose which includes these lines *"I can assure everyone that 99% of the pace of the ball was absorbed by a sensitive part of my anatomy. The next thing I remember through tear-filled eyes was John Boyle lunging in with his outstretched boot following the exact trajectory as the ball had seconds before. Fortunately my private parts were already anaesthetised by the ball, so I didn't particularly feel the six studs gouging their way across them."* There was much more in a similar vein but my own eyes are already watering too much to include further memories.

This was a magnificent victory, a real I-feel-like-a-wet-rag-afterwards affair. My Saturday night celebrations remain a blur on the journey home. Myself, my mates, seemingly everyone on the train, we were all repeating variances of the same mantra to each other – just one more game. Overcome one more obstacle, and we'd be back at Wembley. The aroma of success was as heady as Rackhams cosmetics counter.

Remember our varying fortunes against Nottingham Forest earlier in the season? By coincidence, the Cup match against Chelsea was followed a week later by a Hawthorns League match against the same opposition. There were no celebrations this time. The Pensioners discarded their walking frames, replaced them with running shoes and won comfortably 3-0. Disappointing, but we'd all got Wembley in both nostrils and everything else just didn't seem to matter that much.

The three other clubs remaining in the FA Cup were Manchester City, Everton and the weakest of the three – Leicester. Naturally the press wanted a potential re-match of the 1968 Cup Final but when we drew Leicester I was more than happy. The Foxes were marooned in a relegation spot en route to losing their top-flight status.

So onto Hillsborough. What a bitter, depressing and miserable experience. My pre match optimism faded away at a rate of knots. Albion's 18,000 ticket allocation had been eagerly snapped up. And no one could possibly entertain the thought of a defeat. How wrong could we be? Albion put on a dismal performance. Even so, thoughts were turning to an unlikely replay venue of Middlesbrough when John Osborne dropped an 87th minute clanger by fumbling a routine effort from Allan Clarke. It was the most crucial in an afternoon of constant errors which sent me and the huge army of Albion fans back home immersed in abject despair.

I really had been spoilt with our cup runs and it was hard to accept they were over for another season. It's the hope I can't stand. We were so close and blew our chance. My anguish lasted for the best part of a week. Optimism replaced by 100% negativity.

The next game saw a 2-1 defeat at Old Trafford but after that we had some sort of consolation, and a vastly improved league placing. From the last eight games, a welcome return to form saw five wins and 3 draws, topped off with a 5-1 defeat of Newcastle.

The end result meant another mid-table position. Highlights were the blooding of Asa Hartford, an International in the making; and the first look at another promising youngster in Len Cantello. Graham Lovett was back to his best. John Kaye and Doug Fraser always battled and, as always, the incomparable skills of Bobby Hope. The midfielder had set up so many of the 26 goals scored by Jeff Astle and the 23 of Tony Brown.

The defence was still the main weakness for me. Sixty-four goals scored compared well with the League Champions Leeds United who managed 66, but as we conceded 67, compared to their miserly 26, it was clear where the discrepancies lay.

The reserve team enjoyed a good season, finishing second in the Central League. During this period, attendances often ran into several thousands, partly because the bar remained open (a rarity on a Saturday afternoon) and also as it was the only way to get regular updates on progress of the first team. For a couple of the home games, I managed to introduce our fast-growing Old English sheepdog puppy 'Holly' to the joys of watching the Baggies. I smuggled her in using an above average size bag through the Hawthorns turnstiles. Mercifully, her behaviour was impeccable (well she was an Albion fan) to the extent that I exercised her on a lead at half-time. I seriously considered enrolling her as a Supporters Club member!

# 1969/70
My (and Albion's!) "Annual' Cup final outing

In late May, Albion suffered a major blow. Graham Lovett, who had so courageously battled his way back after that horrendous car accident, unbelievably discovered that lightning can strike twice. Returning home from the airport, he met a double-decker bus coming towards him on the wrong side of the road. Following the collision, the bus agonisingly toppled over onto his car. With the limited technology available at the time, "Shuv" was trapped for over two and a half hours. In a desperate state, he faced months of intensive recuperation.

Alan Ashman was eager to move the club forward from its inconsistent, score-a-lot, concede-a-lot status the previous term. Out came the cheque book, partly enforced due to the prolonged absence of the brilliant Lovett.

Albion broke their club record, signing striker Colin Suggett from Sunderland for £100,000 though at the Baggies, he became a midfielder. Local-born Suggett was popular at the Mackems but they felt unable to say no to the biggest fee they'd ever received for a player. Without him, Sunderland went on to be relegated.

Arguably costing even more than Suggett was Danny Hegan. The Scot was a very experienced professional with Ipswich Town who signed for £88,000 plus Ian Collard. He was a potential 1960's Willie Johnston, though to everyone's frustration he played only in fits and starts. He built a reputation as a notorious pub-goer and quickly management realised they'd make a bad mistake, presumably not picking up just why he was on Town's transfer list for so many months. 1960's Albion directors are very similar to modern day counterparts in that they consider money is not plentiful and needs to be invested wisely. As Hegan years later admitted to reporter Dave Instone, *"It was the wrong time for me to go there and the wrong time for them to sign me, and it just didn't work out."*

Suggett and Hegan weren't the only newcomers into a team in transition. Another £30,000+ was invested in goalkeeper Jim Cumbes from Tranmere Rovers. Jim was famously one of the last footballer-cricketers though was almost as well known for his enormous hands. Aided by his cricketing skills, he thought nothing of throwing a football accurately to a team mate on the halfway line. It was an extraordinary weapon and briefly confused the opposition. Cumbes was officially to provide senior competition for John Osborne. I often wondered whether privately Ashman thought that the ever-nervous Ossie would never fully recover from the trauma of his FA Cup Semi-Final mistake.

Alan Glover, a winger cum midfield player, also joined from Queens Park Rangers. Part of the deal meant that 'Chippy' Clark would be returning to his old club after spending nine great years with the Baggies. At times, it hadn't been all sweetness and light, and on more than one occasion he'd requested a transfer after disputing happenings at the Hawthorns. But on the field, I thought he was tremendous. Quick and tricky on the ball, I saw him mesmerise the finest full backs in the country. That was "Chippy" the Baggie fans revered, the one I will always remember with his trademark rolled down socks and no shin pads. He was painfully kicked and kicked again but always got up without complaint. What state his lower legs were in during later life doesn't bear thinking about. I was so saddened when he left as I knew it would be a long time, if ever, I saw another wide player of equal talent.

Percy Freeman was also in the team. He was big, strong and almost absurdly enthusiastic and what a character. Any opponent in possession would feel the human battering ram bearing down on him. Unfortunately for such a likeable person, that was the limit of his talents. He was way out of his depth, only playing in a trio of senior games before being transferred to Fourth Division Lincoln City, where his strengths were more suited.

Both Suggett and Hegan were in the team on the opening day. Albion won 2-0 at Southampton with Suggett scoring both. Despite their good start, the Baggies lost their first home game. And their second. And their third. For me, it was a massive let-down. There was a buzz around the area with over 30,000 people turning up for the first three games and to be defeated in all three was a massive let-down, especially as they were partly self-inflicted.

There was a worrying disharmony between Jeff Astle and the board over wages. Jeff believed regularly enduring a battering from defenders deserved more reward while the Board were offering. Take your pick between taking a strategic view around increasing remuneration for just one player or just being tight-fisted. The popular view around me favoured the latter. The King was dropped but his absence merely strengthened his case as without him, the side couldn't manage one goal in 3 home matches. Local media summarised the situation succinctly: *"Astle is clearly one man Albion need back in the side - and quickly. He is not only wanted for his ability to score goals but to bolster the confidence of a sagging team."*

Once a settlement was agreed, the King put his body on the line again. His six goals in September steadied our ship somewhat but the Hawthorns men went to secure just three points in their first seven home games. By then Albion were just one point clear of a relegation place.

The first home win was a narrow 2-1 over Manchester United at the back end of October. Apart from a massive sigh of relief all round, the fixture was noticeable as a young defender Alistair Robertson played his first game. He was tough for one of such tender years. One In One Out – expensive new signing Hegan was out of favour and into the reserves, never properly to return.

Fortunately, nine more home wins followed before the end of the season to ease relegation concerns or as the newly launched Monty Python might say *"and now for something completely different."* Sadly a finishing position of 16th (conceding another sixty-six goals) wasn't at all different. The considerable investment in the squad had not improved the League form and made Alan Ashman vulnerable. Albion remained heavily dependent on the King scoring goals. His 25 made him top scorer in the First Division. But throughout most of the season, he continued to be overlooked by Sir Alf Ramsey for England selection. Quite why this was so was, for me, a mixture of extreme frustration and disappointment. What more could he have done to persuade the reluctant England supremo to give him a chance to prove is worth? The cynical view was that he wasn't wearing a Manchester United, Liverpool, Leeds or Tottenham shirt.

But in the meantime, Astle and company were keeping their manager in a job, thanks to another, almost taken for granted exciting Cup run, this time in the League Cup. And who happened to have the honour of being our first victims? None other than the Claret and Blue residents from the area I knew so well. Where Dot tended to the needs of a blind mother and where we spent many hours playing 10 pin-bowling.

Yes, Aston Villa was languishing in the lower depths of Division Two. For all that, I knew only too well that in a local derby form can, and often does, fly out of the window. But not that night. It was Villa's misfortune that the 'King' had settled his wage claim just before we clashed at Villa Park

It was a messy, untidy and often ugly spectacle but who cares in a local derby cup match, providing you win? Albion only fitfully demonstrated their higher class and gave the majority of the 40,000 crowd some hope of a shock outcome. That was until a classic Jeff Astle headed goal ten minutes from time. From then on, Albion demonstrated their power while Villa supporters streamed out early once more. The score sounded close at 1-2, but the final minutes were actually a stroll.

A favourable Cup draw is always crucial. Generally, the Baggies were fortunate to avoid all the big names. In the next round, we drew struggling Ipswich away, drawing 1-1 before beating them 2-0, courtesy of goals from Astle and Hope, in the replay. Good fortune continued to smile bringing Third Division Bradford City to the Hawthorns. Lower division opposition at The Hawthorns generally wilted. Scoring first was the key. Once we'd done that, more followed and we strolled to a very comfortable 4-0 win without any problems.

In the Quarter-Final, there was some opportunity to get revenge over now Second Division Leicester City for their role in our Hillsborough demise. The Foxes no longer had their Semi-Final goal scorer and ex WBA supporter "Sniffer" Clarke in their ranks. He'd decamped to Leeds after relegation. Again, Albion needed two games but even so, City's demise helped a little bit. *"You're not going to Wembley"* wasn't a terrace chant in those days but I was certainly thinking just that.

The other surviving clubs were Manchester United, FA Cup holders Manchester City and Carlisle United of the Second Division. We got Carlisle! The route to the Twin Towers was wide open.

For two key Albion men, the Semi-Final was a grim prospect. The Cumbrians were special to Alan Ashman and so whatever the outcome, he was onto a loser. For the Baggies often brilliant but permanently nervous goalkeeper Ossie, the pressure to not make a mistake sat like an albatross on his shoulders. He knew his error in the last Semi-Final cost Albion a Wembley trip and the nearer the first leg got, the worse he felt.

In United's six League Cup matches, they'd only conceded one goal, including a 1-0 victory over Chelsea. Against this success was a modest showing in League games so in theory, there wasn't that much to concern Albion's hard-nosed professionals at Brunton Park in the First Leg. Unfortunately Ossie's nerves overwhelmed him. Carlisle won the leg 1-0 and so easily the deficit could have 3 or 4 goals. A warning shot had clearly been fired across the bow of 'SS ALBION' as we approached the vital Hawthorns second leg.

Very quickly, the match began to resemble a warmer re-run of Dunfermline. The Baggies were chasing the game against frantically hard-working opponents. Albion started with one jittery player in Osborne and by the interval those jitters were spreading rapidly through the whole side and the nervous fans.

Other than in the away end, the ground was silent. Alan Ashman was white-faced. Carlisle looked comfortable and almost scored on the break. The Baggies had lost a defender and bravely reshuffled into a 3-3-4 formation. Yet despite the four man attack, the visitors appeared calm and unruffled.

But there was one key difference to our European frustration in the presence of Bobby Hope. Our midfield maestro made the difference. His shot through a tangle of legs turned the game in the 56th minute. Thank God, what a relief! The visitors sagged, lost concentration and Hope set up two more goals in six minutes to settle the game. Final score was a comfortable-sounding 4-1 but it was anything but that. The emotion at the end was far more relief than joy. Most of the modest crowd headed for home immediately. Only a handful of youngsters, oblivious of the nervy proceedings, ran onto the pitch. But we were at Wembley again – three times in four years. Could there be any supporters in the land that weren't envious of that honour?

With a twin towers trip already guaranteed three weeks before Christmas, to even consider a second visit via the FA Cup did feel a tad greedy. In Round 3, we had to return to Hillsborough once more, this time to play host side Wednesday. The routine felt quite familiar. Train to Sheffield Midland station, then a football special bus to the big old ground. Painfully, the result was also familiar, thanks to a frankly awful refereeing error.

The score was 1-1 when Colin Suggett found himself completely unmarked in front of goal with only the keeper to beat. Referee David Smith then amazingly blew for offside despite the linesman keeping his flag down, and when John Kaye led the protests, he immediately admitted to making a mistake: *"I'll just have to live with it. I just didn't see the Wednesday full back playing him on, on the far side of the field."* He wasn't the only one who had to live with it.

Perhaps Suggett would have missed the chance. But I somehow doubt it. Ironically the free kick award led to the winning goal at the opposite end and that really did rub salt into an open wound. This completely took the shine off what has been generously acknowledged to be one of the finest goals ever scored by any player. And as this was the opinion of Bobby Charlton who more than most, knew something about this art form, it would be hard to argue with his view. Yes, *that* goal.

The ball was floated forward to Tony Brown and as it dropped over his shoulder in full flight, he volleyed the ball like a bullet past the keeper. The Bomber always agrees it was his best ever goal. But as Albion lost the match, he admitted much of the satisfaction was lost.

With no more jam for two months, I sustained myself on what felt like routine bread and butter League matches. We were now regularly winning our home matches and losing nearly all the away fixtures. By a quirk of the fixtures, there was a League Cup "rehearsal" at The Hawthorns when our Final opponents Manchester City were in town. That season, City were just an average Division One side, finishing tenth.

With Asa Hartford acting as conductor in midfield, The Citizens were never in the game as the Baggies demolished them 3-0. In this fine exhibition of swift, decisive and accurate passing, goals from Asa, Astle, and Suggett were no more than the performance deserved. I was convinced the Baggies would need a bigger trophy cabinet.

Five weeks later, it was a very confident, or was it overconfident, group of players and 34,000 supporters making a very familiar trip to London. And wasn't it cold that day! Snow on the ground and temperatures below zero but at the time, I was grateful the match was still on. Three days earlier, 18 inches of snow was dumped on the Midlands and South. Everyone was taken by surprise as the weather forecasters had predicted only light snow showers. I was fretting fearing a postponement. Had I know what was about to enfold....

I did some window shopping, then took the tube to Wembley but this time there was no Henry Cooper to welcome us back home. As usual, I was in the small non-drinking minority. Many of the rest had convinced themselves the more they drank, the more they would enjoy themselves. I saw many crates of booze on the train, bottles all over the floor on the tube and inside Wembley. There were simply no restrictions then. Many young people around me were "skinheads." They had close cropped hair-memories of my National Service days resurfaced! Skinheads always wore big, ugly-looking boots (again, very army- like), jeans with deliberately short legs to show off their boots and big overcoats. Such a get-up just made me feel old.

There was much banter with City fans as we 'charmed' each other as to why our team was certain to win. For me, there was no way following that Hawthorns 'stroll' that we could possibly lose, so outclassed had been the blue half of Manchester.

Then I had my first shock. Unbelievably, the Wembley officials had allowed "the Horse of the Year Show" to be held on the hallowed turf the previous weekend (when the pitch was already sodden), leaving it in a dreadful state. Add the heavy rain and snow was it any surprise the playing surface could only be described as disgraceful. *"A pig of a pitch"* as one reporter aptly put it.

The ground staff covered the surface with straw in an attempt to soak up the mud and water and hopefully help protect it from the anticipated frost. However several inches of snow and sub-zero temperatures just added to the mess and the outcome was a very muddy and uneven surface. Yes it was the same for both sides but even now I still feel this had much to do with Albion's performance.

Yet we had a great start. "King" Jeff brilliantly beating Joe Corrigan in the air after just 5 minutes, and duplicating his arms raised FA Cup winning goal salute. (This goal meant a unique first for 'King Jeff. He'd become the first player to score in both League and FA Cup finals at Wembley. Mildly satisfying but as he said himself it didn't mean a lot without winning the Cup). Arthur Mann was one of two City defenders who immediately vented their spleen at the deflated Corrigan.

City fought back, equalising through Mike Doyle, so at the end of a bruising, niggling 90 minutes, extra time was required. Albion's main tormentor had been wide man Francis Lee. An aggressive, cocky player who rival fans would unanimously claim had to be high on any list of the game's supreme 'Con Men'. The number of penalties he gained with blatant dives was legendary, and after one clash he so frustrated Doug Fraser, the Baggie skipper, swung an arm in his direction. He failed to make contact, but as expected, Lee threw himself on the mud in an attempt to have Fraser sent off. It was a nasty incident from a player who had talent in abundance and didn't need to resort to this cheating tactic. Lee was City's top goal scorer five years in a row so maybe cheats do prosper.

In extra time, Albion ran out of steam and it was the Manchester fans that watched their team carry off the trophy after full back Glyn Pardoe notched the winning goal.

So for the second time in three seasons we'd missed out. And although the supporters could at least try to lift the player's spirits with sympathetic applause, there was absolutely no one who could offer similar consolation towards the fans.

Every supporter appreciates the thrill and pride of seeing their team play at Wembley. I had begun to believe, unrealistically, this now resembled a second home. If I'd had known then I would not return for 23 years, my mood would have been near suicidal. Tell me that Albion would be trying to escape from what I still call the Third Division; I'd question the sanity of the messenger. Albion in the Third Division - Impossible! Not Albion ... never. But Villa... oh that was different.

There was so much amusement among the Hawthorns regulars that Aston Villa., (the biggest club in the Midlands, don't forget) were relegated again, this time into the murky depths of Division Three. Three wins and a draw in their last five games wasn't enough to keep them up. The world was about to end according to their supporters. I suppose League matches against Rochdale, Halifax, Torquay and Walsall tend to give that impression. *Just never got over being beaten again by Albion in the Cup..."* was a much-used line of knife-twisting banter.

I knew the Baggies were never going to be a Manchester United, Leeds or Liverpool. But we were still one of the leading second tier clubs, with resources to acquire sufficient quality players that meant we'd always be in with a chance of challenging for honours. How naive was I?

With nothing left to play for apart from pride, (and sometimes I believe players do not have as much pride in their club as the fans), the season petered out without many redeeming features. Only two matches were won, and in the final fixtures we witnessed an embarrassing 7-0 drubbing at Old Trafford, followed by a 3-2 defeat at Stoke. Same old story, a leaky defence undoing all the efforts and bludgeoning at the opposite end. The King found the net a remarkable 30 times and was well supported by Colin Suggett (15) and thirteen from the Bomber.

On a much wider scale, UEFA made a long-overdue policy change. Drawn matches in their European competitions would no longer be settled by replays or the appalling concept of a coin toss. Instead, there was a new idea – the penalty shootout. This would be definitely something to bear in mind for our next European campaign.

Away from this long overdue football policy change, I'd taken a major personal decision. It was time for me to get a new job. I was fed up with having to catch 3 buses in each direction (or, if the weather allowed, a 50 minute bike ride).

For weeks, I scanned the 'Evening Mail' job vacancies pages. There was plenty of choice but one vacancy did stand out, an office-based position at the world-famous HP Sauce factory. I applied and was selected for an interview but something inwardly said this job was not for me. Travelling to, of all places, Aston and being just down the road from Villa Park was probably the key factor.

Why the heck hadn't I thought of applying at another even more famous factory a mere 10 minutes walk from home, I asked myself? So I did and passed the interview with flying (blue and white striped) colours to join the home of the best chocolate in the world... Cadburys.

## 1970 World Cup Mexico

Surely it hadn't been 4 years since I'd celebrated England's World Cup triumph? All that roaring, cheering and hand-bruising applause as they defeated West Germany at Wembley followed by the magnificent reception at Kensington Town Hall. But no, the calendar wasn't lying. Four years had elapsed. Naturally, I'd have loved to have travelled to see the trophy defence but cost made this impossible. Travelling to Manchester twice a season was one thing but the difference in cost and difference between Manchester and Mexico was something else!

Brazil were clear favourites but England were also short odds to win. Six of the 1966 World Cup winning side would travel and so too would Jeff Astle. He'd finally had a chance to make his mark on the world scene. This he did, but unfortunately for the wrong reason.

Famously, England and Brazil were drawn together in the same group and the match between them was huge box office, even though in reality both were highly likely to qualify for the Quarter-Finals. This remains to this day one of the few matches where a whole generation have clear memories of the major incidents such as that astonishing save by Gordon Banks. The calm assured display by Bobby Moore. How hard England really pushed one of the greatest teams the World has ever seen. And Jeff Astle's miss. On as a substitute, "The King" was busily winning header after header with Brazil in retreat. Everaldo panicked when yet another high ball was slung in the box and headed down to Jeff standing all alone in the penalty box. Although sitting in my living room on the far side of the world (adorned in my 1966 '.World Cup- Winning Willy T shirt and cap', I leapt to my feet to greet his first World Cup goal. Even now, I remain devastated that his left foot shot was way off target to leave me bitterly sad for Jeff. A goal would have given him worldwide status and pressured Ramsey to keep him in the team and who knows where his career might have gone.

Later Jeff told Baggies fans it was just one of those things. He had the chance and missed it. End of story. It cost England a draw, but name me any striker who hasn't missed a sitter? But whether he really believed the "stiff upper lip" message himself is something I will never know. Opposition supporters subsequently taunted him endlessly with the nonsensical chant that "Astle lost the World Cup." Curiously Bobby Charlton, who also scorned a chance before being substituted, didn't receive the same treatment.

It had been a great game but as England went on to beat Romania and Czechoslovakia, there was still the possibility the teams could meet in the Final.

Again, reference books show West Germany beat England in the Quarter Final to end our interest. My recollections are that it was tactical errors by manager Alf Ramsey that eventually cost a Semi-Final place. Winning 2-0 and seemingly cruising, Ramsey took off Bobby Charlton and Martin Peters, replaced by Colin Bell and Norman Hunter. England began to lose control and with Peter Bonetti in goal (Gordon Banks missing due to food poisoning) having a poor game, the Germans equalised to take the game into extra time. The coup-de-grace was administered with a winning goal from Gerd Muller and England's reign as World Cup holders was over.

Enlarging on the enforced absence of Gordon Banks, many years later a theory was advanced that the best keeper in the world had been a victim of 'foul' play. Just like a racehorse in a Dick Francis novel, someone had deliberately added a substance to his food with the intention of making sure he'd miss this vital game.

Whether anyone took this seriously 33 years down the line is questionable, but when Gordon Banks was a guest at a Supporters Club meeting, I couldn't resist asking the question. His reply; *"At the time it never entered my head but looking back it was strange as I ate the same food as everybody else, but I was the only one taken ill. So it does make you think there might have been something going on"*.

He didn't say he actually believed the story, but then he didn't discount the possibility either. But unless the alleged culprit actually confesses, we will have to continue believing what we want to believe, and perhaps that's the way it should be. Everybody loves a conspiracy theory and this one has to be up there with the best. If he had played instead of Bonetti, I believe England would have beaten the Germans. In the semi-finals, Germany came up against Italy, and in a classic encounter they lost 4-3, again in extra time.

Meanwhile those supreme artists from Brazil booked their place in the final beating Uruguay and this resulted in what even today has been described as the most complete World Cup victory ever. Brazil in irresistible form put on a dazzling display to light up television screens. They "murdered" Italy 4-1 to win the Jules Rimet Trophy for the third and last time, being allowed to keep the trophy forever in recognition of such a magnificent achievement. They were truly awesome, possessing players with individual skills that moulded into a unit, were almost unbeatable. Would the World Cup ever see their like again? I'm still waiting.

Top Left – Teenage Terry. Top Right –"Left. Right." Endless drills at Tilehurst Barracks in 1951. Can you see me- front centre? Middle – 81 Platoon team picture at Tilehurst. I'm lurking 8th from left on back row Bottom – The Dilwara – hosting my 6 week free cruise courtesy of the Government

Top Left- Taken at the famous Singapore Barracks. I'm the one standing in the white shirt

Top Right – Doing my bit, literally supporting Hong Kong children with Toc H.

Middle Left: Then known as *"Brummie Terry"*, enjoying Silvermine Beach in Hong Kong with Terry Thomas and Jock Watt

Bottom Left: At ATV Studios with Billy Wright promoting Animal Welfare.

Our big day – Dot and I looking very newly-wed. Wootton Wawen, here we come.

On assignment for Radio Birmingham. meeting the Birmingham Brummie's Arthur Brown in 1976. Crazy World!

Definitely one of my favourites. It's the 1973 Lord Mayor's Parade and I'm "on duty" with Henry Cooper and Holly.

The FA Cup – at West Brom Dartmouth CC x 3. Me, me with Holly and Dot and me with Graham Williams. A holy trinity of photographs which remain on proud display in our home.

Some of my favourite people –
the late, great Derek Kevan
(*top left*), Catherine Zeta Jones
(*top right*) plus Dot and Gordon
Banks (*left*).
*Below left* is Sir Stanley
Matthews and *right* - 3 1954
Cup greats Barlow, Nicholls
and Allen

## 1970-71

After the General Election in June 1970, Edward Heath became the new Prime Minister of a Tory Government. From an Albion perspective, this is apparently a bad omen. The theory goes that the Baggies only win the Cup under a Labour Government. In reality, the theory doesn't quite stack up. I enjoy the intrigue of conspiracies myself but it is very hard to look beyond mere coincidence with our Cup victories.

The demise of Harold Wilson did raise concerns about whether the UK would become more involved in the Vietnam War. This hopeless, brutal struggle had already run for 14 years and it was never far from news headlines. Officially at least, Wilson refused to send troops to Vietnam. Mass demonstrations continued on both sides of the Atlantic, against what considered was a war impossible to win.

Inflation wasn't just confined to the number of goals conceded by the Albion. The annual rate of inflation in 1970 was 7% which would rise to an alarming 10% a year later. Motorists were now paying just over 6 shillings (31p) for each gallon of petrol.

Fuel had a strong link to the major matchday change – the Hawthorns at last was connected to the motorway network. The new Junction 1 of the M5 opened in May. The "missing link" between Bromsgrove and Walsall had taken several years to bridge, with bridge being the key word as most of the section was raised on stilts – then a major engineering headache. As a non-car driver, much of the detail was wasted on me. My car-owning acquaintances were thrilled that their trip to and from the ground was so much easier and couldn't help sharing their excitement with me over and again. I tried to feign polite interest. Several of my pals, part of the traditional post-match refugee-like march to West Bromwich town centre, were less than pleased that the narrow Birmingham Road had swollen into a huge motorway junction. It felt much further to walk. Worse still they needed the assistance of a Bobby to actually cross the very busy slip roads.

A single gallon of petrol still cost more than a game at The Hawthorns, despite the Football League raising the minimum price of admission. Entry to the Brummie or the Smethwick was now 6 shillings (30p). Unwelcome at a time when average monthly earnings were only £150. But if the additional money was invested in a quality defender, we'd collectively stop moaning. That's what I told irritated fellow supporters over the summer only to be confounded by Alan Ashman. He'd gone back to Carlisle to buy winger George McVitie but a new defender didn't appear to be on his shopping list .I wasn't alone in being completely baffled.

Twenty- one goals were conceded in the first six away games. That more or less was the story of our whole season. Losing 4-1 at Manchester City wasn't that much of a surprise. Conceding 6 at Arsenal was embarrassing (even if they did win the Double) and so too was a 3-0 defeat at relative new boys Crystal Palace. Alan Ashman at last took action. Perhaps remembering how effectively he'd once shackled Jeff Astle in a Cup match, Ashman purchased defender John Wile from Peterborough. Years later, Wile recalled he was on £27 a week with the Posh and hoped that the move to the big time would increase his salary to maybe £35 a week. He was pleasantly surprised when the Baggies offered almost double (£65) plus an unexpected but very welcome £5,000 signing-on fee. As a long-term investment, Wile was a masterstroke. But in the short term, the rookie was hardly going to change fortunes by himself. John Osborne continued to add backache to his other ailments.

A final league placing of 17th was much too close to the relegation spots for comfort. The last two away games were 3-0 and 2-0 defeats respectively at Newcastle and Derby so it was hardly surprising the ball had been picked out of the net no less than 75 times, the highest number conceded in the Division.

The attacking options still leaned heavily on the scoring ability of just two players. From their 42 League games, Albion had scored 58 goals. Not brilliant but still more than twelve teams that eventually finished higher in the table. However the worrying aspect was that Tony Brown had scored 28 and Jeff Astle 13 with the rest of the team mustering a miserly 17 between them. A worrying statistic should either pick up a long-term injury.  There was an old joke doing the rounds at the time which tied in with a record by Pickety Witch *"I still get the same ol' feeling."*

*"Knock Knock"*
*"Who's there?"*
*"Astle"*
*"Astle Who?"*
*"Astle get the same ol' feeling."*

I guess you just had to be there to appreciate it.

Albion's away record was frankly embarrassing with only one match won, and that, against massive odds at Elland Road. Leeds United were feared across Europe. Two years earlier, they were League Champions, second the year after and were an excellent bet to win it again, with only 4 games remaining when the Baggies hit town.

Albion's extraordinary 2-1 victory was front page news. Not so much for the shock score (though it was remarkable), more so for the near-riot after the visitors' second goal. This was a tense, bad-tempered match throughout with both sides making errors or kicking lumps out of the opposition. A Jack Charlton error gave the Baggies the lead. More errors by United gave glorious chances to Suggett and Brown, both of which were missed. Thus it wasn't such a surprise when another Leeds pass was intercepted giving the Bomber space to run on goal. But by normal definitions of the era, Suggett was offside as he was in the opposition half beyond the last defender. The linesman's flag went up immediately. The Leeds defence en bloc stopped, waiting for referee Ray Tinkler to blow the whistle. Tony Brown also stopped with the ball at his feet. But as the signal failed to materialise, he ran forward, before slipping the ball to Jeff Astle, also probably offside, who promptly tapped the ball into the net to give Albion a two-goal lead. Uproar!

As commentator Barry Davies had it *"Leeds will go mad and they've every right to go mad."* But there are ways and means of making a protest. Leeds players took out their frustrations on the referee. He was shoved, pushed, pulled and abused. Not only by players but also by dozens of supporters who invaded the pitch. Some of them were definitely *"old enough to know better"* as my folks used to say. Play was held up for five minutes as the Police battled for control, arresting over 30 of the pitch invaders, though sadly not Don Revie. The linesman collapsed after being hit on the head.

Albion players and supporters could only stand and stare at the carnage. We fans were horribly mindful that we'd have to find a way to get to the train station.

It's very rare in my 2,000+ games that I feared for my safety but right then I was very nervous.

Amid a mutinous atmosphere, Leeds tried to rescue their season. Alan Clarke squeezed one goal in from a ridiculous angle to create a nail- biting last few minutes.

The final whistle only partly relieved the tension. Some United watchers wanted to take out their frustrations on somebody and any visiting supporter would do. So it was off with the colours, sub-divide into small groups and try to look anonymous. I was lucky but I fear some of my fellow travellers had a thoroughly painful return home.

Don Revie's team had an "us against the world mentality". They took cynicism in a whole new direction added to which was the violent reputation of United supporters.

For these reasons, neutrals thought the events at Elland Road were just highly amusing (it was alright for them, they weren't trying to get away in one piece). Too many had been on the receiving end of United's tactics or their supporters to have any sympathy.

But yet the referee was wrong. By the rules of the day, to decide that Colin Suggett was not interfering with play was a most unusual interpretation. To this day, Tinkler maintains that Suggett was not offside because he was nowhere near the ball and that he'd always had a reputation for playing advantage.

That decision was decisive in changing the outcome of a match. Even today, Leeds claim that this defeat cost them the title. Further, with part of their punishment being to play their first four home matches of the following season away from Elland Road, this also fatally damaged their chances of becoming Champions the following season. Allegedly.

I would never react with that degree of loutish behaviour, but for sure I'd have wanted to vent verbal 'revenge' on someone. The pain and fury from that palpably wrong decision still haunts United. To be an Albion supporter at Elland Road from then on was always a little more difficult. There was always the risk that some drunken redneck would shout abuse or worse about the events of '71. The players didn't forget either. At a Sportsman's' Dinner several years later, plain speaking Jack Charlton bellowed across the room *"that bastard there cost us two League titles."* But Jeff Astle always had a riposte ready. With one of his trademark grins, he responded with *"You know as well as me Jack, you always play to the whistle."*

In the calmer climate of Cup competitions, Albion's and my interest, ended early. We did manage four FA Cup matches but even so were knocked out in early February.

The Cup started with a dismal goalless draw at home to Fourth Division Scunthorpe United, which was put right in the replay following a 3-1 victory. Famously, a very young Kevin Keegan turned out for the Iron but I'm afraid that I was so focussed on our inability to score a goal at home; I didn't pay any attention to individuals among the visitors. In the next round, another poor defensive display saw us 3-0 losers at Ipswich, again after a draw at home.

Interest in the League Cup was at least stretched to the 4th Round. We'd dealt well enough with initial lower Division opposition, beating Charlton 3-1, and Preston 1-0. Our reward was a trip to Spurs, not exactly ideal! However, strangely I was content with the draw as White Hart Lane is my favourite London ground even though I'd seen the home side demolish the Baggies all too often. There is something indefinable about the place that appealed to me. Given the porosity of the defence, I suppose I shouldn't have been surprised that we crashed out after another poor display. But a 5-0 defeat, whatever the reason, is always teeth-grindingly painful. I did take some little consolation later that we'd been beaten by the eventual Cup winners. Spurs went on to (thankfully) defeat Aston Villa in the Final. A game made more satisfying as I journeyed among hundreds of Villa supporters.

En route they were convinced that there was no way they could possibly lose. On return, there was a totally different scenario. Despondency ruled. I just sat quietly listening as I knew how they felt .After all, hadn't I painfully endured similar feelings returning from Wembley after losing Cup Finals? .Feelings that can never be erased from the memory box. Not that this left me sympathising at their demise!

In January, the Ibrox Disaster focussed the whole country's attention on football not just for days but weeks. Infamously, as an Old Firm match came to an end, Celtic led by one goal. Dismayed "Bears" were making an early exit down a long flight of steep and straight stairs. Amid a huge roar, Rangers scored a last minute equaliser. Amid the distraction, somebody fell and started a chain reaction. The result was carnage. Thousands tumbled down the steep steps leaving over 200 injured, but even more tragically, 66 lay dead. There had been previous examples of injuries and even deaths on the same stairway but Rangers shamefully had not made any improvements.

The horrors of Ibrox reminded me that the steps to the Rainbow Stand were straight, steep and uncovered. I used to skip up and down them in all weathers. I was fit, young and thought nothing would happen to me. I was more cautious post-Ibrox at the Hawthorns though thankfully the club were also more aware of the dangers. They installed a ramp at the side of the Rainbow Stand and also improved signage. I was very relieved.

Cup Final tickets were always in short supply, even for season ticket holders. Ticket allocations for the two finalists were always inadequate, particularly as prices were inexpensive. There were rules that players should not sell their personal allocation on the black market, but the practice was widespread and, at that time were rarely, if ever enforced. Rightly or wrongly, it was considered a perk of the job. It was Jeff Astle's bad luck to be singled out, just one among the many. He'd claimed £200 profit on Cup Final tickets to the press and was hung out to dry. His protests that his words were theoretical and that his tickets went to his family were not believed. The FA could not see beyond the press reports. He was subsequently stripped of the captaincy, fined £200 (the equivalent of 600 gallons of petrol), and banned for receiving FA Cup Final tickets for life. There weren't many Albion fans prepared to condemn him. This was the King, a down- to- earth hero who willingly spent so much time with supporters and boosting local good causes.

Dot and I rounded off the season by attending another European Cup Final at Wembley. Obtaining tickets was no problem even though this was the great Ajax team which provided so many "Dutch Masters" such as Cruyff for their national side. Dot didn't need much persuading as she enjoyed trips to the capital as much as I did. Ajax beat Panathinaikos 2-0 in a dull affair.

For Albion, this was another nine months of "work in progress". Everyone knew our defence was far from the best at the start of the season so to be still making the same comments nine months later really did make me wonder what the heck was going on. We did have young players close to regular first team action like Wile, Robertson, Reed and Cantello but there were no guarantees any of them would succeed. Some of my fellow Rainbow Stand inhabitants were increasingly strident in their criticism.

Then the "time bomb" that had been ticking away finally exploded. Alan Ashman was sacked. It was the manner of his sacking that reflected so badly on the board. Poor Alan was on holiday abroad in July and only found out via the press that Don Howe was being lined up as his replacement. Everyone, supporters and press alike, were united that this was an appalling way to treat such an essentially decent man. Under pressure, the board apologised and blamed the leak on everyone and anyone but themselves. Alan always mused that one of the reasons given for his removal was because the directors, while appreciating the cup exploits, wanted a manager who could win them the League Championship! Unbelievable or what?

Personally, I was dismayed that Alan was leaving at all. He'd given me so many great moments during his period in charge; moments that made me say *"that's why I support the Albion"*. I thought he deserved more time. Many of my mates disagreed, declaring that our goalkeepers badly needed to ease their aching backs.

So Don Howe was our new manager. Superficially, the choice made sense. He was a former player, a Black Country man to boot and a most intelligent one at that. He was an integral backroom part of the Arsenal double-winning team, a club who really knew how to defend. So a perfect match? Not everyone was convinced. Howe had no managerial experience and for me, Arsenal were so boring to watch.

## 1971/72

Albion's first managerial change for half a decade added something extra to the new season. I'd met Don Howe many times of course, and was really impressed by his eloquence. I believe to this day that he was the finest right back in Albion's history. (Contrary to rumours, I'm far too young to have seen Jessie Pennington!) He had 23 England caps to his name.

On his appointment, with a four-year contract tucked into his suit, he said all the standard phrases expected of a new manager. *"I will be happy to see Albion finish in the top seven to qualify for Europe again. All the players here will get the chance to show me what they can do. There are some very talented players at the club etc".*

Talented they may have been, but my hopes weren't long in evaporating.

Brewers Watneys were keen to make their name in football and set up a novel pre-season knockout tournament with a twist. The two clubs in each Division who'd scored the most goals without winning anything were invited to participate and Albion were happy to accept. The £4,000 fee plus bonuses probably explained their keenness. The twist was an experimental rule around offside only applying within the penalty area. It was perhaps fortunate that Ray Tinkler wasn't chosen to officiate, given his obvious confusion about the existing rules.

The twin bonuses of extensive media coverage and fixtures against opposition we'd never previously played created more interest than usual. An FA Cup match in 1930 apart, our visit to the Racecourse Ground in Wrexham remains our only competitive visit there. A fair number of Baggies enjoyed a sunny day and a narrow 2-1 win. In the Semi-Final, we made a rare midweek visit to Halifax and won 2-0. That brought Fourth Division Colchester United to the Hawthorns for the Final. It was good to see former Baggie Bobby Cram leading out the U's. The TV cameras were on hand as they assumed there would be a feast of goals. Indeed there was but not enough were in the U's net.

4-4 was a ridiculous 90 minute score mainly due to our still colander-resembling defence, who were confused further by the offside flexibilities. The presence of the cameras added both pressure and embarrassment. Why could we not beat an ordinary Fourth Division side at home? I was, to put it mildly, very irritated. The whole country was rooting for the underdog and I'd had quite enough of it. The game would be settled on a penalty shoot-out, the first one I'd witnessed such a scenario. The experience was not a pleasant one. Colchester won. I left hastily, not in the best of moods.

By Monday, I'd regained my sense of perspective. It was basically a friendly, with experimental rules and would bear no relation to League reality or so I told myself sternly. I was still reasonably optimistic that Howe was capable of changing matters around come the big kick off.

We had an encouraging start, with two wins in the first two games, 1-0 at West Ham, and 2-0 at home over Everton. We were joint top of the League and Don Howe. Heavens, what an inspired choice.

Lamentably, this fine start was followed by just three draws from the next nine matches. Howe's emphasis on defence and the frequent absence of the King, due to cartilage problems, were a grim combination.

The defence was certainly less generous. Howe was fortunate enough to inherit the youthful Wile and

Robertson and made full use of them from October onwards. When Yorky Kaye was sold to Hull City, Ally Rob was in the team and stayed in for the rest of the season. There weren't many opponents who relished a full- blooded tackle from either or both of them! The young central defenders had ample support from their team mates. So much support that scoring goals ourselves didn't seem to matter. Only 6 goals were scored. And as five came from Tony Brown, and the other a header from John Wile, it was obvious that new blood was needed in this department. Popular music of this era basically went in one ear for me and out the other yet just sometimes a current tune matched the times. The latest big hit Slade's "*Mama, we're all crazyee now*" captured the mood perfectly!

Realising the desperate need for goals, Howe went to of all places-Wolverhampton to sign centre forward Bobby Gould. Our new striker was, in modern language, a "ratter". He'd chase opponents manically, rather like Shane Long but with less skill. I didn't take to him though I had to accept that opposition goalkeepers didn't like him much either. He'd pressurised several of them into fatal errors. The lunging boot of Mr Gould wouldn't be too far away if there was anything resembling a 40-60 ball. Arguably there was also a bit of Joey Barton-esque "foot in mouth" about Gould. One of the King's many anecdotes relates to Gould's first day at training where he accused all of his new team-mates of being "cheats". This was on the basis that when he was lapping at Arsenal, he was one of the last to finish but at the Hawthorns, he was one of the first. How not to make friends and influence people! Infamously, John Kaye had a word, this while Gould was dangling by his neck against the dressing room wall. According to Gould, Howe wanted him at the Albion to shake the place up and break down the resentment towards the manager. Hardly the way to win friends and influence people, Bobby!

If this wasn't bad enough, Leeds United wanted to sign Asa Hartford. Naturally the Scot was very interested in joining one of the most powerful clubs in the land.

Sadly for Asa came the bizarre announcement that he'd failed his medical check due to a hole in the heart. The transfer was off. Given the state of medical knowledge at the time, this could have been identified only by a doctor listening on his stethoscope and is also known as a heart murmur. I'm something of a medical dunce but it seemed to me that Asa had absolutely no fitness problems in an Albion shirt but Leeds were not convinced. I remember ATV interviewing another footballer Dudley Tyler who had exactly the same problem. Dudley was, at the time an outstanding non-League player, who later moved to West Ham. The Londoners presumably had more enlightened medical support. Asa's subsequent non-stop running and grafting in the Albion midfield must have led to the Leeds management questioning their medical team's judgement. I didn't complain - it was Albion's gain and a Leeds loss.

The League position was causing increasing concern. Without a win for ten games, it needed a great improvement to bring anything resembling a smile to my face, especially as we had crashed out of the League Cup at the first attempt. For the second season in succession, it was Cup holders Spurs at White Hart Lane who were our executioners. I took a little consolation that we lost only by a single goal, compared to the five- goal margin the previous season.

Just after Christmas, we won our second home game of the season, a surprising (though welcome) 1-0 over title-chasing Liverpool. Over 43,000 were present, so it was elbows in and don't even think about going to the toilet. Victory felt marvellous and was so much needed. Thank you Bomber Brown for making my Christmas!

A diversion of a Cup run would be very welcome but we didn't get one. The FA Cup was just as deflating as the League Cup, a 2-1 defeat at home to Coventry in the Third Round.

There were non-League clubs who lasted longer in the FA Cup than the Albion. One in particular – Hereford United. They'd earned their Third Round place after winning their Second Round Second Replay at the Hawthorns. I wasn't there myself but I was assured the curious Albionites present got behind the smooth-passing Southern League side who eventually beat Northampton Town in extra time. The reward was huge – a game at Newcastle. Such is the focus on the famous mud-filled encounter featuring, Ronnie Radford, parka-wearing supporters and John Motson's debut that few remember this was actually a replay, following an extraordinary 2-2 at Newcastle. Thanks to endless postponements, the replay finally took place on Fourth Round day. Even as highlights, it made for compelling TV viewing. Newcastle became national patsies, not for the first time, in the FA Cup. I did hear that the manager Joe Harvey was so upset that he had to stop the coach just North of Hereford to be physically sick at the roadside. Interestingly, his assistant manager was Keith Burkinshaw. Perhaps that national humiliation explains his permanently glum expression in later life?

In the same month, the retired ocean liner Queen Elizabeth 2 caught fire, rolled over and sunk in just 43 foot of water. Ships sinking weren't that uncommon but what really caught my eye was the location. It happened while berthed in the 'Fragrant Harbour', better known to thousands of National Servicemen as Hong Kong. A time that I certainly couldn't ever forget, a period of an antiquated wireless system and a torturous wait for letters telling what was happening back home. Had 20 years really passed?

Back in the Football League, the Baggies had rediscovered the art of winning at home, so much so that there was only one more home defeat – and that to Leeds United, who eventually missed the Championship by a single point. At the end of the season, a total of 35 points kept us five wins ahead of the relegated duo Nottingham Forest and Huddersfield Town. Four decades later, Huddersfield supporters still wait for a return to the top level.

Although it was his first season, and perhaps the fans shouldn't have expected too much, Howe was never going to be as popular a manager as he'd been a player. His dull, negative approach clearly upset most fans. Many feeling that while he'd tightened up the defence (54 goals conceded as opposed to the previous 75) this had only come at the expense of attacking capability.

Years later, Jeff Astle told of the time Howe had instructed him not to head the ball so much. As his wife Laraine had it *"Jeff was staggered. He just couldn't believe it."* How any manager could instruct one of the finest heading exponents in the game to restrict his greatest asset was totally and utterly baffling. But then Don had many ideas that not only the fans, but also the players, found astonishing.

With coaching and philosophy of this nature was it any wonder Albion only managed a miserable, pathetic 42, an average of exactly one goal per game. We were used to far better. Of these, 'The Bomber' netted 17, Bobby Gould 12, while Jeff from 22 appearances scored only a couple. A new striker, Alistair Brown, signed from Leicester City on the eve of transfer deadline day. He scored on his debut, finished with 3 goals from 11 outings and was ultimately one of Don Howe's finest purchases. Albeit we had to wait five years before he won a regular first team place.

Overall, it was difficult to see what positive difference the new manager had made. Howe's pre-season comment *"I will be pleased to finish in the top seven to take Albion back into Europe"* was regularly used in evidence against him. Would it ever get better? Indeed, half a dozen fans even asked me to organise another petition. This time to be entitled "Don Howe must leave the Hawthorns." I had sympathy with their view but I just couldn't consider it. Anyone that saw him at his best, as I had, representing West Bromwich Albion and England, couldn't turn full circle.

I was half-tempted to change my mind when I saw that Howe had released both Graham Lovett and Bobby Hope. I was furious, convinced at the time that both were major errors by the manager. In my book, although Graham had never fully rediscovered his tremendous potential following his second traffic accident, Howe hadn't given him any opportunity by denying him a first team shirt. Lovett had gone out on loan to Southampton with a view to a permanent move but the player was returned after just three games. To anyone who would listen, I told them vehemently that this was a tragedy that cost Graham a tremendous international playing career. I was convinced he could have been the next Duncan Edwards.

Releasing brilliant Bobby Hope at just 29 to newly promoted Birmingham City staggered me even more. For some reason, he'd also been out of the first team. I was furious and far from alone. Perhaps Bobby hadn't been seen at his scintillating best, but I thought this had more to do with Don Howe's coaching and approach to the game, rather than Bobby's playing capabilities. Whatever the reason, he was still regarded by astute managers as being one of the finest, most skilful players around. What a pity Don Howe wouldn't, or perhaps couldn't, see it. For weeks, I was on my soapbox telling anyone prepared to listen this was a nonsensical decision.

History shows that Don Howe or more probably the excellent George Wright (the Baggies' first proper medical man) may have made the right decision. Possibly following the Southampton failure, no League club would take a chance on Lovett and he ended up in the Southern League before hanging up his boots. Bobby Hope didn't fare much better. In his four years at the retirement home for old Baggies, the Scot averaged barely one game per month. This just provided some additional evidence for the theory of that era that players are finished at 30. The Albion Old Guard was certainly on the way out. In addition to Yorky Kaye, Graham Williams also left the Hawthorns.

## 1972/73

After such a gloomy 71-72 football season, I needed something or someone to excite me. There were more than enough gloomy events in the World already in 1972 without my weekly fix being affected as well. In January, there was Bloody Sunday when 26 Irish civil rights protestors were shot by the army. Then striking miners briefly forced a three day week and blackouts. Football had to work around the problem as best it could. Albion were obliged to kick off at Maine Road, Manchester at 2.00pm one midweek afternoon. Over 25,000 people managed to get there – burial at grandmothers must have been at an all-time high that day.

On the other side of the world, the horrific, pointless loss of life continued in Vietnam. How many years now? – I'd simply lost count. There were the dreadful events at the Munich Olympics with 11 athletes losing their lives. Inflation was growing, as was unemployment.

Thankfully I did have other interests to distract me. My compassion for Animal Welfare led to my spending weekends working at the 'Hollywood Animal Rescue Centre'. (No, not that Hollywood) I exercised and walked dogs of all shapes and sizes, along leafy country lanes. It was rewarding and enjoyable, unless the heavens decided that there couldn't be a better time to open the floodgates!

In purely football terms, home matches were becoming a chore, an extension of the dullness of the working week, for those who were still in work of course. Also, the increasing off-field aggression was increasingly depressing, particularly with elements of certain clubs like Chelsea or Manchester United. Although I was never directly attacked, I always had to keep one eye out just in case I accidentally found myself between two squabbling tribes of uniformed and booted teenagers. Terraces were segregated now, a necessary but sad development. Bring back National Service!

Don Howe most certainly wasn't raising my hopes of a rosier future. In his programme notes for the first home game, he wrote "*obviously I have an objective for the new term and it is simple, to continue to build on the foundations laid in my first season as manager. I expect to see a significant improvement, particularly in our home results, which were disappointing in the extreme.*" Don Howe expected an improvement. So did the supporters but we didn't get one.

Instead, we witnessed an abject season as the Baggies ended a spell of 24 years in the First Division with a truly appalling series of displays. Over the last couple of years, I'd chatted anxiously with other Baggie watchers about just how dependent we'd become on our big two goal scorers. How would we manage without one or both of them? Last term was a worrying example with Jeff Astle missing 50% of the games. This season, with the King off his throne for three quarters of the season, my worst fears were being realised. We patently couldn't manage without him.

Jeff had a long-term injury. To compensate, Tony Brown was played up front instead. The Bomber was never a striker as such. To use modern terminology, he played in the hole where he could make late runs to be in the right place at the right time. Up front, he was tightly marked and subsequently ineffective. In public, Don Howe spoke about Tony Brown being adaptable and broadening his talents. Privately – who knows? Maybe he thought the alternatives were even worse. Howe's popularity no longer registered on the scale. It was basically zero.

We started the new term as we finished the old one. Dismally. No wins from the first seven games with no goals scored until the fourth match. Just two points from 14 had us holding up the table. We were early favourites for the drop.

I hung onto a glimmer of hope after successive wins against League Champions Derby, Crystal Palace, and Coventry stabilised the situation, but the improvement was short lived. And the lack of goals was, at the end of the season, the difference between survival and the sheer awfulness of relegation. After 24 years of generally comfortable top-flight football, dropping out of the First Division felt really beyond words. A whole new generation of supporters had grown up knowing and expecting nothing else but top flight football. Relegation? What's that got to do with the famous West Bromwich Albion?

By October, we'd bowed out of the League Cup; a win against QPR being followed by a 1-1 home draw against Liverpool and a 2-1 extra time defeat in the replay at Anfield. We'd pushed one of the country's best sides to the limit so there was no disgrace in losing to the Reds. With an early exit from the Texaco Cup (another sponsored competition, this time involving Scottish clubs) criticism of the manager was steadily mounting. Supporters wanted action, not excuses, especially as after Christmas the team were standing just one spot above the relegation trapdoor.

We needed inspiration from somewhere. Albion pushed their financial boat out and bought the most exciting winger I had seen since Clive Clark in Willie Johnston. Our new arrival was signed from Rangers where his reputation had gone before him. Both as an exciting goal scorer with pace and control but was also notorious for being wound up easily and being sent off. This was a most un-Don Howe purchase and perhaps there was much in Johnston's assertion that Howe had never seen him play.

I was both excited and relieved, as were my fellow supporters. So too were Willie's new team mates. But the mercurial winger and Howe were like two pieces of sandpaper rubbing together. This, and apparently the lack of quality golf courses near his new home, left Willie as just another dejected, drooping player along with all the others. We saw so little from him, with many crosses going straight into the crowd. But he was a record signing, and so he was kept in the team.

Johnston bought Gould's orange-painted house in Sutton as the wanderlust residing in Bobby Gould saw him move again, this time to Bristol City. Not for the first time in his career, the selling club personally delivered him to the buyer. I was quietly pleased he'd gone, even though I had to admit his dozen goals the previous season had kept us in a safe position. I expected more from an Albion forward than a mere dozen goals. If only I fully realised what lay ahead.

A home game against Crystal Palace in February felt so significant. Or as the group Sweet had it, a "Blockbuster". Both sides, together with Birmingham City, were dead men walking with 19 points. The metaphoric four points were at stake. Palace romped home 4-0 and after that, I knew relegation was on the way despite positive noises from both the manager and players; I was convinced that we were doomed. This was to be Colin Suggett's last appearance in a Baggie shirt before moving on to Norwich City, and while fans were sorry to see him go, I felt his form had dipped under Howe's management style. Same as the rest of the team!

David Shaw from Oldham was the next arrival, bought in an attempt to boost the attack, but I was certain that only the return of a fit Jeff Astle could save our top flight status. Gloom, gloom and for good measure, more gloom.

Somewhat surprisingly the advent of the FA Cup had seen a more relaxed Albion. The fighting spirit (missing from League matches) resurfaced and I saw signs that just perhaps, this could be a turning point from a thoroughly disappointing campaign.

It took three matches to beat Nottingham Forest in the Third Round. Swindon were duly beaten at the Hawthorns in the next round and then horror of horrors - another trip to Elland Road. The team and supporters, buoyed by the return of the King, travelled in hope but by 5 o'clock, we were out of the FA Cup, beaten 2-0. Leeds went on to Wembley, where they famously lost to Second Division Sunderland.

Did our Cup efforts help our League form? Sadly the answer was no, although in the next match, a 'Bomber' goal saw off Arsenal, and with the return of 'King' Jeff there was still a flicker of hope that we could pull off an escape act that Harry Houdini would have been proud to claim was solely down to his expertise.

There wasn't too much distance between the bottom three clubs. Basically any two from Albion, Blues and Norwich were falling through the relegation trapdoor. The last game of the season just happened to be Birmingham City at St Andrews. Would it all depend on that local derby?

Feeling pressure from all sides, the Baggies rallied a little with back-to-back home wins. Firstly, 1-0 against Leicester (thank you Jeff) followed by a totally unexpected but very luxurious demolition 4-1 of Everton. I dared to hope. As any regular supporter, it is the hope that hurts. It's the hope you can't stand. Just four games remained with two against fellow strugglers. Could we escape?

No. We lost 1-0 to Liverpool at Anfield. The vital home match against the Canaries was also lost 1-0 after a frantic struggle. I'd hoped for rather more than John Osborne having to keep us in the game with a succession of saves. He was finally beaten by David Cross, with Colin Suggett setting him up. The *"easy, easy"* chants from the visiting supporters at the end only added to my end-of-game frustrations.

Thus the penultimate match against Manchester City at the Hawthorns was win or bust. Any fan that has experienced the agony of seeing their team relegated will understand how I, and every Albion supporter, agonised that night. We'd hoped for a miracle, but all we got was the realisation that the team had already given up hope of survival, going down 2-1 to surrender our prized Division One status.

If the scenes on the pitch weren't deflating enough, a supporter in front of me in the Rainbow Stand collapsed, with what I found out later, was a heart attack. All the St John Ambulance crew were based in Halfords Lane so attracting their attention was rather difficult. Even Police radios at the time were hit and miss. One female supporter, presumably familiar with first aid, did her best to keep her fellow fan alive. Everyone else stood around helplessly. A medical team finally arrived to take away the ailing supporter. I heard that he'd died, which put relegation into perspective, painful though it was.

Next day John Wile said, "*At least now we know the agony is over. It's as if a great weight has been lifted from our shoulders*". I understood the sentiment but it didn't lift my mood very much.

We still had to endure that final match at St Andrews, the ground where we'd enjoyed so much success over the years, humbling both their team and supporters. This was to be their payback. Blues had every reason to crow. They were on a run of 8 victories in their last ten games, which moved them up from 18th to a highly respectable 10th. Actually Albion didn't play badly, but were still on the wrong end of a 3-2 score line. It was no surprise as we'd only secured only one miserable point on the road since November. Blues supporters loved it. *"Going down, you're going down"* was a constant chant to which we had no retort. That made me appreciate how Villa fans must have felt when we doomed them to the Second Division thanks to that late Ronnie Allen goal. Even at the death we had to carry on suffering, as Albion, winning 2-1 with just 10 minutes remaining, somehow contrived to concede two late goals. The Evening Mail reported that Birmingham were somewhat lucky to win. Not that a win would have been anything more than a miserable consolation.

Recriminations were soon airborne. Chairman Jim Gaunt, at the club's Annual General Meeting, was blunt. *"I am not standing down. I do not want to be known as the Chairman who got us down and then got out. We have got to pull back the fans by playing the kind of football the fans want to enjoy. We have been driving away supporters, both at home and other grounds. We are one of the poorest supported away teams in the League."* He also made the strange remark that Howe's future with the club was secure although he was critical of the team's playing policies.

For me this was a whitewash. Don should have gone there and then as Albion's form was often abysmal. Gaunt added: *"I do not blame the players but something has gone wrong with our method. We just hope that the fans will be loyal to us if we play the kind of football they want."*

Looking back, I still find it hard to explain Albion's relegation. The obvious answer was that they plainly weren't good enough. It couldn't have been much worse with 9 wins, 10 draws and 23 defeats. West Bromwich Albion amassed just 28 points and deservedly finished bottom. But look at the players we had - Len Cantello, John Wile, Tony and Ally Brown, Jeff Astle, Colin Suggett, Asa Hartford, Willie Johnston etc. All of them bar Jeff would go on to have top flight careers. Yes of course Astle missed three-quarters of the season but with such an array of talent, how could we end up being so dependent on one man? For me, Howe and his stifling of individual skills, was directly responsible for relegating Albion.

Naturally, away from the Hawthorns, things went on their 'merry way'. On the International front, Bobby Moore gained his 100th cap when he led the team to a 5-0 victory at of all places - Hampden Park. A result that didn't go down at all well over the border! Not such good news for his fellow international, Gordon Banks, acknowledged as being among the world's greatest goalkeepers. Banks was involved in a head on crash with a lorry. He stressed that he hoped to play on despite the loss of one eye, was fitted with a contact lens, and picked to play in a representative match on the right wing. Sadly he was forced to admit that that his career was over. He'd played his last game.

At their AGM, the Football League agreed to introduce a permanent 3 up, 3 down, for the top three divisions. This news was significant for all Albion supporters. In theory, there was a better chance of a quick return.  In theory!

Away from the gloom of football, I'd won the vote for the position of Honorary Secretary of the Birmingham Branch of the Animal Welfare Trust. Admittedly, there wasn't a multitude of other applicants.

A vital element of any charitable organisation is fundraising via any possible means. So with my interest in both song and dance music, I thought I could exploit my knowledge to raise revenue for the Trust. Had I realised then how much time, effort and sheer hard work was involved in sourcing a suitable venue, band and ticket selling, I may have reconsidered. But with much gallant assistance from Dot, I battled on and succeeded.

To add more fun to the proceedings, I gradually developed my singing voice. I was never going to be in the class of the Guvnor Frank Sinatra of course. But when the song was suitable and within range, I persuaded the resident 'Coordiners' vocalist to consider a highly unlikely duet.

Encouraged by this modest triumph, I made what I considered to be a brave personal decision to learn to dance.  For too many years, dating back to Hong Kong and National Service, I'd awkwardly avoided the dance floor. No longer!  Dot and I enrolled at a local dance school under the auspice of the International School for Dancing-IDTA for short.  Thus Mr and Mrs Wills took their first stumbling steps learning the intricacies of Ballroom and Latin American dancing. Over the next few months, I discovered that it wasn't only certain Albion players who had two left feet. But more of that later!

## 1973/74

I'd also developed a new interest in local radio. The concept was new, fun, exciting and probably rather raw – radio that featured local people and places I actually knew well. I became firmly entwined in both local stations – the BBC and its commercial rival BRMB. BBC Radio Birmingham was based in Pebble Mill while the BRMB studios were then located in a familiar area to me – Aston.

Jim Rosenthal, now so well known to television audiences, became Sports Editor at Radio Birmingham and he was totally unflappable in front of a microphone whatever the situation facing him - literally! You had to be there to appreciate the antics of colleagues working with him. When Jim was broadcasting, a number of them would sit in front of him making faces or gestures to force a reaction from Jim. No way. Ever the true professional, Jim would ignore all attempts to break his concentration and carry on as if they weren't there. He was a true master of keeping a straight face.

My regular but unpaid contributions to BBC schedules were reporting on the results and fortunes of two of our local Speedway teams - Birmingham and Wolverhampton. I became a Monday night regular at Perry Barr and Friday at Monmore Green. (Cradley was impractical as they rode on a Saturday night, thus overlapping with the Albion) I loved it although changing weather leading to a late postponement was an occupational hazard. The Brummies always will be 'my' team. In my early years, I'd first set off for the Hawthorns, complete with blue and white painted rattle. At the final whistle, I'd cover my raffle with a red and yellow paper insignia before catching two buses to the other side of the City. Could you imagine that these days!? Reformed after many years, they completed a Cup and League double after being admitted to Division Two. There were many memorable evenings that season, which, being honest, were more rewarding than watching (enduring?) the Albion.

One simple pleasure for me was standing next to rival supporters just chatting about anything and everything that took our fancy, a pleasure regularly denied as a football lover. If I had to choose just one highlight, I don't think I could top one extraordinary evening at BRMB. I met and chatted to Ole Olsen, for me, Speedway's greatest ever World Champion. One of those unique experiences which gives you a fixed grin for a full day afterwards.

My official contribution to BRMB had nothing to do with sport although I was a regular on their phone in programmes. One of the regular hosts was Tony Butler, a great character who was perhaps a very early "shock jock". His carefully chosen comments were designed to prompt a response. He invariably succeeded, in winding up supporters of all the local clubs. His broadcasts were hard to switch off. Were my own contribution that compelling! My little niche was as a film reviewer. My weekly taxi trip to the Aston Cross studios was to review new films. Like most people, I loved a night out at the pictures and to be paid for the privilege really was a bonus.

I had no great enthusiasm for the new football season even though my Rainbow Stand season ticket was, as always, ready and waiting. Although I automatically renewed, I couldn't see any genuine hope for progress, and Howe's frightened, defensive football was a complete turn-off. I'd not watched Second Division football in over two decades and, irrationally enough, felt I'd left that behind in my youth. I had much sympathy with a quote from John

Osborne: "*When you get up in the morning thinking "Oh, I've got to go to that bloody place again...when you get to that stage, its pointless carrying on.*" Another part of my personality remained dominant though – the part which reminded me I'd signed up for life as a Baggies follower and that meant bad times as well as good.

The bulk of the players who were responsible for our demise, were handed the opportunity of readdressing the balance. The sagging number of season ticket holders, combined with relegation, meant there was little alternative. So poor had been the majority of individual performances in the relegation season, there wasn't much belief in the Hawthorns stands and terraces. As I discovered from chatting to them in subsequent years, the players were even less confident.

Our first game of the season was an unexpected bonus - Blackpool at Bloomfield Park in August. How good was that? A combination of football and an overnighter at the seaside galvanised the huge away support. No doubt some were seeing at least two footballs but their backing from the huge North Stand terrace inspired the Baggies team to win 3-2.

A week later saw Don Howe's perfect score 1-0 over fellow relegatees -Crystal Palace. For me, the world was feeling a better place. In the programme notes, Albion's captain John Wile wrote: " *One immediate aim is a couple of good wins to restore confidence, not only in ourselves but in the minds of our supporters, because it was plain to see that confidence was lacking in players of known and proven ability. That we have got to alter without delay.*" So there we go. Two wins and its now game on?

If only! A week later, a novelty trip to Swindon was negated by a 1-0 defeat and Willie Johnston enhancing his reputation by being sent off. Four days later came another defeat at Sheffield Wednesday which started another miserable, depressing sequence of losses and scratched draws. Our next win wasn't until late October by which time, the attendance had shrunk to an alarming 12,000. During a period when gate receipts made up nearly the entire income of football clubs, this was a major worry. There would be no buying our way out of trouble. Around me on the Rainbow were empty seats. Not just the big-game hunters were absent, so too were grizzled battle-scarred veterans, people who I considered mates. If I'd had a pound for every time I'd heard "*I can't take any more of this, Terry*", I'd have taken early retirement. I made little attempt to persuade them otherwise because I absolutely understood. We had a team of First Division players regularly being outplayed by Second Division outfits and I was sick of it.

But there was even worse to endure that month. In the League Cup, Fourth Division Exeter City made their first ever visit to the Hawthorns, and on an evening I wished to forget, they won 3-1. Losing at home to a Fourth Division club was a grim experience. Nights like this had me pondering whether I'd ever see a return to what had been exciting competitive games against the countries' finest teams.

League form picked up markedly after this new low with a string of narrow victories. Once again, Jeff Astle was on the operating table with yet more cartilage problems. We were not to see him on the pitch until February 1974. I just didn't want to face up to the reality of what such a prolonged absence meant for Jeff's future.

On Boxing Day, some former rivals were in town. Villa had escaped from the Third Division and fancied their chances at the Hawthorns. Suddenly, we were again a genuine football club with 43,000 packing in. Two goals from Bomber Brown made up all the scoring and I was grinning from ear to ear all night. That felt good. Another victory three days later over bottom side Swindon and Albion were fourth, just one win short of a promotion place. One of the goal scorers against Swindon was Willie Johnston, his first League goal since arriving a year earlier.

There was more good cheer in the FA Cup. In early January, Second Division Notts County were on the end of a Tony Brown hat trick in a 4-0 hammering. The Hawthorns was a great place to be that day. Famously, the Bomber went one better a week later, with all four at the City Ground, Nottingham. After demolishing the pride of the city in a week, allegedly his team mates dared him to cross the Trent without using the bridge.

This was not to be my only memory of Nottingham clubs that season. In a League match against Pompey, 3 different Notts County players all failed to score from the same spot kick. The first was disallowed because the keeper moved before it was taken. The second because the referee had not signalled it could be taken. And lastly the third attempt failed to find the net! It had me baffled. Why change the original chosen player just because the keeper had moved?

Albion drew old rivals Everton away in the FA Cup Fourth Round. It felt like our Cup road had just become a cul-de-sac. Everton were having a reasonable season in the top flight (they eventually finished seventh) and secured the vast majority of their points at home. With another miners strike biting, coupled with an oil shortage and Liverpool also at home, the decision was made that the game must be played on a Sunday. Sunday! Never before had the Baggies played on the Sabbath. This was partly because the law prevented it and also because people then genuinely believed that Sunday was the "Day of Rest". Shops, restaurants and even pubs in some areas were closed.

The novelty served only to raise the appeal. I was just one of a very impressive 6,000-strong Albion army. Good to be back at timeless Goodison and better still to remember what supporting the Baggies used to be like. There were over 53,000 in the ground that afternoon with our Stars in Stripes competing against a very determined and competitive Merseyside outfit. Don Howe's defensive tactics felt more acceptable when up "against it" Pressure on our goal was certainly hairy at times but I wasn't about to complain with a 0-0 draw and the chance of seeing us causing an upset in a replay.

The Baggies moved quickly to secure a generator to avoid an afternoon kick-off just 3 days later. We won. I didn't expect a victory but Bomber Brown's solitary goal secured progress and I was in the proverbial seventh heaven. Losing to Exeter belonged to a different decade.

The match is not remembered for the victory, more so the all-in wrestling simulation on the pitch. Willie Johnston had a disagreement with Everton full-back Archie Styles. Instead of resolving matters, the participants grew more heated. It turned into an almighty punch-up as the pair rolled around the turf punching each other. Most people around me found the incident funny though I disagreed. Our record signing had nearly as many dismissals as goals to his name and at that time I felt this was poor value for money.

Our run ended in Round 5 as a rampart Newcastle took over the Hawthorns. Malcolm McDonald inspired Newcastle United to a comprehensive 3-0 victory. We were completely over- run on the muddy pitch and off it too, as United brought vast numbers of supporters with them. There was a pitch invasion of excitable Geordies after their second goal. The big Cup matches bought home to me just how desperate I was to see us climb back into the top-flight. Once again, there was some consolation that we'd gone out to the Cup Finalists – the Geordies well beaten by Liverpool at Wembley.

Back in the real world, the dogfight for promotion was as fierce as ever, and as a rampaging Middlesbrough were more or less certainties, it left only two places up for grabs. When 'Boro came to the Hawthorns in mid-March, only goal difference kept us out of the top three. Jack Charlton's marauders had won their previous four games, their back line held firmly together by the menacing-sounding combination of Boam, Spraggon, Craggs and Maddren. I defy you to say those names aloud and not conjure up images of gritty, raw-boned Northern defenders. Graham Souness ran Boro's midfield while David Mills was their first-choice forward. Whatever happened to him?

The North-East side strolled to a very comfortable 4-0 win. It was the joint biggest away win recorded in the Second Division all season and the Baggies never really recovered from that drubbing. They only managed one more win in the remaining nine games. I saw our hopes fade away without too much of a fight. There was a final indignity on the last day as we hosted Luton Town. The Hatters had just secured promotion and their supporters, as normal in a final game, set out to enjoy themselves whatever the result. They certainly left in a happier frame of mind than yours truly following a 1-1 draw that could have been worse but for a 'Bomber Brown' spot kick.

Middlesbrough finished as clear champions. Who was promoted in third place for their first ever season in the top flight? Alan Ashman's Carlisle United. This reopened the old argument. Were the board of West Bromwich Albion right to sack him? What I do know is that in company with virtually every Baggies fan, I found the football under his stewardship far more stimulating than the fare Don Howe's teams had served up all too frequently.

Lack of goals was again our big problem. Sheffield Wednesday and Cardiff, who both just stayed up, both found the net more often than the Baggies. Of the forty-eight scored, 19 had come from Tony Brown and 8 from David Shaw. As for the "King" Jeff Astle, this was a third consecutive season to forget. Yet more cartilage operations restricted him to just six appearances and one goal. That was the main reason Joe Mayo had been signed from neighbouring Walsall, and while at times he appeared decidedly awkward, he nevertheless appeared to be a useful prospect for the future. The question was what would the future hold if changes, so badly needed from the fans' point of view, weren't forthcoming? Surely there had to be a radical rethink, and drastic changes, if Albion were to increase their attendances, and most importantly, get the Baggies back into playing First Division football?

A First Division which incidentally would now be minus one Manchester United. They'd had a grim season and the final straw came at Old Trafford when their former star player, Denis Law, now playing for rivals City, backheeled the winning goal. Results elsewhere would have seen United relegated anyway but it was still a desperately unhappy moment for United and for the Law man too. United in the Second Division would mean a huge gate at the Hawthorns but no doubt accompanied by numerous louts and thugs bearing United scarves making everyone's life a misery. Hooliganism was a major problem.

League President Len Shipman, clearly of my own generation, was so short of ideas to combat this problem that he resorted to making appeals for the return of the birch. I shared his view, as did many others, probably out of desperation, but the Government was never going to restore a punishment abolished just after the war. Away from worshipping the Great God football and his Number One disciple West Bromwich Albion, I was most involved in my twice- weekly dancing lessons. What I hadn't realised when joining the school was that at the end of my 3 months of lessons, I was expected to be brave enough to demonstrate whether the time, effort, and expenditure had been worthwhile!

It wasn't mandatory but I didn't want to decline either. After all, hadn't I castigated certain footballers for lacking bravery over the years? Thus having decided to 'bravely' accept the challenge, one Sunday morning Dot and I strode bravely into an empty hall. During those nervous moments, I suddenly realised our tension were akin to that of Bomber Brown stepping up for a crucial last-minute penalty.

We handed over the appropriate forms, tried to breathe deeply and away we went, horribly self-conscious through most of the test. Just finishing was a big relief.

We had to wait several days for the results. I skipped over the marks and comments looking for the result and we'd passed, thank heavens. Goal! The first of 3 Bronze, Silver, and Gold Medals that even now, 40 years on, still hang on a cheap plastic plaque at home…a 'priceless' memento!   I did muse whether any 'Strictly Come Dancing' winners possibly took their first steps on the road to fame for the same reason as this 'nutty' Albion supporter. Was I tempted to carry on? Watch this space!

## 1974 World Cup

I was bitterly disappointed when England failed to qualify for the World Cup finals in Germany. Still under manager Alf Ramsey, they'd missed the opportunity on a dramatic Wembley night, when needing a win to book their place; Poland held them to a 1-1 draw, due to a series of glaring misses added to an astonishing display from the Polish goalkeeper Jan Tomaszewski. The nation sat around their television sets watching in total disbelief as the keeper (famously labelled "a clown" by analyst Brian Clough) defied everything England could throw at him. Yes, he had his moments of luck and good fortune but as the minutes ticked by at an alarming pace, I had the feeling that it was going to be one of those nights. The ball simply wasn't destined to go into the net however hard or accurate the shot or header and so it proved.

Even without England, this was still an enjoyable tournament. West Germany, on home soil, ran out winners against Holland. The Dutch played "total football", an exciting new variant of passing football which apparently all ten outfield players comfortable all over the pitch. Johann Cruyff caught the eye but he was just one of many talented players. With the gift of a first minute penalty, Holland were much the better side but the Germans equalised from the penalty spot, went on to snatch the lead, and the Cup. A 2-1 defeat was rough justice on the Dutch but like England they'd discovered if you don't take your chances, you'll regret it.

## 1974/75

*"It's the hope I can't stand."* Admittedly, that phrase didn't become commonplace until later decades but I can't think of another phrase which better describes my frustration. I'd put up with Howe's defensive dalliances and dared to dream of promotion only to see such hopes slide away from mid-March. This was so deflating. I thought our prospects were grim 12 months before but now with club income reducing steadily and our better players wanting an instant return to the top tier, my rock solid support was being severely tested.

Pessimism abounded. Many long standing Rainbow fans made it clear they would not be renewing their season tickets *"I can be miserable at work, I don't have to pay to come here to do it"* was the most common explanation. Others just stopped attending. I was on the receiving end of so many jokes – the usual stuff around having to shout so that the nearest supporter could hear me. Money was becoming a problem for everyone, with inflation running at a ridiculous 16%. Anyone on a standard variable mortgage was having a wretched time just trying to keep up with payments.

Much like the previous year, there was plenty of gloom around in the world in 1974. The IRA remained horribly active, setting off bombs on a motorway and in the House of Commons in the first half of 1974 and there was much worse to follow. The miners' strike came to an end after Harold Wilson agreed to a 35% wage increase. The rest of the country was just so grateful the strike was settled and there would be no more power cuts. Blackouts reminded me of the War but the younger generation had never experienced life without power before and were overwhelmed. Over the water, President Nixon resigned rather than face trial over Watergate but at least the Vietnam War was finally over.

Back at the Hawthorns, three of our players wanted out. Asa Hartford, Len Cantello and Alan Merrick were all transfer listed at their own request. Cantello was clear that if he couldn't leave, he would rather play for Albion reserves than the first team. Asa Hartford was rather more conciliatory. As he explained *"there is no chance of patching up my differences with Albion but I will play anywhere the manager wants. I still want to move and my plan is to show people I'm fit and worth a fee."* His wish was granted on the eve of the season as Manchester City whisked him off to Maine Road. *"Can we all go?"* asked several Albion supporters on a local radio phone-in. No, I wasn't one of them.

Cantello stayed but only because Aston Villa of all clubs only offered £125,000 while Albion stubbornly held out for £150,000. This was an indignity we didn't need, even at the risk of keeping an unhappy player.

Almost unnoticed amid this squabbling, a truly great Albion career came to an end. After struggling with a series of injuries, and ten years at the club," King" Jeff Astle left to join non-League Dunstable Town. Along with many fans, I thought Astle could still have played a part in trying to get Albion back into the First Division but the club obviously thought otherwise. Anyone with a modicum of interest in the fortunes and history of West Bromwich Albion will surely realise the debt of gratitude owed to Jeff Astle. He had scored 174 goals, gained a ridiculously meagre total of five International caps, and represented England in a World Cup. Truly a splendid record and of course, he would always be remembered for that magical strike in the 1968 Cup Final. For certain, it would be strange realising that the "King" wouldn't ever be seen leading a Baggies attack in the future. His number 9 shirt was shared by Shaw, Mayo, Glover, Hartford, Hughes, Ally Brown and Tony Brown which in itself said much.

A 1-0 opening day defeat at home to Fulham, followed by the same score at Hull was just the same-old, same-old. The Humberside team were managed by Baggies favourite John Kaye. On a spying mission at the Fulham match, Yorky said it was a shame to see his old team in such a state. Meant kindly of course, but when the manager of Hull City is feeling sorry for us, times are indeed grim.

It was a campaign of fits and starts with a winning sequence being followed by too many disappointing results. This consistent lack of consistency meant that although many fellow managers (including England's Don Revie) expressed the opinion that Albion might make a promotion run, in reality they again hovered on the fringe of the pack, unable to force their way up among the front-runners.   These included Manchester United, who invested heavily in hungry Scottish players to ensure they were not going to linger in the Second Division. Right behind them and the source of much angst was Aston Villa. They won the League Cup as well as promotion. Truly, it felt as though we were being left behind.

Albion were out of the League Cup by October. Initially Millwall were beaten at the Hawthorns, but Norwich City, after claiming a Hawthorns draw, beat the Baggies 2-0 after extra time at Carrow Road. Our sequence of losing to Finalists continued.  Norwich reached the Final where they were beaten by a certain team playing in Claret and Blue shirts from just down the road - guess who!

On a personal level, I will never forget the annual 'Radio Birmingham' listeners' get-together at the

'Rainbow Suite' in the city centre on November 21. Everyone was enjoying the night when the wailing of fire engines and ambulances were heard in very close proximity. Their sirens were frightening in their intensity. What was happening? News filtered through that the IRA bombing campaign had reached Brum. Two nearby pubs were blown up resulting in 21 deaths and many serious injuries. Shocked and stunned people quietly made their way home and began to realise exactly what carnage had occurred just 200 yards away.

Next day, the Salaries Office at Cadbury's had a dreadful atmosphere. Hardly a word was spoken as people tried to get their heads around those terrible happenings - an atmosphere that lingered on not just for days but for weeks. Mention of the bombings brings back strong emotions even now.

Four days later the Baggies beat Orient 2-0 at Brisbane Road. A much-appreciated light relief victory but one that could never eradicate the memories of a horrendous night of evil perpetrated against totally innocent people.

Albion didn't fare well in the FA Cup despite progressing to the Fourth Round on the back of a 4-0 replay home victory against Bolton Wanderers. Another mammoth trip to Brunton Park to face First Division Carlisle United was our downfall and after a 3-2 defeat there was the usual cliché from supporters: "*We can now concentrate on promotion!*" I imagine some even believed it.

Despite my criticism of Don Howe, and his apparent inability to instil consistency into the team, at times we appeared well equipped to play and compete if we did return to the First Division. Len Cantello and Ally Robertson were stand-out players. John Wile led by example. Tony Brown was still on the goal trail but his total of 12 was probably a personal disappointment for him. Curiously, he'd only scored three times by the start of March. Joe Mayo with eight and David Shaw with six also had useful seasons. Useful but we needed more.

Thankfully, there was one source of constant entertainment in Willie Johnston. His brilliant, if sometimes erratic, performances were both a joy and relief to behold and if his finishing could have matched his sparkling wing-play, his individual tally of seven goals, and the teams total of fifty four, would have been many more. Willie was a reason to keep supporting the club, in many people's eyes maybe the only reason.

But for all that, the Baggies team still hadn't convinced me they were capable of reaching the First Division. A view clearly demonstrated in early April when apathy reached a new can't-be-bothered low. The gate to see Notts County at The Hawthorns was a pathetic 7,212. Us small Band of Brothers did receive payback with the biggest win of the season 4-1.

Two days later, new-ish Chairman Bert Millichip issued a grim statement. The club finances were in a parlous state, there was no way Albion could afford big fees for new players, although he recognised a desperate need to see fresh faces. I wasn't surprised. Millichip was only stating the obvious. Since the last hurrah of signing Willie Johnston, all incoming players were signed for modest transfer fees or none at all. Seemingly, month- on- month, more and more supporters just stopped attending. Sub 10,000 home gates were commonplace and Villa's success only made matters worse. I almost, but not quite, had a whole row of seats to myself in the Rainbow Stand.

The club's woes were summed up in a lengthy article in the Evening Mail. It was predictable stuff under the banner headline "WHERE DO ALBION GO FROM HERE?" The answer came in dramatic fashion just two days later. The board sacked Don Howe. At last! I rejoiced. In fact, most everybody connected with the club rejoiced including the players. Tony Brown was particularly relieved. Earlier, Crystal Palace had come in with a bid for him and the Bomber was willing to leave such was his level of frustration. Thankfully, the Board refused to sanction a transfer of the Baggies' talisman. No one can say for sure what would have been the long-term effects if the transfer had gone through, but in the short term, could a promotion team be fashioned without him?

The board were clear that the manager's job would be advertised and this time it had to be the right appointment. Now how often had the board shared that line with supporters? Indeed would they ever make the right appointment? Frankly, I'd heard it all before.

The Baggies won two of the final three games against York and Cardiff, before losing the final fixture 2-1 at Forest. Against York, and almost unnoticed, a youngster from County Durham made his debut and scored twice in those three games. Early promise that in due course would bloom into fruition and eventually lead to him becoming Britain's costliest footballer six years down the line. This was a young player of whom the club described as a tremendous prospect. As it turned out this was a gross underestimation for one Bryan Robson.

With the regularity of Coronation Street, the 'dreaded' name of Leeds United continued to make front and back page news. Yes, they possessed some truly wonderful players who could play devastating football. But, as a counterbalance, they would regularly hog news headlines for all the wrong reasons.

At the start of the season, Leeds appointed Brian Clough to succeed Don Revie (he'd moved on to manage the national team). It was a "bold" move given that Clough was openly critical of Leeds United and the players were clear they wanted Johnny Giles to be their gaffer. That said, United staggered the football world by dismissing Clough after just 44 stormy days in charge.

Cloughie, being Cloughie, had come in and quickly began to make the changes he felt were needed. They didn't go down at all well with anybody, basically. He plunged into the transfer market, put established stars on the transfer list and installed authoritarian discipline. Reports spoke of a dressing room revolt with the players passing a vote of no confidence in his decisions. Leeds initially dismissed these reports but just hours later Clough and his solicitor were summoned to a meeting where he was sacked and received a £44,000 pay-off on his four-year contract. The board claimed: *"What had been done is for the good of the club and the happiness of the players must come first".* These words drew a typical Brian Clough response *"I think it's a sad day for Leeds and football."*

The press agreed, with one highly respected commentator asking: *"this disgraceful affair now more than ever raises the question: Just who is running professional football - the management or the players?"* (Now doesn't that ring an ironic bell the bearing in mind what has happened several decades later?).

Thinking along the same lines was Tottenham's very successful manager Bill Nicholson. He resigned in August 1974 after Spurs had lost their first four games but stressed this wasn't the reason for him quitting. He was disillusioned by wage demands of players, and hooliganism – notably in a European Final against Feyenoord. Famously, he was in dispute with Martin Chivers who'd described the clubs offer as "*rubbish*". He was put on the transfer list and Nicholson's attempts to sign a replacement were thwarted by several players demanding under the counter payments. When he left, Bill Nick outlined what he considered to be the problem. *"Players have become impossible. They talk all the time about security but are not prepared to work for it. Players abuse me. There is no longer respect."* Perhaps not wanting to go out on a sour note, he later retracted these thoughts, writing in his autobiography *"I resigned because I sensed I needed a long rest, I had no more to offer. It was really nothing to do with Martin Chivers or anyone else.'*

On a lighter note, and stop smiling as you digest this, the FA match committee suggested players *'kissing and cuddling'* after a goal could be charged with bringing the game into disrepute. But surprise, surprise, the FA rejected the ideas as being impracticable.

Two other measures were introduced which subsequently changed the game. Firstly, the Football League decided to switch from goal average to goal difference from the start of the next season. For me, this was common sense. Goal difference required a calculator to work out.

The same body also agreed to freedom of contract. No longer could a club retain a player after their contract expired. If they wanted to move, they could. Obviously they wanted the same rights as employees in any other profession and how top end players have taken advantage of it since.

Returning to Elland Road, as the media invariably did, it was palpably unfair to brand all United fans as being little more than hooligans but the sizeable group among them who had regularly disgraced the name of their city finally went one step too far.

Leeds United had reached the European Cup Final to face Bayern Munich. At the time, this was an extraordinary feat, only previously achieved by Manchester United in 1968. The venue was Paris and this turned out to be a night that shamed not just Leeds but led to the foreign press labelling hooliganism as the 'English Disease'

Both sides were struggling for form domestically (Leeds had much recovering to do after Clough) and this was a no holds barred clash to turn a season around. Leeds supporters had developed a "No One Likes Us" mentality over several years and were convinced that here was another referee who was giving them nothing at all. They'd conveniently overlooked the savage tackling by their team which put two Munich players out of the game in the first half. Twice United claimed penalties against Franz Beckenbaeur and the second claim did have a lot of merit as the German international blatantly tripped Allan Clarke.

In the second half, Peter Lorimer put the ball in the net. The referee initially gave the goal and then changed his mind after Beckenbaeur spoke to him. Bremner, who was running away from goal, was deemed to be offside. In a fit of rage, a section of supporters showered the pitch with debris ripped from the Parc des Princes. The match was halted as Leeds skipper Billy Bremner appealed for calm. As the French Police battled with hooligans, United completely lost concentration and Bayern scored twice in late counter attacks to win the match. In the minds of the hooligan element, this was reason enough to go on the rampage across Paris.

This ultimately led to UEFA, thoroughly sick of English hooligans, banning Leeds from competing in Europe for four years, which was later reduced to two years. It was ultimately academic as United went into decline and didn't quality for Europe anyway. Sad for English football as a whole, but there were very few fans of other clubs who had an ounce of sympathy for their cynical play plus the truly thuggish behaviour of some of their supporters.

One of United's men that day had just played his last game in a Leeds shirt. It's unarguable that over the years the board of West Bromwich Albion have made some "strange" managerial appointments. But the announcement in June that Leeds United's Irish maestro Johnny Giles would be taking over in a player/manager capacity was greeted by a combination of amazed speculation and expectation. Had they at last managed to make the right appointment? Giles had been an integral part of the ruthless Leeds machine, honed to perfection in the art of what is now commonly known as "professionalism", slowing down a game, subtly wasting time, antagonising opponents and pressurising referees. If it wasn't specifically forbidden by the rules, Leeds would do it.

On his appointment, Giles said: *"I know it's going to be hard work playing and managing but I would rather be joining Albion than a lot of First Division clubs. They have a First Division background but there is plenty to work to be done. Can I cope with the dual role? I'm perfectly fit and feel I have a year or two left in me so it would be a waste if I did not play"*. His last sentence left me with an added spring in my step. There was a possibility that he could remove the deeply implanted negative thoughts that Baggies fans had endured courtesy of Don Howe.

But that was for August. Before then, I savoured not having to be concerned about football trials and tribulations even though I had much else to think about.  There were numerous animal fundraising functions, carnivals, dances, etc. Dot and I had enough on our plates to fill all our waking hours. Encouraged by our initial dancing success, we'd taken the plunge and moved on to more intricate formations. Moans, groans, and curses but at the end of the year…. another 'GOAL' …a First Gold Bar. Time to invest in a trophy cabinet!

# 1975/76
## The Unbelievable Johnny Giles Era.

We had a new season to enjoy but with the same old hooliganism problem. So-called Chelsea fans, having failed to get their match abandoned at Luton when losing 3-0, staged a pitch invasion, attacked the Luton keeper, rampaged through the town and, to cap it all, destroyed their train on the way back to London. Over 100 of their number were arrested. On the same day, another train was halted at Crewe when hooligans set it on fire. British Railways response was to stop running Football Specials for the rest of the season and refusing to sell cheap tickets until after 3pm on Saturdays. If fans wanted to travel by rail, their club would have to charter special trains and be responsible for any damage meaning all decently behaved supporters were forced to suffer the consequence for such unforgivable actions

Violence was actually far from universal though newspaper readers were force fed a different impression. Casual supporters and those with children were deterred from going to games. There were lots of ideas to counter this problem but none of them worked or were feasible. The tired cliché of 'Bring back the Birch' was trotted out yet again. England manager Don Revie was in favour saying "we have tried everything else, we may as well try this drastic deterrent." The referee of the Luton v Chelsea match agreed. So did I, thinking of my disciplined days of National Service, even though I fully understood corporal punishment would never be re-introduced.

The Police Superintendents Association even suggested that matches should be classified in the same way as films with fans under the age of 16 banned from 'X' rated games unless accompanied by an adult! Never an option, but Chelsea who had some of the worst problems, were not impressed with such a ridiculous proposal. Their chairman Brian Mears asked: *"Who would decide which matches were selected?"* Any involving Chelsea or West Ham, Brian!

Chelsea had been relegated to the Second Division (join the club!) and they provided the opposition for the Baggies first home game. Fortunately, it was a night match. This and heavy rain were, at the time, the most effective anti-hooliganism measures. Ray Wilkins played in midfield while Kenny Swain came on as a late substitute but the rest of the Londoners side relied heavily on youth. The game finished 0-0 which was acceptable. Johnny Giles was not able to install any early miracles. Our first game at The Dell was a sad curtain raiser. Mick Channon & Co stormed to a comfortable 3-0 victory. Our curious looking combination of green and yellow with blue shirts looked rather limp that day as did the team.

Indeed a streaky 1-0 victory against Luton was the only win from the first ten games and by the end of September the Baggies were again sprawling among the strugglers. I'd believed anyone other than Don Howe could do a better job but now I was far from sure. Away from home, we had collected just two points and some press hacks mentioned Albion dropping into the Third tier.

Giles had found no solution to our lack of goals and just as under Howe; we relied on our defence to keep us in matches. Still, I had to keep telling myself that a top form Giles had to mean better times ahead. He was 34 but very fit and tough as befitted a former Leeds man. Being a player-manager, he was a core part of his own tactics, which often consisted of *"give me the ball."* Given that he was possibly the best passer of the ball in the Division, this was simple logic. However, not even one of the best footballers the Republic of Ireland had produced could do everything by himself. He needed new recruits. The new manager was shopping at the equivalent of Aldi rather than Waitrose. (Metaphorically, we all were as inflation was rampant, standing at 25%. Difficult times!) The Baggies' meagre funds were all invested in securing our new leader.

Giles had the choice of either bringing in either callow youth or experienced old pros. Mainly, he chose the latter, starting with England's hat trick hero of the 1966 World Cup Final, Geoff Hurst from Stoke City. In retrospect, he was a gamble that simply didn't work. He only made ten appearances, scoring two goals in the process.

Fortunately, this was a rare poor signing. Two "old" Irish team- mates joined the club. Mick Martin from Manchester United was followed by Paddy Mulligan, an overlapping full back. In addition, John Osborne was rescued from third team obscurity. Slowly the Giles way, honed by so many years as a winner with Manchester United and Leeds United, began to bear dividends. Eleven games without defeat lifted everybody. Pick of the bunch was a 2-0 win at Ashton Gate over the then League leaders Bristol City.

The quality of football was much improved; possession football became our trademark, the ball being stroked around albeit sometimes to excess. The philosophy of our new leader was *"If we have the ball, they can't hurt us."* As the players explained to me, both at the time and later, Giles gave clear information to everyone. There were not many instructions but if they didn't deliver to the required standard, they would not play.

His philosophy slowly began to pay rich dividends and come December the Baggies had climbed into a dizzy top eight position. And, along with other fans, I was actually beginning to believe this diminutive, genial Irishman could be the magician to take us back into the big time. If he hadn't yet worked a miracle, he was certainly pushing his claims to be recognised as a leading contender for the 'Magic Circle'

When asked for his mid-season perspective, Giles readily conceded the sluggish start but pointed out that changing philosophy, playing style and belief all needed time. Key to the improvement was his expectation that all of his team would self-analyse their personal performances and work on their shortcomings. Improved discipline, an Elland Road expectation, was the other major key. (At this point, I could easily imagine a few conversations between player manager and a certain Scottish winger).

To reinforce this message, he'd set up a players committee comprising senior pros in Tony Brown, Len Cantello, and John Wile. The committee would be judge and jury on their team mates' misbehaviour on the pitch. The Baggies, by necessity, had a slim squad and needed every deterrent to avoid incurring disciplinary points awarded against the club. The FA had introduced a code of conduct under which a club that reached 100 points for bookings and sendings off would be called before their disciplinary committee to explain their actions. There was a scale of points for bookings, depending on the severity of the offence and a fixed point penalty for dismissals. The Players Court worked well until the Baggies played at Kenilworth Road. We had a player sent off for the first time that season. Embarrassingly, it was our player manager. For a man who built a reputation as being "hard", it was surprising to note this was his first ever early bath.

Albion had fallen behind but was beginning to control the game when Giles was involved in a clash with Ron Futcher. Out came the red card, off went Giles, and despite a battling display, Luton held on to poach an undeserved two points. This was no accidental clash. Giles had a grudge against Futcher and basically wanted to "take him out." His team mates pronounced judgement of a £5,000 fine, mainly because of this personal vendetta.

Incidentally, Albion's equaliser from Mick Martin came straight after the break. So fast that many of the Press corps, still ambling back from their half-time 'cuppa' in tardy fashion missed the action. Whoops – bet the Players Court would have loved to pass judgement on that lack of alertness.

I was joyfully celebrating just below the press box when Nick Owen appeared. I'd worked with Nick at BBC Radio Birmingham and he was well known for supporting Luton. Decades later, he was to become their Chairman. He now had to report a goal he had not seen.

*"What happened, Terry, who scored?"* A quick word in his ear and a few seconds later back in the studio, the famous 'Goal Horn' broadcast to warn listeners that a goal had been scored, were followed by the smooth tones of a Luton devotee using my words to describe a Baggies equaliser. Spoken like a true Beeb professional. Nice one Nick! Ten men Albion battled feverishly in the attempt to snatch an equaliser to no avail. Team and fans felt that the Hatters were fortunate to hold out.

The following week, the Baggies painfully lost again to Southampton, this time at the Hawthorns but after that, we went game after game without losing.

I had my hope and optimism back. Going to the Hawthorns was no longer a chore, on a par with mowing the lawn or weeding. This was Football – a pleasure to be both anticipated and savoured. I felt an inch taller and I'd tell anybody who'd listen how proud I was to be a Baggie again. Yes, we didn't score that many goals but our sophisticated brand of possession football was very easy on the eye. My habit of reading every newspaper possible was renewed and they mirrored my optimism. I still have a Birmingham Post cutting which reads *"Revie cannot have failed to notice how Giles has attempted to mirror the formula of building Albion into a promotion winning team"*

Albion saw off fellow Second Division outfit Carlisle 3-1 in the FA Cup, drew 0-0 with new League Leaders Sunderland, won at York and then just hung on against Graham Taylor's Lincoln in the FA Cup Fourth Round. Lincoln led the Fourth Division and under Taylor thought they could overpower anyone with their hit and chase football. We won narrowly and breathlessly 3-2. The reward was another home game but against bogey team Southampton.

Before the Fifth Round, we'd won 2-1 in most enjoyable fashion at Chelsea and then crushed Bristol Rovers 3-0. As The News of the World had it *"towards the end, they showed touches of First Division class as they sprayed the ball around with an ease that took their unbeaten run to five games."*

Being in the FA Cup last sixteen against a decent team felt exciting, had the opposition being anyone bar Southampton. The Saints "had our number" and were content to take us back to The Dell for a replay. Once again, we were second best in Hampshire and were thrashed 4-0. Yet again, our victors went on Wembley and this time, they won the trophy by beating Manchester United 1-0. Being able to concentrate on the League was rarely more meaningful. I could smell the "p" word. No, spell it out Terry - PROMOTION.

The Giles trademark was clear for all to see. He may have lacked real pace but his close control, tactical ability, and most of all, his passing skills were astonishing. Those soul-destroying displays perpetrated under Don Howe had been put to rest. The only question was "*could Johnny work the final miracle?*"

March looked crucial. We won well at Notts County "*Albion had so much class they played County off the park*" was another headline which I just had to keep.. My optimism was rising week by week. Those early season comparisons with Don Howe were in the distant past. Mid-month successive games against promotion rivals Bristol City and Bolton Wanderers looked crucial. We lost to City but beat Bolton. At the top of the table, Sunderland, Bristol City, Bolton, Albion, and Southampton were battling it out for three places.

It's a sobering thought that with anything resembling a reasonable start, we could have been top. But we couldn't buy a goal scorer with our meagre budget so we had to grow our own or make do with what we had. Sunderland were clear favourites to win the Division, Bristol City would probably follow them but Bolton were feeling the pressure. Echoes of a certain other side decades later,The Wanderers had started the season very well but a FA Cup run distracted them significantly.

Bolton were definitely wandering rather than concentrating and with just a few games to go, we were breathing down their necks. Matches became bi-sensory with radio updates on Bolton Wanderers given equal weight to events on the pitch.

West Bromwich Albion had the attention of the whole West Midlands. Villa, Blues and Wolves were all involved in a moribund struggle to avoid relegation, a struggle that eventually cost the other Wanderers their top Division place.

The day after the Burnden Park Wanderers had inexplicably lost to York; the Baggies had a chance to take their promotion spot and grabbed it with a 3-1 victory over Fulham. This was the Nuremberg rally revisited, 90 minutes to make you loud and proud. And I was definitely both. The press were raving about Albion's display, summed up in the Birmingham Post: *"On an occasion when they might have been expected to show deep intense pressure of chasing promotion, they overwhelmed a Fulham team who had already beaten them twice this season. Add to the fact that Bolton are succumbing to tension and it's no wonder the happy Albion fans were loudly singing "Villa, Villa, here we come".*

We went on to beat Nottingham Forest 2-0 amid much tension. Bolton had a horrible match at League leaders Sunderland. The Mackems were unbeaten at home all season and much to the delight of our part of the West Midlands, the Lancashire side were sent packing with a 2-0 defeat. Our route was clear now – we needed 3 points from our remaining 2 away games to go up. The Baggies had the best away record in the whole Division but when the prize is so big.... I reassured myself that two shut-outs and just one solitary Albion goal would be enough.

The 'first leg' was a predictable tense affair at Orient. The O's were in lower mid-table with nothing at stake but they played with spirit and great determination. Defeat was unthinkable, defeat would be death to our hopes but at the end of 90 so tense minutes, we'd done just enough to escape with a 0-0 draw. All my fingernails were bitten to the quick, and I swear one supporter was chewing anxiously on his scarf. We'd achieved our objective and this set the scene for one of the greatest and most joyful days in the history of our great club. Anyone who was lucky enough to be there will never forget it.

To be certain of promotion, Albion had to win their last game at Boundary Park. .A draw, coupled with a Bolton win at Charlton, would see the Wanderers take the prize. After the Everest-sized Mountain we'd climbed to get so close to the summit, it would have been heartbreak on a grand scale. During the previous day, I'd tormented myself with ifs and buts. I wanted that prize so badly. Saturday May 24th was also Dot's birthday. What better present could she possibly want? It's a cliché I know but we all revert to them in times of stress.

A mass exodus along the M6 started early. A caterpillar line of coaches and cars, all sporting flags, scarves and banners from windows, filled the motorway. So much so, the Police had to rescue the team coach and force a passage through the invading army. By kick-off time, Black Country hordes had taken over this windswept corner of Greater Manchester.

The tension and expectation felt overwhelming. So much relied on these 90 minutes that the thought of failure hung like a black ominous cloud shroud over our heads. At half time, the game was goalless, and with Bolton in front, we had to score.

"Come on you Baggies" was chanted relentlessly and in the 55th minute 'the Bomber' obliged. It was tremendous, marvellous, wonderful - choose any adjective you like. This was a goal worthy of winning any game. Picking up a knockdown from Ally Brown, he juggled the ball from one foot to the other before unleashing a brilliant left footed volley into the net. The players swamped each other. Three quarters of the ground erupted.

The news that Bolton were beating Charlton 4-0 racked up the tension further. It was now down to the defence to put up the shutters, and how we agonised in those final 35 minutes. 'The Bomber' almost made the game safe with a second goal but as a counterbalance only a great stop by Ossie preserved the lead. It was clear that Albion were the better team but nerve ends were jangling as one error could undo everything we'd set our hearts on.

Time dragged on. Had the referee's watch decided it was it was time for a go-slow? A pounding heart and knotted stomach refused to go away. There was no slip up and as the final whistle ended our torment, the scenes demonstrated the sheer joy of fans released from emotional turmoil. Make it a historic day. Eureka. Mission accomplished.

Thousands of the `green and yellow' clad army ran onto the pitch while those in the stand wished we could have joined them. It was as if Wembley had been moved to Oldham. We cheered, we sang, some cried, many just looked stunned. We had done it. We were back in Division One and the 'big boys' had better look to their laurels!

Normally, the end of the game means a mass exodus at Boundary Park. Get up, get out, and start for home as quickly as possible. Ice Station Zebra is not the most welcoming. But this was an exception and if the players had celebrated all night from the balcony of the main stand, we'd have stayed there with them.

Eventually we wended our way out to start our fervent homeward bound journey. Occupants of a cavalcade of vehicles were in joyous mood. Sports

Report' had a sing-along special magic that night. The team coach was right in the middle of the convoy. Royalty never had an escort this big. Most visible was a grinning Willie Johnston who'd clearly had "a few drinks" and was keen to acknowledge everybody all the time.

For Giles to have steered the Baggies to promotion in his first season was a tremendous achievement. For the fans, it had been the coming of the new Messiah. "*Johnny Giles walks on water*" he was told in unison, over and over again. Despite the comparatively few goals scored with Tony Brown finishing as top scorer with 12, our new gaffer had given us cultured football. His cut-price signings, Martin and Mulligan, (sounds like a comedy duo!) adapted to his style. The whole squad looked as if they were enjoying themselves while the promising young Bryan Robson, on the strength of his fourteen appearances, seemed set to distinguish himself back where all the fans were convinced we belonged - the First Division.

Later came a fine chance to offer personal thanks to the players at the Adelphi Ballroom in West Bromwich. Everyone was in high dudgeon including Dot and myself. Johnny (Mr Maestro) Giles made a point of visiting the delighted Baggies supporters' tables to pass on his thanks for the magnificent support he and the team had received. He stressed that historic day at Oldham could never be forgotten. As I eagerly told him - ditto Johnny -a thousand times over!

What was I expecting back among the Big Boys? Raging optimists spoke of challenging the top sides. I'd be more than content with merely stabilising a place in the First Division after three years of waiting.

Oldham's Boundary Park may now be my "favourite" ground but I wasn't keen to go again.

Ahead of Dot and I was an eagerly awaited holiday in Bournemouth. Sun, sea and dreams about who would be our first victims of this rejuvenated Johnny Giles Division One team.

## 1976/77

The music of your formative years always stays with you. Thus I could think of no better song that Guy Mitchell's *"Cloud Lucky Seven"* to reflect my post-promotion idyll. I hummed it; I sung it often and played the record even more frequently. I cocked a deaf ear to all laments about its 1953 vintage.

Dot and I enjoyed a well- earned holiday in good old Bournemouth. We didn't need to go abroad to Spain, Greece or wherever for sun – the heat came to us.  Such was the heat that talking in the shade over drinks was the only sensible solution. Every day, for nearly a month, the temperatures varied between 80c and 90c.

With replica shirts now commonplace, it was easy to identify and strike up conversations with supporters of other clubs. I was always keen to chat to discuss respective fortunes and, if we got on really well. I'd give them a rendition of Cloud Lucky Seven. I earned respect among the younger elements by casually mentioning *"last time I was here for a match, Albion were the Cup holders."*

As well as mentally replaying Albion's promotion run-in, it was hard not to be concerned about our immediate top flight future. We'd just scraped into the First Division with a very mature team and we had no funds to buy in younger players. Goal scoring was a problem in Division Two, so without additional talent, we'd surely be firing a lot of blanks. By common consent, WBA were in for rough baptism. I feared the worst, considering that finishing outside the relegation places would be a success. That's what my head said. My heart believed that Giles was a shrewd operator and would surprise everybody. Hadn't he proved it?

The balance of power in the top tier had tilted slightly since our previous membership. QPR were now a "name" having finished just a couple of points short of winning the Championship. Ipswich, Leicester and Derby all had decent teams, which finished in the top seven.

Who were the first team to test our capabilities? None other than our Irish maestro's ex club, Leeds United at Elland Road. This seemed a brutal, not to mention cursed, start for us top Division rookies, mainly because of the legacy of the infamous 1971 game. Yes, three years had passed and yes we'd played there several times since but there was a concern about a very hostile reception. Naturally, the media angle was around the return of Giles to one of the clubs where he'd made his name.

Despite the anxiety, I was so looking forward to the return to the big time. We'd been away for 3 years but it felt so much longer. I was early onto the Elland Road terraces among what I'd term an expected crowd of 40,000 plus. And was it hot! The pitch looked hard due to the blistering summer. But the conditions didn't bother the Baggies. Surprisingly, we out-passed Leeds demonstrating our disciplined possession game was just as hard to combat in Division One. The natives were becoming very restless as the upstarts from the Second Division went two goals ahead thanks to the 'Brown Brothers,' Tony and Ally. We thought the points were ours until United snapped back by scoring twice in the last five minutes. It hurt then but by the time I got home, I'd convinced myself that we'd secured an excellent point. I wasn't to know then that Leeds were to have a miserable start to the season and would eventually finish in mid-table, their glory days over.

Our very satisfactory start would be tested further. In what seemed like downright sadistic fixture planning, next up were League Champions and UEFA Cup winners Liverpool. Not only were they to be our first home League game but we'd also drawn them away in the League Cup. This was the classic Reds side with all the big names – Keegan, Toshack, Heighway, Emlyn Hughes and Phil Thompson.

Once more, this fixture felt big, an instant payback for their labours last season. No need to shout to my nearest neighbour now, with just shy of 30,000 people descending on the Hawthorns. Even the Post Office got in on the act issuing a First Day Cover. I savoured the recognition but could have done without them printing the final score of West Bromwich Albion 0 Liverpool 1.

If this was a shock that perhaps truthfully we should have expected, the next development stunned everyone. At the AGM, Johnny Giles announced he was resigning to take up a full time paid directorship with an Irish club, an illegal position in England. He also warned that although the club had done wonders to gain promotion, if they really wanted to establish themselves as a true contender for greater honours they would have to spend big money. At the time, I hoped this was a hollow threat, arm-twisting by the manager for a bigger transfer budget, particularly as Giles was persuaded to stay for the rest of the season. I had no idea that Giles had bought into a vision to transform his home-town club Shamrock Rovers into a European power.

In the short-term, we remained surprisingly respectable in the League even though goals were in short supply. The first home win came courtesy of a 2-0 against Norwich with an attendance barely half that for Liverpool. This was normal for the period though made worse by rampant inflation standing at an average 16%. At one point, it reached a simply impossible 24%.

The first away success was also early in the season – at St Andrews, thanks to another Tony Brown winner. Remembering how they'd been mercilessly in their sarcastic mickey-taking in 1973, this was sweet revenge indeed. The status quo was restored and we'd put City back in their place. I was more than content to share my views with local radio. What was I worrying about in the summer? A stream of disillusioned Blues supporters rang Tony Butler to share their troubles but after Tony had subtly twisted the knife, they rang off even more enraged.

There was an astonishing start to the League Cup campaign. Firstly, in what the national press unkindly called "*the battle of the oldies*", the Baggies battled manfully to earn a 1-1 midweek draw at Anfield. Giles himself scored our goal. Just a few months ago, we'd struggled to keep out Orient and now we'd held both Leeds and Liverpool on their own turf. Time for Guy Mitchell again.

*"You never know, you never know, you never know.*
*There's no way that you can detect it*
*It can happen when you least expect it.*
*You never know, you never know, you never know."*

Much better still, in the Hawthorns replay, we put the mighty Reds out of the competition. Mick Martin scored the only goal. In high dudgeon I didn't, as normal, travel home on public transport. Instead, I swear I floated on a cushion of air! We'd beaten the double winners, a mighty feather in Giles' cap. Even if the feeling that he could walk on water was a slight 'exaggeration', I felt he was capable of swimming the channel in both directions - without taking a break.

But after beating the 'Pool', we disappointingly went down 2-0 at home to the Albion team who hailed from Brighton. Not for the first time we'd underestimated an in-form Third Division club, who went on to be promoted. Alan Mullery was a canny manager, Peter Ward a hot goal scorer (36 that season) and a team urged on by a large support.

This was the infamous match in which wee Willie Johnston was sent off for aiming a kick at the referee. His effort in front of the Rainbow regulars missed the target. He immediately found himself making his way back to the dressing room to enjoy a warm early bath. As this was his 10th sending off, he received a five game suspension for bringing the game into disrepute. ("*Nice one Willie, Nice one son, nice one Willie, Lets have another one*") Yep instant forgiveness, such was Willie's status at the time.

Giles then made another very shrewd and typical purchase. An Irish team mate in his thirties with some fuel left in the tank. Ray Treacy was the new arrival, to be sure. Perhaps second time around might be more accurate as "Paddy" had played just five games in his first period with us in the early sixties. On his second debut, he bought the house down by scoring both goals in a 2-2 draw away at Derby County. Despite the goals, Ray's biggest asset was holding up the ball, key to the Albion's possession game.

Johnny Giles and his organised, motivated team was turning heads and making critics look foolish - particularly at the Hawthorns. First Division side after First Division side roiled up with expectations and left soundly beaten. Spurs were seen off 4-2. Docherty's Man United were outplayed and thumped 4-0 with West Ham escaping with a mere 3-0 defeat.

The Manchester United win was particularly satisfying. The Reds were not yet the all-conquering force of later decades but they were at the top end of the table and under Docherty were considered "sexy. To make our triumph complete, BBC's Match of the Day' cameras were present so we could watch extended highlights the same evening, a real "Proud to be a Baggie" night.  There was Giles at his imperial best, directing the Albion midfield like an orchestra leader, not to mention scoring himself from long range.  It was to be his only goal that season but what a strike – and against his former club too!  In that moment it felt OK to swear in pure delight.

'Pride comes before a fall' is an old truism, so too is "you're only as good as your last game." Both phrases were bandied around after the infamous match at Portman Road. Albion lost 7-0, their highest ever defeat to Ipswich and even now I find that score hard to comprehend.  True, our record in Suffolk was far from great but this took some swallowing on what was then a 4 hour coach journey. In truth, it was just one of those games where nothing went right though of course it was weeks or even months before I could reach that sensible perspective. The home side were flying that day, with a team about to become their best ever, featuring internationals like Paul Mariner, Kevin Beattie, John Wark and one Brian Talbot. They were having a serious go at winning the Championship (they eventually finished third).  Five of their goals were spectacular long-range efforts. Goalkeeper John Osborne later admitted to being so down about the result that he didn't try to stop the last goal. Giles directed the team coach to a remote country pub and ordered the team to get drunk and forget the defeat. In that period, a beery team-bonding session was considered a perfectly sensible activity by a top-division side.

Possibly Giles used the defeat as leverage for within a fortnight the Albion Board had agreed to what was then a major incoming transfer for the club. Target man David Cross was neither Irish nor in his 30's, yet WBA still purchased him from Coventry – for £150,000. That was seriously big money at the time for us but the reassuringly higher gates (average attendances were up 7,000) softened the blow. Cross made a cracking start, finding the net four times in his first seven matches.

One win was particularly satisfying, coming as it did at the Victoria Ground, Stoke just before Christmas. Our record in the Potteries was grim even then. Our previous victory was way back in 1949 and if I did go, I have no memories of it. Thus any win was to be savoured but best of all was both goals in our 2-0 triumph were scored by home grown players. Growing our own talent – the perfect solution to not having a big transfer budget and I do need to acknowledge Don Howe's foresight at this point. The previous season, the Albion Youth team won the FA Youth Cup, thumping Wolves 5-0 over two legs. I enjoyed that! One of the stand-out players was left back Derek Statham, who had fully earned a first team debut against Stoke City. And what a debut! Not content with his primary role to keep out the opposition, Derek rampaged through the City defence in fine style to score – past Peter Shilton of all people.

Full backs don't normally do that on their debut but his style and speed created a perfect *"I was there"* moment. Fellow scorer John Trewick was reasonably well established by then but it was Derek Statham made all the headlines. A new star was born that day, an exciting 300 game man who was always more comfortable running at the opposition than the other way round.  With left back duties shared between Cantello and young Bryan Robson, the club ultimately needed a specialist No. 3 and Statham was the right man at the right time.  He was given a run in the first team later in the season and after that, the number 3 shirt was copyright Derek Statham.

Being a smoker, Derek was no doubt made particularly welcome to the first team squad by the other smokers who included Ossie and Willie Johnston.  Smoking was considered a stress-busting activity at the time though other members of the squad did resent the smell. Keeping both the smokers and non-smokers happy during an away trip was tricky and did become quite a saga.

At the turn of the year, holding tenth place in the table was highly satisfying, so much more than I'd dare hope for but any hopes of an FA. Cup run quickly disappeared in the Third Round. A Willie Johnston strike at Maine Road meant a 1-1 draw but in the replay it was City who notched the deciding goal. No shame in this defeat as the blue half of Manchester were only just beaten to the title by Liverpool at season's end.

Still the critics expressed doubts as to whether Albion could hold on to their prized First Division status. For me, these views were beginning to sound desperate, spiteful and vindictive, a sort of wish fulfilment if you like.  We'd demonstrated over and over again our controlled intelligent football, delivered by a combination of experienced professionals blended with exciting home-grown talent could compete and often beat the best.  As I'd tell anyone prepared to listen, only Liverpool had beaten us at home in the League though Leeds did spoil that record in late January.  And then came a Sunderland shocker which had our knockers bouncing up and down saying "*I told you so.*"

That debacle was an almighty shock for the expedition-travelling faithful as Sunderland handed out a 6-1 hammering. Not since Ipswich in November had anybody scored more than two goals past us and given that the Roker Park club were rank bottom of the First Division at the time, to concede six was quite simply embarrassment on the grand scale. There was no sparkling conversation to be had during the tedious long journey home.

Whether it was this setback that spurred Albion to their best run of the season had to be a consideration. But whatever the root causes an unbeaten run of nine games, seven wins and two draws, shot them up the table.

And it was during this period that Johnny Giles signed who I personally consider was the Baggies best ever player despite the sad fact that we'd lose his services after two short years. That was the incredible Laurie Cunningham, a player of infinite skills, pace and true athleticism albeit often combined with being an outsider who lacked an innate discipline of most footballers. Giles had picked up on a recommendation from Chief Scout Ronnie Allen.

Laurie was tipped to become the first black player to be capped by England even before he joined Albion from Leyton Orient. This was a common misconception, as another young player with black skin had already won an England schoolboy cap.

The national press were startled, not to say amazed, that a Midlands team had snatched him away from under the noses of the many London clubs keeping a radar watch on his progress. But it is easy to watch, far harder to overcome the blind racist perceptions particularly noticeable in London. In fairness, Laurie had served a brief but unhappy apprenticeship at Arsenal where his laissez-faire attitude to time-keeping had him out of the door inside a year with a negative entry on his cv.

Ironically Laurie made his debut at a London club (Tottenham) when the team were in the middle of their splendid run and he more than played his part in a 2-0 victory (our fourth straight win). Laurie was Albion's first ever black player, in an era when the colour of a players' skin was not only noteworthy but the subject of much debate and often outright hostility. There was another debutant in this satisfying win - goalkeeper Tony Godden, who was a very cheap purchase from Ashford Town, presumably another Allen spot. He replaced John Osborne who at 36 was finding recovery from injuries more difficult. Ossie was one of those rare people who seemingly age before their time and thus had apparently been in his mid-30's for at least a decade already.

It didn't take Laurie long to open his account. In the next match he was on the mark as we gained revenge for that thrashing at Ipswich by winning 4-0, and I remember screaming for another trio of goals to level up the seven they had knocked in against us at Portman Road. Ipswich sat second in the League at the time. There was a fine hat trick for Bryan Robson, a feat rather overshadowed by the dancing figure on the touchline. The *"Laurie, Laurie Cunningham"* chant had its first airing. Albion had a man who had different coloured skin but could play football very well indeed. This came as a shock to many football supporters and the National Front campaigners who regularly haunted the Brummie Road on match days (never the "posh seats" in the Rainbow). The racist abuse which Laurie constantly endured, mainly though not entirely from the opposition supporters, was shameful. And yet it was deemed to be acceptable behaviour at the time. There was no channel for protest, no legal recourse.

With the Baggies riding on the proverbial crest of the wave there was a distinct possibility Albion could qualify for Europe. And, if this could be achieved, supporters naively hoped this would be sufficient motivation for Johnny Giles to reconsider his decision to leave.

By early April the Baggies lay fifth, just six points behind now shock leaders Ipswich Town. Unfortunately the run-in proved our undoing with three successive home defeats serving as a painful poke-in-the-eye to our Albion pride.

This was redressed a little in a satisfying 5-0 away win at Leicester City. Giles considered this was his best ever game for Albion. Said he *"That display, particularly in the first half when we led 3-0, had everything a manager wanted to see from his team. I was always looking for perfection and when I was at Leeds on a few occasions we were almost there.*

*When I went into management at the Albion I was looking to reach that level of performance. And when we played at Leicester we reached it that day. It was simple, it was good, we had pace, we had power, it was effective and we just wiped the other team off the pitch."*

But following that demolition at Filbert Street, the unpalatable truth was that in the last home match against Stoke City, Baggies fans would be waving goodbye to the mercurial Johnny Giles. It was emotional. On the eve of the game, Giles commented: *"I will leave Albion with a greater sense of achievement than in all my years at Leeds. All my memories are fond ones. I have experienced a most enjoyable stay here. Happily the club succeeded in winning promotion, and now we are on the fringe of European qualification. Relatively speaking I would say that this has been as significant as winning two championships, F.A. and League Cup wins and European honours. There is a great collection of players here - a mixture of experience and potential. I am convinced that even without me Albion can achieve success in top class football in the future."*

As to the match- won 3-1- the Birmingham Post reported *"the Hawthorns was an emotional place to be. It had little to do with football but with Johnny Giles last appearance. "Johnny don't leave us", yes there was euphoria about the whole thing"*

*They were still rejoicing in the skill of the little Irish wizard. The truth hadn't really sunk in that they would go into next season without Johnny Giles".*

Giles admitted the fans had been tremendous, calling him back to the director's box to wave goodbye. But he added: *"there is nothing in the back of my mind. I'm just pleased to go out on a high note and glad it wasn't an anti-climax for the fans. We haven't been too far away from a European spot when most people thought we would be lucky to finish half way up the table."*

The last two games were away at Everton, which finished 1-1, and a grim Villa Park finale. A thoroughly miserable Cunningham-less performance (dropped for poor time-keeping) leaving me reluctantly admitting the villains had been very comfortable 4-0 winners. When I'd calmed down several days later, I took solace that overall the season was richly enjoyable. After universal doubts about retaining our top flight status, Albion finished seventh, achieved through a widely admired brand of football, topped by sparkling individual performances.

We didn't yet have a notable goal scorer. David Cross topped the list with a modest dozen. Bomber Brown was still a key performer with eight. But more excitingly once young Bryan Robson had overcome his injuries, he found the net eight times. Sumptuous new boy Cunningham managed six in a limited number of games. The future was very bright – for the right manager.

To this day, supporters of my generation still reminisce about Johnny Giles and wonder what might have happened had he stayed. But Giles was frustrated by the brakes on spending. He wanted to make his own decisions. There was no precedent for a manager to sit on the Board and Albion's notoriously conservative directors had no wish to start one. So Giles went home to Ireland. He was to return to the Hawthorns years later but the circumstances were very different.

In later years, Johnny explained his frustration through examples. He wanted to purchase the outstanding Plymouth Argyle striker Paul Mariner but was informed by the board there was no money to buy new players.

A week later Chairman Tom Silk approached Giles saying, *"I think we should go for Paul Mariner."*

Giles replied wearily: *"There's no point in going for him because I've been told we haven't got the money to buy a £200,000 player."*

*"I think we can get the money."*

Giles' reply? *"So what you're telling me is that if I fancy a player but you don't, we have no money but if you fancy a player then we have the money?"*

Sadly Tom Silk's response is not recorded. Albion did bid for Mariner but he chose Ipswich and became a full England international within six months.

Giles shared another example. In the summer of 1976, he asked the Board to buy Brian Kidd from Arsenal. He was available for £100,000, and £200 weekly wages. The Board immediately baulked at the weekly wage, some 30% higher than the top earners at the Hawthorns. "*No way*" was their instant response. The Board were fearful of opening the doors to a higher club wage all round but for me it was a chance missed. Instead Kidd went to Manchester City, where he scored 44 goals in 98 games. A fair return methinks and I still muse as what were the hidden feelings of a Board responsible for this proven error of judgement?

Of course, Giles didn't share his less successful transfer targets with me. But because they couldn't persuade the fiercely ambitious Irishman to stay, the club directors had the terribly awkward job of finding a replacement.

Who would be next for the hot seat? Would he be a popular choice? Would he have the same ambitions as the fans? All the usual questions asked by a supporter when a new appointment is in the offing. Managers and players come and go, many of them never giving their old clubs a second thought, but for a supporter there can be no such change (unless you're David Mellor) you just soldier on regardless. Hoping and praying the appointment will be the right one.

While Albion's board deliberated, their counterparts at the Football League reached a verdict at their Annual General Meeting that at the time had limited impact on most football lovers. After winning the Southern League Championship three years in a row, Wimbledon FC were finally elected to the Football League, under the "old pals" act of that period. Woe betide any struggler who were geographically isolated. Outside Merton, Wimbledon were well-known only for holding Leeds United to a 0-0 draw in the FA Cup Fourth Round, at a time when Leeds were at their pomp. At the same meeting, delegates agreed that red and yellow cards would be introduced to add clarity to the disciplinary process. Club hopes of a new revenue stream via shirt advertising were temporarily blocked, primarily because of the objections of TV companies. It was only a short-term respite - there was too much new revenue at stake.

On the International front, this was a wretched year for England. Wales won their first ever match at Wembley 1-0 but in comparison to Scotland's visit to Wembley on June 4 that was hardly worth reporting. Scotland won 2-1. The Scots, including one Willie Johnston were on top throughout, supported by tens of thousands in kilts, from North of the Border. To 'commemorate their rare victory, their fans celebrated by charging on to the pitch, tearing down goalposts and ripping out the nets. They topped this by cutting up pieces of the Wembley turf into pieces to take home as souvenirs. Damage amounted to £180,000 with the arrest count standing at almost 300 that weekend. It certainly left me considering whether it was worth the hassle and possible aggravation attending any big matches in London unless of course Albion were involved.

The hooligan stories ran for weeks on end linking with other recent episodes such as the Villa v Rangers friendly the previous October which ended in a riot. It was the same old problem, same tired old solutions and sadly a prime reason to keep away from football.

This embarrassing defeat to the Scots was pretty much the swansong for 'Three Lions' manager Don Revie walked out on England after press reports he'd secretly, and deceptively, found himself another job as manager of the United Arabic Emirates. In club management, being tapped up was just part of the game but this was England and a nation already in pain. Revie was the first ever England manager ever to resign and the tabloid press worked themselves up into a righteous fury, secure in the knowledge that Revie, with his Leeds past, had few admirers. The FA levied a 10 year ban on him for bringing the game into disrepute. To me and many others that seemed perfectly reasonable but in legal terms the ban was dubious. Subsequently, on appeal in 1979, this was overturned but taken all round there weren't many administrators or fans who cared one iota what happened to Revie who had been a far from successful national team manager.

After so much football frustration, I was pleased to try something new. In what was a personal first for me, I travelled to Poland for the World Individual Speedway Final, in the company of two other regular Birmingham Brummie watchers. I was keen to discover whether my pre conception of Poland being a cold austere country was correct. I couldn't have been more wrong. Following a long, tiring coach journey, we arrived in glorious hot sunshine. The locals were sporting casual and colourful clothes, many of them enjoying ice cream. I didn't expect that! Was I really in Chorzow or back in Alum Chine, Bournemouth?

Rounding off a memorable venture, Peter Collins, a rider who never knew when he was beaten, was crowned World Champion with another English rider, Malcolm Simmons in the Silver Medal spot. What could possibly top that? Albion winning a major honour admittedly but that apart.....

For Dot and I, fund raising reality meant endless manning of stalls at local carnivals or jumble sales. More significantly, we organised and participated in sponsored walks. All these events had to be carefully planned to avoid clashes with Albion games. Fortunately in those days, 3pm kick offs stayed at 3pm.

Sponsored walks, oh yes! How could I possibly forget when together with 'Holly' Dot and I decided to participate in the famous London to Brighton Walk. The full 44 mile walk was impractical because of the time factor and our levels of fitness! We settled instead for the early morning train to London. Once there, we changed to a stopping train and get off at appropriate station to join in for the last 10 or so miles. We met up with glamorous fashion model Celia Hammond, another tremendous animal welfare campaigner. We swapped details of various campaigns before at long last we caught a welcoming sight of our destination-Brighton's renowned Pier.

There were greetings and congratulations from the Lord Mayor. After final chats we were off back home. Back to London, onto Brum and mission accomplished. Our tiring challenge was overcome with a fair amount of sponsorship money raised that made it a well worth exercise. Not that I was anxious to repeat the process. Time to wonder what lay in store in Albion's next challenging season. Please, please let it be good.

## 1977/78

The first match was overshadowed, in some people's eyes, with the death of Elvis Presley. Personally I was never a great fan but I do remember the shock generated. For me, after numerous reports of drug dependency, I just can't help believe that the only question was when would he die? Elvis was just 42.

Despite the focus being elsewhere, the football show rolled on. The Board hadn't been overburdened with success in their choice of managerial appointments. All too often their first choice went elsewhere. I was downright perplexed by the latest Thanks but no thanks, this time from Graham Taylor.

Taylor had led Lincoln to a record-breaking Fourth Division title-winning season and come reasonably close in the Third Division to a second straight promotion year. The Baggies was a prestigious job with a settled First Division side but to universal surprise, Taylor said no to WBA in favour of Fourth Division Watford. This choice was a universal jaw-dropper. What a magnificent selling job Elton John must have done on Taylor to take on an average basement side who, at the time, had a greyhound track around the pitch. Money was a factor - with the Hertfordshire club offering more of it.

Albion's board instead offered the manager's position to a safe pair of hands in their Chief Scout Ronnie Allen. But, as if to doubt their own judgement, the job was only offered on a temporary basis. The former No. 9 had decent credentials. He'd managed in both Spain and Portugal plus Wolverhampton and Walsall locally. The securing of Laurie Cunningham demonstrated his talent spotting on a budget, an ability keenly desired by club directors. But there was no permanent deal on offer.

Initially, the Board could bask in a decision well made. On the opening day, regular strugglers Chelsea were sent back to the Bridge on the receiving end of a 3-0 defeat.

A satisfying away draw at Leeds proved this was no fluke and despite a first defeat away at European Champions Liverpool the pattern had been set for a satisfying season. Indeed from the first fourteen games only two were lost with both Newcastle and Manchester United suitably chastised on the backs of 3-0 and 4-0 defeats respectively. Not bad for a caretaker manager.

Early into this spell, many of us were privileged to see the début of another number nine who today is revered as a true Albion great - Cyrille Regis. Famously, Ronnie Allen was so utterly convinced that Regis was the man for the job that he offered to pay the small transfer fee to Hayes himself. The directors clearly took some persuading! Allen had made his move at just the right time. Regis had just passed his examinations to become a fully-fledged electrician. Had Allen delayed much longer, Cyrille's joint income from building sites and part-time football pitches would far exceed what West Bromwich Albion were willing to pay him and he may never had a professional football career. How many clubs would take a chance on a black player who would inevitably "go missing" in the depths of winter? This sadly was a widely-held belief in the late 1970's, a myth which persisted well into the next decade.

First choice striker David Cross was injured for an early-season League Cup match with Third Division Rotherham and with such talent elsewhere on the pitch, Ronnie Allen thought he could give the 19 year old rookie a game.

And such a rookie! Part-time footballer, full time sparkie with a few reserve games with a professional club behind him now turning out in Albion's heritage-rich no. 9 shirt. Not to mention his walking to the ground from his accommodation. This just couldn't happen nowadays. Cyrille was remarkably big and remarkably powerful, so much so he could outmuscle and "out head" any of his senior colleagues in training.

These attributes compensated for his lack of technical know-how. He was as yet incapable of holding the ball up as was expected of a main striker in Giles's team. (To me, it was still Giles' team even though Allen was the manager)

Third Division central defenders are robust by law but the new boys' combination of immense physical power and pace was too much for them. For a Hawthorns crowd, first impressions often count. Fuelled by our rich tradition of powerful strikers, Cyrille became a favourite within minutes. He was different - very raw but very exciting. I wasn't the only one making comparisons with Jeff Astle that night.

With Rotherham already two down, crowd pressure earned Cyrille the chance to score his first ever professional goal from the penalty spot. This he did before scoring the fourth and final goal against a not-at-all Merry Millers side. He was roared off the pitch and in the traditions of the era, Cyrille and most of the team strolled to the Hawthorns Hotel and got merrily drunk with the supporters. Mine host organised a lock-in until the early hours of the morning. Easy to imagine Cyrille *thinking "is it always like this"?*

In the short term, it was. Just four days later, Middlesbrough were in town and Regis kept his place, even though David Cross was fit again. There was one awkward conversation for the manager. *"Yes, you are the club top scorer David but I'm going with this kid who's never played in a professional League before..."* It was the first of a series of difficult debates which ultimately led to Cross leaving the Hawthorns before the year was out.

News spread quickly and had a positive effect on the gate. The 'Boro remained notoriously dull opposition and the attendance was quite modest for what, unexpectedly became an "I was There" moment. The magnificence of Cyrille's goal that day, since enhanced and exaggerated, safe in the knowledge that no TV footage exists. Exaggerated to the point where the younger generation might believe that 5 defenders, their manager and several supporters were hanging onto Regis during his lightning charge. The reality, whilst not that quite spectacular, remained memorable. The debutant picked up the ball in his own half and just ran straight at goal, the sort of direct route that only a novice would consider. The Teesiders were completely foxed by this unorthodox route. Their men were outpaced or outmuscled as our new striker finished the job with aplomb. Such a marvellous moment was greeted by a tidal wave of noise around the ground. Everyone, except a few bigots, were on their feet to applaud and cheer Regis. Good times!

A week later, the Baggies travelled to Newcastle and Regis found the net again, the most positive way he had of combating the volume of monkey noises and hurled bananas.

With a new goal scorer completing a talented line-ups, I had hopes this could be our season. Promotion was enjoyable but for a long-time supporter like myself, I wanted more marches on Wembley. I missed those Twin Towers.

But slowly, the absence of Giles off the field became more pronounced. Giles was charismatic and a fine man-manager. Ronnie Allen was more distant and didn't inspire his charges in quite the same way. There was a sequence of poor results,

The stand-out game was a League Cup tie at Third Division Bury. On a miserable foggy night, Albion were easily defeated 1-0 in a shameful display. The pressure told on the dressing room. Rumours circulated about big fall-outs between the players, manager and staff, including some horribly unpleasant racist overtones. This would not happen with Johnny Giles. More poor results followed including a painful hammering by Villa. Losing consecutive derbies heavily to the claret and blue is never acceptable. The Baggies didn't find the net for five games before struggling to a 1-0 win over soon-to-be-relegated West Ham.

Suddenly we knew the reasons why. Frustrated by his lack of a long-term contract, Ronnie Allen was looking after himself first, using his head not his heart.

Saudi Arabia offered him a £100,000 contract per annum, presumably tax-free. Compare that with his non-contractual arrangements at the Hawthorns and from his pragmatic point of view, his departure was wholly understandable. The public response from the Board varied from the obvious to the puzzling. Bert Millichip's thoughts were that Albion had no chance of matching the oil-soaked Saudis while Vice Chairman's Tom Silk's quote was of the "*Stop messing us about*" variety. Perhaps he was deliberately misquoted. It is hard to see such an observation, with its overtones of the country squire addressing his peasants, being terribly helpful. My own thoughts echoed those of the majority. If Ronnie Allen had been given a long-term contract, the situation may never have arisen. To misuse a famous quote *"to lose one manager is unfortunate but to lose within six months is careless."* In best supporter tradition, we brushed aside the troubling run of mediocre results on the pitch which implied that Allen wasn't actually the right man for the job anyway.

We natives were getting quite restless. We had a decent and settled team holding 4th place in the top flight so why was it so hard to keep a manager? The players were putting forward a case for John Wile, the dominant senior voice in the dressing room, to become player manager. Better the devil you know. The Board weren't keen on such a young and inexperienced choice (and hindsight suggests they were right to do so). In the short term, they gave Wile temporary charge over Christmas and into the New Year.

So pick again! The bookies money was on another young manager Colin Addison who'd made his name with Hereford United and Newport County but he didn't get the nod either. Instead, the new incumbent was Ron Atkinson of relative new boys Cambridge United. He was reputed to be an aggressive character. One that encouraged United to play attacking football. That was music to my ears!

From the first day of his appointment, I was privileged to witness some of the finest football played in the clubs history and I don't say that lightly. At their peak, Atkinson's Albion were up there with the near double-winning team of 1953-54. What a pity that Big Ron's time at the Hawthorns would ultimately end in acrimony. Not once, but twice.

After feeling his way into the job, his influence began to take effect with Tony Brown and Big Cyrille cracking 29 goals between them. Laurie Cunningham was back in the side having being dropped under

Allen. There was a definite feeling among fans that we were on the verge of achieving something big. *"Don't bore me"* was Atkinson's public plea to the team. Who can resist such a line? I couldn't.

We were not bored! Shortly after Atkinson's arrival came the FA Fourth Round against Manchester United. The Reds had recent Wembley experience and expected to beat the Baggies with their inexperienced manager. Albion so nearly beat them at Old Trafford, thwarted only by an injury time equaliser. The replay, on a sea of mud, was one of the greatest Albion matches of the decade. Cyrille was at his powerful best during a dramatic two hours of tension, scoring the winner in a fascinating 3-2 triumph. Another *"I was there"* moment with every potential of more to come. In the Fifth Round, Derby were defeated 3-2 on their own mud-heap pitch, much to the delight of the packed away end. Most of us could see most of the grass in between the fences and the endless pillars.

The Quarter-Final draw did us no favours. We'd drawn Nottingham Forest, the runaway League leaders who were unbeaten for a quite ridiculous 42 games. Even though Albion were at home, Clough's team were overwhelming favourites. It was the biggest day of the weekend, a complete sell-out with many supporters disappointed. Lennie Henry wrote a comic sketch around unorthodox ways to get into the Hawthorns.

Clough's men dominated the Quarter-Final. They had more possession, more attacks, more shots but it was the Baggies who joyfully scored both goals and otherwise grimly defended. As a fine early example of the panache from Atkinson's men, Willie Johnston trapped the ball with his bottom. It was a beautiful moment, made even better by Clough's scowl but the best moment of all was the final sounds from the referee. We'd put the country's best team out of the Cup and we were in the last four. I floated all the way home (again) and I may even have had a celebratory sherry during Match of the Day. If the neighbours objected to repeated playings of "Cloud Lucky Seven" that night, they were too polite to mention it.

Albion were surely on the march to FA Cup glory. We'd had several rotten draws along the way and overcome all the challenges. In the Semi-Final, we drew Ipswich Town at Highbury. I believed I could smell and feel Wembley on my Semi-Final ticket. It felt so close.

I wasn't alone. Getting horribly carried away, Big Ron was filmed holding a replica of the FA Cup at Wembley prior to the Semi-Final. His players were appalled. The Ipswich manager Bobby Robson probably couldn't believe his luck - no need to construct a pre-match team talk now.

Atkinson's actions was terribly naive. Years later, I took the opportunity to ask Big Ron why he agreed to the filming. His response was carefully worded. *"I was led to believe that officials from both Albion and Ipswich were asked to have photographs posing with the Cup. Why only mine was shown came as a surprise. I certainly didn't intend to claim Albion felt the Cup was as good as won. We respected Ipswich. We knew that they were a good team and if we did win, it would only be after a very hard game."* Behind his crafted diplomacy, Atkinson was stitched up and I'm sure he knew it. Without this gift to Ipswich, who knows what the score might have been. In reality, the Suffolk side were grimly determined and the stars in stripes wilted. Most froze, one (Mick Martin) was sent off with others injured in their desperation. The one lasting image from that sad afternoon is an injured

John Wile battling on with a bloodstained bandage wrapped around his forehead.

My huge balloon of optimism had a hole in it. I'd been chatting to Asa Hartford before the game who was just as confident as I that the twin towers were next. Oh, it was such a horrible ending to the afternoon. Almost too numb to move, I stayed in my seat for the full 90 minutes though many others left very early. Nine and a half men do not retrieve 3-1 deficits in Cup Semi-Finals. To add one final insult, a lot of windows of the Albion coaches were smashed by persons unknown. Yes, I was there but I almost wish I wasn't. Semi-Final defeats take a lot of getting over. It wasn't as bad as losing to Villa in 1957, I kept telling myself.

Atkinson acquired an emerging team. His only addition was Brendan Batson, picked up cheaply from Cambridge as a youthful replacement for Paddy Mulligan. Where Atkinson made a difference was by taking the brakes off, encouraging more attacking play. By careful cultivation of the media, he raised the clubs profile and naturally his own as well.

Albion enjoyed a satisfying League end of season thanks to six wins and two draws from the last nine games. The only reverse coming at home where we painfully endured our third heavy defeat by the claret and blues. More carpet-chewing that evening.

I went to Wembley for the Cup Final even if the Baggies didn't. I'm not sure that I enjoyed the occasion too much as I couldn't easily get away from the "What ifs" and "it should have been me" type thoughts swirling round my head. I was so envious of the Ipswich Town players showing off their new trophy. I took some consolation that a former Albion great in Bobby Robson had won the day. Remarkable how much he picked up from training me and the other Nomads all those decades ago.

On a happier note, I thoroughly enjoyed watching Liverpool retain the European Cup beating Club Brugge at Wembley. Liverpool were so impressive, especially when they were overcoming the infamous Belgian Astle-kicking club of nine years earlier. There was a more prosaic reason for Albionites to get behind the Reds. A Liverpool victory would mean they wouldn't need their UEFA Cup spot. That would instead go to the club in sixth spot who just happened to be WBA. Europe, here we come! This was a reasonable balm for our FA Cup pain.

And so to the World Cup in Argentina. Scotland were going to win it. Apparently. Their very loud (irritating?) manager Ally MaCleod told everybody this would happen so it clearly must be the case. As England had failed to quality again, it was difficult to query this claim with any Brummie-based Scots without our own shortcomings being raised. With our very own Willie Johnston being part of the Scotland squad, I felt I couldn't be too critical of their over-the-top boasts. No doubt they had a decent team but the concept of them ever beating Argentina in their own backyard, I found quite comical.

Scotland made an awful start, losing to a decent-looking Peru. That blew a massive hole in their qualification hopes. Worse was to follow with a miserable draw with Iran but far worse was Willie Johnston failing a routine drugs test conjuring up headlines all over the world. Poor Willie. He'd innocently taken Reactavin to ease his hay fever. This included a banned substance and from then on, he was labelled a "junkie". Other Scottish players were using the same hay fever remedy but their name wasn't called. The Scottish FA acted quickly, presumably with the intention of sacrificing an individual to save the team. Willie was given an immediate life ban and ordered home immediately. There was no support for the wide man or any challenge to the allegations. Perhaps Willie's track record was still uppermost in their mind. Johnston was to endure a media circus for weeks on end. In the months to come, he'd become the target of endless, mindless abuse from opposition supporters Would Albion fans react accordingly if faced with a team possessing a similarly accused player? Good question. But such is the nature of the beast, I suspect that bigoted fans who want to see their team win at any cost, would adopt the same attitude.

The World Cup continued without him though the Scotland team weren't that far behind him in seeking a plane home. Their only hope of qualification was the highly unlikely scenario of beating the mighty Holland team by three clear goals. To their credit, they nearly pulled off the sensation of the tournament as they did run out 3-2 winners. It wasn't enough but some face was saved.

It was Argentina who ultimately triumphed, not at all to my surprise. Argentina had always been confident in their ability. For me, their philosophy bordered on arrogance. They, not Brazil, were the true masters of South American football, and this tournament would prove it, even though there appeared to be some skulduggery along the way. European hopes rested with Holland and it was Argentina and Holland who lined up in the Final. The game went into extra time but again when the referee blew the final whistle, Argentina had consigned the Dutch to a second successive, massive, World Cup setback. Amongst the latest batch of World Cup winners was one Osvaldo Ardiles.

## 1978/79

Was this West Bromwich Albion's finest ever team? I think so but I do accept the counter argument that if they were so great, why did the trophy cabinet remain empty? It's a fair point but everyone across the country knew they were an exciting team to watch. Can you rattle off the team? I can. Tony Godden now established in goal, the classic back four of Batson, Wile, Robertson and Statham, midfield trio of Robson, Cantello and Bomber Brown and then the forward line of Cunningham, Brown and Regis. Doesn't that tell you something?

The Albion were off to a cracking start. First up was some petty revenge over the Cup holders Ipswich Town. Trying to ignore their songs of FA Cup triumph, we won 2-1. Wins at QPR and at home to Bolton followed. Wanderers were soundly beaten 4-0. This fixture was also notable as this was the first Albion game that my publisher Simon Wright attended. Oh, these Johnny-Come-Latelies, passing themselves off as veteran supporters.

However, when you've been visiting the Hawthorns for decades, it is easy to take your surroundings for granted so I was interested in Simon's first encounter with the Birmingham Road. "This is not a great viewing terrace. I know I'm not the tallest at 5ft 10 but surely that ought to be sufficient. There's a fence across the front, several pillars and terrace steps which are far too small. Other than the easy demolition of Bolton, my keenest memory is moving from place to place, just to get a clear view of the play. I expected better, frankly."

After Bolton came the first of the matches against Leeds United. The Whites, now under Jimmy Adamson, were desperate to retain their status. Without many star names, they relied on blanket defence for results. They were the exact opposite of WBA - dour, ugly, ruthless and boring. It was our misfortune that the Baggies played them an extraordinary seven times that season. Their negativity was so draining for me, I did wonder what it took out of our small squad to battle against them so often. United's massed ranks of obdurate yellow-shirted defenders remains an enduring image for me even to this day. Annoyingly for this purist, the tactics worked. After two goalless League Cup draws, Leeds edged us out 1-0 at Maine Road in a second replay. Only 8,000 travelled to Manchester to brave this cure for insomnia. Leeds went on to reach the League Cup Semi-Final and also finished fifth in the League.

Willie Johnston played in two of these games, a rare outing for him. Our favourite Scotsman was constantly hounded for his "drug-taking" which was difficult to deal with but even more of a problem for him was the in-form Laurie Cunningham had his shirt. However much Albion supporters bellowed *"Willie, Willie Johnston on the wing",* his Baggies career was coming to an end.

In the short term, the League Cup slog, not to mention our return to Europe, did impact a little on results in these pre-rotation days. But we did bring back a point from League Champions Nottingham Forest and drew with the mighty Liverpool at home. We were so close to beating the Reds too before Tony Godden dropped an almighty unforgettable rick

Kenny Dalglish, who'd unsuccessfully chased a long ball, continued running to finish behind the keeper. Godden gathered the ball. He looked around and not noticing any opposing players (remember Dalglish was behind him) casually put the ball on the ground prior to belting it upfield.

Enter the unseen Dalglish. Never one to discard an early Christmas gift, he simply ran around Godden, gathered the ball and tapped it into the empty net. Looks of varying astonishment. Baggies keeper wondering what the hell had happened. Defenders glaring at each while at the same time making it plain who they felt, no knew, who was to blame. As for King Kenny, he trotted upfield sporting a very broad smile resembling a cat that had lapped up a dish of unexpected cream.

Not surprisingly, the Hawthorns was packed for Bob Paisley's men but attendances did vary wildly accordingly to the reputation of the opposition. With inflation rampant and jobs very hard to come by, it was only natural that many had to pick and choose their matches.

The first defeat came at Derby in mid-September. I vaguely remember the Rams being the stronger side but honestly I just wanted to get away from a place that resembled a doomsday film set. Massive fencing inside and outside, concrete pillars obstructing views, crammed and cramped seating, aggressive supporters, aggressive Police with dogs, a narrow guarded high-fenced alleyway for an exit. Had football really come to this? Thankfully, there were so many better games to appreciate so I didn't dwell on this afternoon for too long.

Such as the annihilation of Coventry City. This was the pre-runner for many more Sky Blues slaughters but at 7-1 remains the piece de resistance. It was hard to know what was more amusing - City's chocolate brown mess of a kit with twin tram lines (where they'd been run over?) or the ragged ranks of their so-called defence. Their strip always features in the Worst Kit of all time debates. City striker Wallace had permed red hair at the time - imagine that with chocolate brown kit and the opposition sniggering audibly in the tunnel. Cue another evening with "Cloud Lucky Seven" on auto-repeat.

There was a price to pay for that heady afternoon in that Albion's potency became very much public knowledge. Opposition outfits were set up to block out the Baggies leading to a November with very few goals. Of course, our exciting and novel European adventure was also impacting on fitness levels for our tiny squad. Galatasary were far from the European power they are these days and the Baggies had little trouble defeating them 6-2 on aggregate. The home leg felt strange. This was our first Black Country European night for far too long yet the match was largely already safe after the trio of away goals in Turkey. Still, there was a highlight provided by the excited and very noisy bunch of Turks in the Halfords' Lane Corner Stand. They seemed unaware of the football convention that supporters keep quiet if their team is being well beaten and thus were the subject of much mickey-taking.

Next up was Sporting Braga and again with the "heavy lifting" already done in Portugal, a 1-0 home victory to open November was most acceptable. It was the first of four wins, all by the same score, as Atkinson's men kept up the pressure on two fronts in the face of a wall of opponents.

Our European reward was a big-name opponent in Valencia. They'd won the competition twice before and had hugely famous players in their team - namely Mario Kempes, the Argentinian centre forward and West German midfielder Rainer Bonhof.

For the third time, the Baggies enjoyed the advantage of playing away first. Valencia were clear favourites to win but after a pulsating vibrant encounter, very notably an extraordinary display of wing play from Laurie Cunningham, we bought them back to the Hawthorns with a grin-inducing 1-1 draw. I was unable to travel so had to rely on Tony Butler on local radio. Butler's routine reference to prayer mats and "Hail Albion" may appears terribly cheesy now but in the simpler 70's, it made for compelling listening. He had much to enthuse about that night.

The Evening Mail reported: "*the Midland side were marvellous. They tamed the world's No1 footballer Mario Kempes, won the admiration of a hostile crowd and produced a valuable public relations exercise for English soccer abroad*". The Spanish press described Albion's display as "El Magnifique'" It was this display that ironically led to Laurie eventually leaving for Real Madrid. He had set out his credentials for all to see on the European stage and no one surely ever did it better.

Despite their hugely boosted European profile, Albion still couldn't beat Aston Villa. I'd become a little fatalistic after all those consecutive defeats so I was almost pleased to secure a 1-1 draw at home in front of a full house. It was after all, only 3 days after the full-on effort in Spain. I realise I was so much in the minority. All around me and on the phone-ins, the big question was "*Why can't we beat Villa with the team I've got? Why? Why?*" Us football supporters - we always want more and better. Spoilt already but still wanted more.

In December, we got even more and oh my, did I dare to dream. Not surprisingly, everybody wanted to be at the Hawthorns for the return match to see the world-class football talent on show - and Valencia too. There wasn't a space to be had in the house. The second leg was played in a frenzied atmosphere. Spanish passion and skills were not only matched but also exceeded. A foolish handball by a Spanish defender led to Bomber Brown scoring after just five minutes which set the tone. The visitors looked rattled and there was much niggling trips and shirt pulling. We urgently wanted a second goal to seal the deal but had to wait almost to the end when Laurie Cunningham skipped past his marker and set up Bomber Brown to find the far post. Albion had served both club and country proud. That took us through to the Quarter-Final and with a clash with Red Star Belgrade next, I was beginning to feel we could go all the way and actually win the competition. But I'd got carried away before... That thought however would stay on the back burner until March. Before then, the players only had to win matches in the League and the FA Cup.

Middlesbrough, in front of a half-empty Hawthorns, were the next victims, seen off 2-0. After that, it was the neighbours turn to be on the receiving end. Not for the first time, Wolves were having a dreadful season and in private at least, I'm sure their followers were fearing the arrival of the imperious Baggies. Be afraid... But in fairness, I gave Wolverhampton credit for defending more stoutly than their relegation spot suggested. Their morale sagged after conceding a second goal and were rather fortunate to lose by only 3-0. The Baggies' final goal was a peach, with Ally Brown putting away a chance set up by a smooth passing movement. I was bellowing *"We're going to win the League"* along with the rest of the Albion support standing on the vast but largely open South Terrace.

After Wolves, Arsenal tasted Boxing Day dust 2-1 on their own Highbury pitch. This was a notable back-to-the-wall triumph often overlooked because of a certain visit to Manchester a few days later.

The 5-3 was a never-to-be-forgotten part of this month. With the footage of the lavish victory endlessly available, it's hard to imagine any Albion supporter who hasn't repeatedly seen the highlights and boggled at the skills on offer and Gerald Sinstadt's "Oh, What a Goal" enthusiasm. It is our riposte to Brazil in 1970 though I'm keen to add some perspective. Both Old Trafford and the team that played there were more modest than in later decades. This was United, the regular underachievers, despite their ever-ready cheque books. It was a shame that there were so little money available to improve the lot of the away supporter. The small-stepped terrace was at pitch-level, split into tight pens surrounded by high fences on all four sides. We struggled to see the action, not least because of the mass supporter jogging and shuffling on their spot of numbing concrete. This was a desperately cold Saturday with frozen snow on the ground. Apart from the obvious abundance of goals in United's net, my strongest recollection was the cold and United's 'keeper Gary Bailey. Firstly, his comic mime to supporters that he'd lost count of the score and secondly his remarkable save where I'd swear that Bailey was diving full length to stop a shot while only being a foot or so below the crossbar.

Whilst marvelling at the score, this was definitely not a game that I wanted to carry on for ever more. I was seriously cold and really, really wanted to get indoors somewhere.

The harsh winter of 1978/79 was a twist of fate which to this day I consider instrumental in Albion's failure to lift the First Division title. On New Year's Day, virtually the entire fixture list was wiped out. Many supporters would not or could not travel to the Hawthorns (the M5 had only one open lane) and famously WBA v Bristol City played only because Atkinson's men discreetly wore imported moulded studs. Their on-pitch mobility in turn conned the referee that the pitch was playable. Predictably, City players were sliding all over the pitch and were easily defeated in what I felt was a shivering, joyless spectacle.

The next Saturday was a wipe-out all round so it was largely a relief to get the FA Cup on at Highfield Road one week later. Steaming after their 7-1 massacre, City were determined not to roll over again. Teeth-chattering on an open terrace, I am sure those around me were not really geared up to offer full support. The game finished 2-2, far better than a defeat of course, but the Baggies really didn't need another fixture.

Still the ice and snow continued to play havoc with everyone's lives in what was the coldest winter for 16 years. For the players, getting to the training ground was one issue. Another was actually finding a surface on which to do any useful work. Not all the country was equally affected. East Anglia was blessed with slightly warmer temperatures and this enabled mid-table Norwich to host the Baggies. With Liverpool unable to play their away game, any kind of positive result would see West Bromwich Albion go top of the pile. And top we went, after a modest-looking 1-1 draw. This felt great to me and had been a long time coming. *"We are top of the League"* was a phrase I'd drop into any conversation possible.

Coventry reluctantly rolled up for the FA Cup and were sent packing once again. Albion Supporters Expected Every Man to do Their Duty and they were ultimately not disappointed. Only 4-0 this time, but how City must dislike West Bromwich Albion. And then the weather bit back again. Atkinson's imagination could only overcome for so long and our juggernaut ground to a halt. Meanwhile, Liverpool, with their undersoil heating, got their noses back in front. Three weeks passed before the Baggies could play proper football again and it was our ill-luck that we had a top of the table clash at Anfield.

Although the Baggies were among the favourites to win the League after 19 games unbeaten, doubts remained. Liverpool manager Bob Paisley made all the polite noises via his programme column. *"Over the years, people have become accustomed to seeing Liverpool victories on this ground but the interest today will be centre on West Brom's performance. The simple fact is that this season, Albion had emerged as one of the most enterprising teams in the First Division. Not only that - they have strung together results in an impressive way and made progress in Europe in reaching the Quarter - Finals of the UEFA Cup. Certainly when West Brom are on song, they are exciting to watch and their results this season speak for themselves. And this is why, in places far removed from Anfield, people will be looking to see how Albion have fared this afternoon".*

*For Liverpool, too, it is a stern test because we are in our own stronghold and the match is a four-pointer. Victory for us can peg back very real rivals in the championship race. And make no mistake, West Brom ARE real challengers".* I doubt any Anfield regular was at all interested in such polite musing. They were Liverpool and WBA were just the latest in a series of challengers to be sent packing.

The Reds recent record was quite modest with 3 defeats in their last eight games but even so, Anfield expected...

A huge number of Baggies fans were desperate to see the match. To minimise supporter interaction, the Police escorted a fleet of free buses to and from Lime Street station. I was quite content with this arrangement. Some Scousers had a nasty little trick of asking you for the time and then responding aggressively when you replied in a less-than-accurate Liverpudlian accent. Sailing along serenely behind glass with a Police escort had me imagining this is what being a Beatle feels like.

The genuine Match of the Day status ensured a 52,000 full house. As usual, the match wasn't designated all-ticket so there were literally scrambles to get through the turnstiles before they were locked at a ridiculous early time. The away section was the first to be closed so many visitors had to hid their colours, keep silent and 'bravely' mingle with the 'Pool supporters. In reality, people were jammed too tightly on the terraces to violently interact.

With the quality of the opposition, a baying Kop, and Albion 'ring-rusty', it was always going to be difficult to get a result. Both Liverpool strikers Dalglish and Fairclough found the net in the first half and it looked all over. But gradually, we upped the tempo, begin to dominate, suitably rewarded as a goal from Ally Brown narrowed the deficit to give us a fighting chance.

Hopes were raised but as valiantly as we cheered, shouted and implored, an equaliser simply wouldn't come. Despite the handicap, it was a tremendous performance but there was no doubt that the enforced break had significantly contributed to the 2-1 defeat. Liverpool secured the result they wanted and they were only to lose only one of their 19 remaining League fixtures, conceding just 6 goals along the way. Ally Brown was one of only four opposition players to score at Anfield all season. How does anyone compete with that?

But back in February, we still dared to hope. Having another three week break because of the weather conditions were another barrier to team fluency. Having to play bloody Leeds United again and again did nothing for morale either.

Already having played them three times in the League Cup, we managed to come out of the hat together for the 4th round of the FA Cup. But before that we had the dubious pleasure of hosting them in the League. On a pitch which was two thirds sand, the visitors recovered from a Tony Brown thunderbolt to lead 2-1 and there was no way back against a United side already familiar with every one of our attacking gambits. I may have sworn aloud. Our League Championship hopes were badly dented by an anti-football team.

Just two days later came the FA Cup match. The last thing our fatigued supporters and players wanted was yet another replay. Albion overcame the routine intimidation and close marking to grab a decent lead but to my intense fury, didn't have the fitness to hold out on our beach. The score ended up 3-3 forcing yet another match. This time I really cursed and on the way home, I pondered what sin I'd committed to deserve this football equivalent of Groundhog Day.

Leeds were just maddening. They had decent attacking players like Arthur Graham and Tony Currie but they hobbled them into a negative and aggressive formation. With United banned from playing home matches in the FA Cup, we had the dubious pleasure of hosting the dour Yorkies again in the replay.

This was the third meeting of the clubs in six days and to put it frankly, the teams were knackered. No doubt both sides were sick of each other by then. I was certainly weary of United's tactics.

Ninety minutes of tedium were rewarded by another strength-sapping half an hour. Somebody had to score to end this marathon and thankfully it was the visitors who cracked, Albion finding two goals to everyone's relief. But the knock-on cost for the next fixture, the no small matter of a UEFA Cup Quarter Final in Belgrade - I was concerned how much energy had gone from our players.

Most positively, European fare couldn't be any less frustrating than playing Leeds United three times surely? Our opponents were the pride of Yugoslavia, Red Star of Belgrade. They were a serious European power, competing regularly in the European Cup. They'd already played and defeated Arsenal in an earlier round.

At the time, Yugoslavia was a communist country still ruled by Tito. They weren't part of the Iron Curtain but even so the trip was nowhere near as appealing as Valencia. A couple of hundred determined Baggies travelled but were presumably all but invisible in the enormous 90,000 crowd.

I was almost literally glued to my radio and Tony Butler. Somehow I'd convinced myself that the closer I got to my bakelite box, the better were Albion's chances. Bizarre, I know. Our fatigued warriors held out well until a goal just ten minutes from the end meant a narrow defeat. I'd had loved an away goal - so would everybody else of course - but hey, we were still in there pitching.

Before the return leg a fortnight later, there were both FA Cup and League commitments. Just three days after the match in Yugoslavia, Southampton took advantage of the Stars in Stripes weariness - in fact, they added to it earning a replay just two days later on the South Coast. On that Monday night, the Baggies Cup dream ended in a narrow 2-1 defeat. But there was no time to waste in recriminations as Chelsea were visiting on Wednesday night. Somehow, the Baggies found just enough energy to overcome the struggling Londoners 1-0.

March 21. The second leg at the Hawthorns with almost 32,000 willing them on with every fibre in their bodies only to see it end in massive disappointment after clawing ourselves back into the tie. The Baggies went for the equaliser with all guns blazing and the strong-arm tactics adopted by Red Star were nasty, crude, and cynical. Our pitch, with much of the sand now turned to mud, didn't help.

The ball simply wouldn't go into the net and even Cyrille Regis, with his speed and strength, was kicked from pillar to post in a desperate attempt to stem the flow. Finally, he had his revenge, lashing in a first half equaliser with a tremendous strike. Supporters went wild. We scented blood. The game was there to be won. Let's go for it!

Sadly, that proved our undoing. On reflection, it was Atkinson's attacking policy that rebounded with a vengeance. Albion went flat out for the winner and the almost inevitable happened. Red Star broke away from deep in their half, a stretched defence was caught out, the visitors got lucky with a divot bounce and they were level.

That was the killer blow. We were out 2-1 on aggregate. My European dream was over. Yes, we'd been the better team but as we'd lost that was a hollow consolation. And how many times has that happened over a season to any team, not only Albion? Red Star went on to reach the Final, which they lost 2-1 on aggregate.

The immediate response to this disappointing setback was three more League successive wins, making six straight victories. But then, as if the realisation that our European dream was over and Liverpool could not be caught, the players seemed to be visibly affected and full of self-doubt. They were also, quite frankly, knackered. There was an away League match on Good Friday, another game the following day and a third on Easter Tuesday.

We drew five out of six fixtures, and a petering out of the season seemed to be on the cards. We were still favourites to claim the runners up spot behind the eventual champions Liverpool but it was a terribly modest secondary target, bringing with it just another entry into the UEFA Cup.

Going into May, our weary, very weary side had to play their final six games in just eighteen days. They managed to win the first four somehow including a - can you believe it - 1-0 victory at Villa Park. Villa Park! John "Tucka" Trewick did the damage. Yes, the title was beyond our reach but I so savoured reminding the Claret and Blue persuasion who were now Kings of the Midlands. Hard to resist joining in the two-part harmony so often heard that term.

> *"Oh, I do like to be beside the seaside*
> *Oh I do like to be beside the sea*
> *Oh I do like to walk along the prom prom prom*
> *Where the brass bands play ...*
> *"West Brom, West Brom*
> *We HATE Villa..*
> *West Brom, West Brom "*
> *"We HATE Villa"*
> *(repeat endlessly)*

There should be a gallery somewhere featuring every Albion hero who scored winning goals against Villa. Were that to become reality wherever the location I'd be more than happy to pay to visit every day. As would our Aston neighbours if given a similar opportunity to gaze on their heroes!

Our penultimate game was at Spurs but it bought no joy for the leg weary losing 1-0 so our League position went to the final game which was Nottingham Forest at the Hawthorns. Forest themselves could pip the Baggies for the runners up spot if they could snatch a win but as far as I was concerned, I was having none of that. We simply had to round off a great season, despite the obvious disappointments, with a win. I roared, pleaded, groaned and moaned. We craved to see a winning goal. *"Come on you Baggies. Come on. Come on."* But agony reared its ugly head. Along with every crestfallen fan, I was forced to endure a single goal from Trevor Francis took all the points. The striker was the first £1 Million transfer after moving from Birmingham City, courtesy of Brian Clough. The Nottingham Forest manager insisted Francis was the player he needed and he was prepared to outbid all other interested clubs to prove it. That defeat hurt badly, strangely almost as much as losing to Red Star. That second spot was ours. It was absolutely deserved after a ridiculously long season and it was snatched from us 9 minutes from the end of the season. I really felt, as the saying goes, as miserable as sin. Three-quarters of the Hawthorns emptied in virtual silence, jeered by those from the East Midlands. *"It should have been us"* I told myself *"it should've been us."*

I could take only minimal solace from the fact that we'd finished behind two of the best sides not just in England but in Europe. Nottingham Forest went on to win the European Cup, beating Malmo 1-0, thanks to a goal from the £1 million man.

It's almost impossible to believe that the previous highest amount paid for a player, £500,000, was when Albion splashed the cash to bring David Mills from Middlesbrough to the Hawthorns. Alas, poor David. A lovely chap to talk to but he was way out of his depth and bombed on the pitch. He was the first of several expensive Atkinson transfer flops.

Yet there was so much to saviour from this WBA side. Ally Brown, an ever present enjoyed a tremendous season with 18 goals. Cyrille Regis, full of pace and power scored 13, Tony Brown managed another 10, and supremely talented Laurie Cunningham chipped in with 9, while one of most talented young players in the game, Bryan Robson, finished with 7.

Robson's potential was so obvious it was incredible the England selectors had yet to choose him for the national team. I vividly remember his performance in a 1-0 victory over Everton when his tackling strength, reading of the game, vision, and passing ability, shone through like a beacon.

On one occasion, it seemed the visitors would break through to equalise an Ally Brown goal. An Everton player found himself in space midway between the halfway line and the Albion penalty area and when he sped off the situation appeared to be fraught with danger. As if from nowhere, Bryan arrived on the scene and with a magnificently timed tackle, won the ball fair and square before calmly setting up a counter attack with an exquisitely weighted pass. It looked so simple but that was the essence of Robson's game. If he had a weakness, it was probably a lack of pace but that `handicap' was more than compensated by his other talents.

No Cups for the Baggies, but there was a plate. To this day, I have stashed away in my drawer an official Albion souvenir plate. It's an impressive souvenir being both large and heavy. There's an image of each member of the 1978-79 team plus their printed autograph. Decades later, it's my reminder of the Nearly Men.

Speedway time saw we usual suspects at Perry Barr when the Brummies faced Eastbourne. For this meeting to gain publicity, we sponsored the event. The Brummies ran out winners and as was normal during the interval, we were driven around the track on our Carnival truck together with the celebrating riders. As a bonus, Dot enjoyed (I think) her ride on the back of the Brummies leading point scorer. Just two laps - track record never in danger!

## 1979-80

Rather like the modern Premiership, our fate was largely settled during the summer. We'd lost the gritty midfield talents of the shamefully underrated Len Cantello, who decided that a move to Bolton Wanderers was best for him. Worse, Real Madrid came a knocking for Laurie Cunningham. For me, still the most talented player ever to don an Albion shirt. We now had to pay the price for his exquisite showing in Spain against Valencia. Laurie generally kept himself to himself apart from a few people he allowed to get close to him. Thus most of his team mates were shocked when he packed his bags and travelled to Spain to negotiate a lucrative transfer to one of the worlds' top clubs - Real Madrid. There was no way Albion could have retained his services against the contract the Spanish giants could offer. Laurie subsequently helped Real to both European and domestic honours though it came with the heavy price of goldfish-bowl living.

On paper, Ron Atkinson signed the best possible English replacements for his departing stars. Midfielder Gary Owen was an England B cap and Man City regular. He was an excellent passing midfielder with one foot. The other was purely for standing on and it was sometimes a little embarrassing to see a top flight player turning a circle to get the ball onto his best foot. Also joining us from City was Peter Barnes, the wide man who'd largely kept Cunningham out of the England team. He and Owen were close, which was handy as Gary Owen was often the only person who had a clue what Barnes was going to do next. At his best, the winger could move like a Champion greyhound but for other games, particularly on the road, he'd vanish. For me, my first comment was "*I remember his Dad*" before realising just how old that made me sound.  Ken Barnes was born in Birmingham and played around 250 games for Man City in the 1950's.

Joining us from the neighbours were the ageing Gary Pendrey from relegated Birmingham City. Gary was to put in some solid shifts as cover for our back four. Less happily, the club chequebook was out in September for £500,000 man John Deehan of Aston Villa.  That we needed more goals was undeniable ... But to go to Villa?  There was much muttering among the regulars. Me, I was willing to let him show off what he could do for us but the majority found the concept of one of them becoming one of us being hard to grasp. Whilst with Villa, he'd been nicknamed "Rubber." I hadn't the faintest idea what spawned this nickname but whatever the reason provided he rubbed up the opposition by scoring those badly needed goals I'd consider he was worthy of wearing our famous Blue and White striped shirt..

During pre-season, there was a routine 4-0 victory over China, who claimed to be playing the game in the true spirit of friendship. There was nothing friendly about the tackle on Cyrille which put him out of action for 3 months with a knee injury.

Lacking Cyrille's power and goals, Len Cantello's ball winning and Cunningham's consistency, Albion managed to win only two of their first ten games and when Nottingham Forest, again, plundered the points in a 5-1 win at the Hawthorns early in September, I was already convinced that Albion wouldn't be among the likely contenders for honours. There was a never a hint of a consistent winning run materialising underlined when after beating Fulham and Coventry in the League Cup, we lost 3-0 at Norwich after a frustrating goalless draw at home.  That night, I fumed aloud that City had more jam than Hartleys as somehow their goal remained intact. Admittedly, 39 year old Kevin Keelan in goal enjoyed a tremendous night-albeit with the aid of what could only be described as the Fortune of the Gods. Whatever divine inspiration befell him, the blunt truth was staring me in the eye. If a team can't score goals, they'll continue to struggle.

The UEFA Cup campaign was an even greater disappointment. Crashing out at the first hurdle after two defeats at the hands of Carl Zeiss Jena from East Germany - 4-1 on aggregate. Most of the damage was done with a 2-0 defeat in the away leg, a game described by Atkinson as *"positively the worst 90 minutes football from any team I have ever managed."* Any chance of recovery at the Hawthorns was torpedoed at half time when Ally Brown was sent off for elbowing an opponent in the tunnel. As he's reminded me a few times over the subsequent decades, Ally has yet to serve his 4 match ban. Less than 20,000 attended, below the average for a League crowd.

Our lack of goals was painful. Of the newcomers, Peter Barnes in particular was little short of infuriating. He had skill and pace in abundance. Indeed, at the end of the season he top scored with 15 goals. But in truth, he only appeared to play one good game in six. What a waste of genuine talent for himself, the team, and supporters. By mid-October, the Baggies had won only twice - beating Man City and Man United. Cyrille's return and the club recruiting a resident cat called "Lucky" did steady the ship but only to move the club out of the relegation zone into mid-table. Some results were horribly predictable with an easy defeat of Coventry (4-1) and in turn being beaten at Stoke City with several of our team injured. The Baggies were yet to secure an away win, though were broadly happy with draws at Villa Park and Molineux. The strongest memory of what was a grim struggle at Wolves was a shameless dive by Emlyn Hughes, pretending that Ally Brown had hit him. At the time, this was perceived shocking behaviour and I was so sad that such a distinguished player resorted to such a pathetic act. The incident made national headlines.

The second half of the season followed a same undistinguished relegation-dodging pattern including another depressing Cup exit. Second Division West Ham won 2-1 at Upton Park following a 1-1 draw at the Hawthorns. The bookies had Albion at 14/1 to win the Cup and West Ham at 80/1. Of course, the Hammers went all the way to ultimately beat Arsenal at the twin towers. Wonder if anyone was sweating on their 80/1 bet coming in that day?

For the Baggies, there was future optimism in the shape of new young talent, notably Remi Moses. The Mancunian was small and stocky but don't let that fool you. He was a fiery tackler, exactly what the Baggies needed. No longer could the opposition run through our midfield and our points gathering improved as a consequence. We lost just once in 16 games (to Villa), though many were drawn, including 6 goalless draws, finishing in a highly respectable 10th position It does beg the question, why wasn't Moses in the team before the tail end of January? It was plain Moses had "something about him" with a great future. We didn't know yet where that future would be.

The other long overdue prize was being at Wembley to see Bryan Robson gain his first, long overdue international cap against the Republic of Ireland. This had been inevitable since he'd forced his way into the team. Bryan was a ferocious tackler who never shirked a confrontation, despite suffering three broken legs and a multitude of other injuries. Just a few months earlier, he'd signed a new five-year contract which Chairman Bert described as *"a wonderful event for the club."* Oh, if we only knew ... Other players breaking into the team included Barry Cowdrill, who stepped in when Derek Statham was injured as he so frequently was, plus Martyn Bennett and Derek Monaghan. The Albion youngsters reached the FA Youth Cup Quarter Final before losing to the eventual Cup winners.

The season petered out with very few highlights although a 4-4 home draw against Bolton was a game to savour, featuring a waterlogged pitch, monsoon rain and a Peter Barnes hat trick. Such were the conditions that only 11,600 people paddled into the Hawthorns. But that was very much a one off as, from the last six games, fans 'enjoyed' four goalless draws, a 1-1 draw away at Arsenal and a final mind numbing 1-0 defeat at home to Stoke City. Our great attacking team were simply no more with no less than 10 goalless draws that term. Leeds United would be happy with that but I certainly wasn't.

ITV shocked the football world when announcing they would be showing 'Match of the Day' on Saturday nights rather than the BBC. This news was greeted with incredulity. The clubs could hardly believe 'The Snatch of the Day' had happened. Jimmy Hill, the then Coventry Managing Director, in addition to being a 'Match of the Day' presenter, said: "*it wasn't an honourable deal, it was railroaded through. The clubs didn't even know whose bid they were accepting*" Naturally the Beeb weren't about to take this lying down and court action became inevitable. The corporation won a respite when the Office of Fair Trading banned the agreement because it broke the rules regarding restrictive practices. A £10m, four - year compromise, dubbed the 'Swap of the Day', was reached with the two networks sharing coverage. The BBC having Saturday football the following season and then the coverage would alternate. This offer was promptly rejected. Club Chairman said they didn't want to commit themselves to such a long-term deal. But warned by Alan Hardaker that they faced the prospect of no coverage of all and the consequent loss of revenue, the clubs finally backed down at the League's Annual Meeting.

Just to prove 'nothing' rarely changes. Rival fans fought on the pitch after Celtic beat Rangers in the Scottish Cup Final leading to the Police calling for all future matches to be played behind closed doors in addition to having their scheduled Glasgow Cup Final postponed. However, there was a new record to marvel at with Colin Cowperthwaite of Barrow scoring against Kettering after just 3.58 seconds. Hard to believe! Shell-shocked Kettering went to lose 4-0. And how about this quote from Malcolm Allison after he received a lifetime ban from the touchline? *"I've served more time than Ronnie Biggs for the Great Train Robbery!"*

I do have other interests apart from trawling up and down the country supporting the Baggies. I'd caught the Disco bug, inspired by John Travolta in 'Saturday Night Fever', Dot and I decided to join a weekly disco dance session, ignoring all our friends who laughed openly at us. Disco was very different to our ballroom and Latin experiences but after collecting a third gold Statuette in these formal routines, we both wanted something different. Something lighter, less hard work and more informal hence disco.

It was different alright as we gallantly attempted to wiggle our hips and point arms while listening to the Bee Gees singing *'More like a Woman'*. Our class was a large one at first and generally very youthful too but as time passed inevitably some began to drop out. No staying powers these youngsters!

One raw winter's night, Dot wasn't keen on catching a couple of buses, knowing the timetable could merely be a figment of the imagination. So I went by myself only to discover that the rest of the 'regulars' thought along the same lines as Dot. But one other person had made the effort. The young, very attractive dance teacher. And so it came to pass that this 'Recycled Teenager' enjoyed a private lesson in an attempt to emulate Mr Travolta's gymnastic moves. 'Night (even overheated?) Fever? You bet. Ah, those were the days!

## The Depressing 1980's

Hardly a happy decade on so many counts. How could it be with war in the Falklands, the murder of John Lennon, inner city riots in Birmingham, London, Liverpool, and Bristol, plus the Lockerbie Air disaster? On the sporting front, Steve Davies was the immaculate World Snooker Champion and in Ice Dancing would there ever be another Jayne Torville and Christopher Dean?

The continuing cavalier approach to supporter safety led inevitably to loss of life at Valley Parade and Hillsborough. In Heysel too, where aggressive hooliganism, combined with another ramshackle stadium, led to many more deaths. The Government had to act but this was an administration who had no understanding or any belief in the beautiful game. Their blundering, knee-jerk responses drew such fury from football aficionados that the fanzine movement started.

For Baggie supporters, it was surely the period that heralded the demise of West Bromwich Albion. From a team that had produced great football at the highest level, had a thriving youth policy producing the likes of Hope, Bomber Brown, Cantello and Robson, and expected to challenge for honours, we would witness the slow, lingering decline of a once proud club.

## 1980/81

This season gave little indication of the decline and stagnation waiting in the wings. There weren't many significant team changes throughout a season that finished with a creditable fourth position. Although as Aston Villa won the championship, with a team showing less flair than the Baggies and we helped them on their way, I considered this scant consolation.

Six wins and only two defeats from the first eleven games meant the team were always there or thereabouts and with Moses, Robson and Regis continually performing consistently, Ron Atkinson's outgoing personality reflected the team's style of play.

There were no cup exploits. In the F.A Cup after a 3-0 win over Grimsby Town, we almost inevitably met our Waterloo at Middlesbrough. As soon as the draw was made, the outcome was inevitable. The Baggies did not win matches at the home of the Smog monsters. Decades were to pass before this situation would change.

But the early stages of the League Cup did hold possibilities. Leicester and Everton were seen off, as were Nobby Stiles' Preston North End after a second replay. Then a 2-1 defeat in the fifth round at Maine Road put a brake on any hopes of a Wembley appearance despite a battling display. This after a Tommy Booth own goal after 3 minutes had me dreaming. Later, I was cursing Joe Corrigan who not for the first time trashed my silverware hopes. He was a big- not to say huge –figure filling up the goal most effectively. Just one of those games where you can't believe your own eyes. Albion were 11 games unbeaten, were well supported in the echoey massive Kippax terrace and really went at the home side. Yet we were out.

Overall, we couldn't really complain about the season. But naturally I did as I was used to better. There were 7 goalless draws to endure, another wretched home defeat by moribund Leeds and possibly worst of all, an embarrassing 3-0 defeat by our whipping boys Coventry. Is the world about to end?

The most bizarre game of the season was at Molineux, which was fog-bound. Apparently we lost 2-0. The only evidence of this were roars from the North Bank and my trusty transistor as we South Bank residents could see nothing but fog. I have no idea how the referee managed as my vision was limited to the South Bank goal and about half of the penalty area. Gallows humour prevailed with on occasions loud but bogus cheering from the away end, celebrating an imaginary goal. If the Albion contingent could be believed, we'd scored at least four times in the first half alone. The Mail reporter produced a highly coherent report two days later. Heaven knows how - maybe he was being as economical with the facts as the Albion supporters. What was the Tommy Docherty quote? Ah yes - *"I've always said there's a place for the press but they haven't dug it yet!"*

Our Stars in Stripes eventually finished eight points behind Villa so another four wins could have won Albion the title. Easy to surmise but realistically this was never on the cards. Four straight away defeats at the end of the season was probably key. Instead, by beating leaders Ipswich and then losing 1-0 to Villa, we did much to divert the trophy to Birmingham. For 85 minutes at Villa Park, we'd defended stoutly, frustrating nervous locals before infamously Brendan Batson erred with a suicidal back pass and Peter "Werewolf" Withe stole in to score the winner. It was a horrible, horrible moment which I've never quite forgotten.

That season, Cyrille Regis top scored with fourteen, with both Ally Brown and Bryan Robson chipping in with ten. One in particular stood out, in the match against Liverpool, when the rapidly maturing Robson cheekily back-heeled the ball into the net, much to our delight, and the astonishment of the Liverpool team. That was Robbo at his best. A supremely confident player who was surely destined to become one of England's greatest players. To some alarm, he'd put in a transfer request at Christmas but withdrew it in March claiming he was now happy to stay.

Yes overall, a satisfying campaign. The team was maturing nicely and with the prospect of a return to European football we could sit back and enjoy the close season. How little we knew and how naive we were.

Taking a closer look at this season and some of the happenings that occurred off the field, I suppose I shouldn't really have been surprised that people, who didn't have any interest in football, had begun to believe that anyone wearing a football scarf should be avoided at all costs.

But that did happen and looking at some of the appalling scenes that appeared to be occurring on a weekly basis, it was hardly surprising. Examples? A random selection that sadly became a common feature. A Sheffield Wednesday player was sent off at Oldham and visiting fans ran amok. The game was held up for 30 minutes and the incident reduced Jack Charlton, the Wednesday manager, to tears.

On the same day, a young Middlesbrough fan died when his head was smashed in outside Ayresome Park after the match against Nottingham Forest. West Ham were forced to play the second leg of their

European Cup Winners Cup match against Castilla behind closed doors due to the outrageous behaviour of their so called fans in Madrid. Mike Carter, a Bolton Wanderers player, was fined £100 for throwing grit at QPR supporters. Brian Clough, as ever, had his own view. *"Football hooliganism? Well, there are 92 club chairman for a start."* Classic!

Attendances everywhere were sinking, particularly in the middle of another recession. Many clubs were forced to sell star players at a loss to raise money. Among the casualties were the Home International Championships as only England v Scotland were drawing significant crowds. The biennial invasion of the rowdy Scots to Wembley had become more than just an irritant. The troubles in Northern Ireland caused the tournament to be cancelled this season. It did re-start in 1982 before finishing completely two years later.

In February, the member clubs of the Football League voted in a new proposal to encourage clubs to go for wins, rather than draws by giving three points instead of two for each League victory. There was a tentative agreement to play a few matches on Sunday to see whether higher attendances would result.

That summer, I achieved another personal first. I'd always fancied visiting Scandinavia and so the lure of Speedways World Championship at the Ullevi Stadium in Gothenburg was too strong to resist. In order to keep costs down. I had to sacrifice sightseeing opportunities but the main event was well worth concentrating on. Cambridge-born Michael Lee was arguably the World's best speedway rider and proved it by winning the World title. Fellow Kings Lynn rider and Brit Dave Jessup was second - what a night to be British.

Shortly after my return, I'd visited the NEC for Indoor Speedway Championship. Bizarre? You'd better believe it. One inevitable accident saw Lee taken to Hospital where I took the opportunity to visit and wish him a speedy recovery. Marooned in an unfamiliar city with few visitors, he was most grateful and happy to chat about the sport in general and his winning the World Championship in particular.

Michael was most impressed that I'd travelled to Sweden to support him and was generous in his praise of the entire hooter-honking and flag-waving English support. *"They really helped me to achieve my lifetime's ambition."* To which he added *"next time, I'm riding at Perry Barr remember to come down to the pits for another chat."*

Never one to pass up an opportunity, I subsequently had a mutual shout in the pits (it's not an area for discreet conversations) and possess a large, colourful photograph with the World Champion in his yellow and green leathers of Kings Lynn. Was I peeved that Lee didn't ride in the red and yellow of Birmingham? Oh yes!

## 1981/82

Before a ball was kicked in anger, let me share with you a unique memory. Invading a pitch together with supporters of Midland rivals in joyous celebration! I'm talking about Edgbaston in July. England versus Australia with the Ashes at stake. The Aussies, who were leading the series thanks to a win and draw so far, looked set to rub it in. All they needed on the last day was a miserly 142 runs to win. How could they possibly fail? Astonishingly, a certain Ian Botham thought otherwise. Against all hopes and expectations He produced an unbelievable spell of bowling taking 5 wickets for 1 run. England had triumphed. Hence the undignified (for cricket) sight of fans running on to the pitch to join in a common cause. Plenty of Blues, Villa and Wolves colours alongside my striped Albion shirt. England went on to win the series 3-1.

For me, this season started Albion on the long slippery road to nowhere. Nine months of rancour involving managers and players, a poor League campaign but bizarrely, we were so close to two Wembley trips.

The aggravation started pre-season as Manchester United targeted Ron Atkinson as their next manager. Atkinson was clear he wanted this job above any other, and despite claims and counter claims revolving around contracts and compensation, he went as fast as his legs could carry him. He refuted allegations that he'd left the club in the lurch, commenting that Albion had a team capable of winning the Championship, with or without him at the helm. Perhaps so but it was largely a team that he'd inherited, a side who subsequently were frankly the poorer for his lavish transfer activities.

Finding themselves in the now familiar position of seeking another new manager, the board re-appointed Ronnie Allen who'd left Panathinaikos to return home.  This also had fans arguing for and against, but as Ronnie was available, and still a true Baggie at heart, in the main, I felt the club had made the right appointment. The bitterness of fans towards Ron Atkinson intensified within a few weeks of the big kick off. Not content with taking the backroom staff with him to Old Trafford, he immediately set sights on the engine room of the team itself.

It wasn't long before Bryan Robson and Remi Moses joined him at Old Trafford. I was seething. Even before Robbo went, many wanted Albion to dig in their heels. Refuse his transfer request, and play him in the reserves if necessary to prove a point. That was never realistic and when he did leave it cost United, what at the time, was a British transfer fee record of £1.5 million. Sounds impressive but for me, I've not seen another player to match Robson at the Hawthorns since.

In the middle of a depressing start to the League campaign came the draw for the UEFA Cup. When Grasshoppers of Zurich was paired with Albion, many supporters fancied travelling to Switzerland for the first leg. This was a country I'd longed to visit but could I justify the cost?  Flying was £239, an executive 4 day coach trip was £100 with the basic straight there- straight back trip priced at £47. I could afford the basic trip and judging by the number of fans turning up at the Hawthorns car park at midday Tuesday, that was definitely the number one choice.

We set off with destination Zurich being a mere 24 hours away. Initially we chatted excitedly but after a cross Channel crossing and several hours of Autobahn travel, the novelty wore off. Most tried to sleep with varying degrees of success as the night drew on. When daylight broke, there was much scenery to take in - though truth be told, the never-ending travel created a level of fatigue that stunning chocolate-box scenes were wasted on the now grey-faced contingent.

This was my first visit to beautiful Switzerland but unfortunately the mid-afternoon arrival left little time for sightseeing. I wandered around the immediate areas of the ground, admired the picturesque views but all too soon it was time to get inside the modest Hartturm stadium.

We'd expected Albion to put on a show against the Swiss. The home side regularly competed in Europe but almost always made an early exit. Admittedly, they had reached the UEFA Cup Quarter Final the previous season but they'd never previously beaten an English club. Sad to relate, Grasshoppers won 1-0 after a miserable showing by our team who were reminded at some length of their shortcomings by tired and emotional supporters. Ahead was a wretched slog home. The delights of the Alpine region were all too quickly forgotten!

Our form generally was grim. We kicked off with a 2-1 defeat at Maine Road. There were only two wins in the first twelve games which included an early exit from the UEFA Cup. A 1-0 loss in the away leg didn't sound too bad but losing 3-1 at home felt pretty grim. Several decades later, WBA remains the only English club that the Swiss outfit have ever defeated in Europe.

With Peter Barnes sold and Bomber Brown crudely farmed out to Torquay, there was an obvious lack of attacking options to support big Cyrille. Regis scored hat tricks against the Bluenoses and surprise top Division arrivals Swansea but couldn't be expected to carry all the attacking impetus by himself. Allen needed to spend and quickly. He bought in yet another Manchester City star, Steve Mackenzie, and from Dutch club Twente Enschede, Martin Jol. Both were talented players with good passing skills, but Jol's game was laced with more than a hint of aggression, frequently leading to clashes with referees due to his over-physical approach. The old joke was resurrected about booking Jol in the dressing room to save time. Jol was both tall and willowy lacking a hard man demeanour yet his tackling was pure 1960's bone-crunching.

The only bright spots came in the League Cup. Second Division Shrewsbury were defeated - just! - in the two-legged Second Round. We'd endured an uncomfortable 3-3 at a packed Gay Meadow before doing enough to win 2-1 at the Hawthorns. Three full-on battles followed against West Ham before Regis, ignoring the shameful racist taunts, scored the winner. The reward felt dubious - another midweek trip to London, this time Second Division Crystal Palace barely a week before Christmas. It wasn't a fixture to enthuse about and the bare 10,000 who turned up were swamped in the wide-open spaces of Selhurst Park. Once again, it was our one-man forward line, Cyrille Regis, who made the difference, scoring twice in a 3-1 victory. The game is best remembered for Allen giving a debut to 16 year old Mickey Lewis.

Then we went head to head in a Fifth Round battle with of all teams, Aston Villa at Villa Park. As always, this was a match every Baggies supporter wanted to win- especially me. Wish granted as Albion won 1-0. Tony Morley was sent off for the home team, as we reminded them throughout the second half - *"where's your Morley gone?"*

Surprisingly, it was Derek Statham who scored which for me, was probably his finest ever game. He unanimously earned the vote as Man of the Match. Quick and skilful, with a magnificent left foot, it was a travesty that due to a series of injuries, and the continuing selection of Arsenal's Kenny Sansom, 'Dekka' only received three full England caps.

Derek was also on the mark in the F.A. Cup as, after a third round win over Blackburn, he netted the game's only goal at Gillingham just days after his heroics against the Villa. This was a classic FA Cup match with a Third Division side hosting one of the "big boys". Incidentally, a young Steve Bruce was in the Gills team that day.

The ground was tightly packed with 16,000 people. Indeed, it was so crammed on the open away terrace, I could barely move my arms. I was part of a huge away support that afternoon and I particularly remember the high volume of coaches from the Black Country that completely bottled up all the narrow streets nearby. With just five minutes left and Albion not making much headway, 'Dekka's out of the blue long range effort was enough to ensure our name would be in the hat for the 5th Round draw. The 'Baggies' travelling faithful enjoyed a contented journey home, I loved the anticipation of a Cup run.

With a two-legged League Cup Semi-Final coming up against Spurs, we'd almost forgotten that Albion also played in a League. We'd played just two League matches in December and only one in January, winning the lot. Impressive but this was far from a fluent Albion side. We relied heavily on our back four to defend and attack - particularly Statham and Cyrille to find the net.

The League Cup Semi-final first leg at the Hawthorns was dull, sterile, and goalless. Tottenham were determined not to be beaten and even the double dismissal of Spurs Galvin and Albion's Jol didn't open up any more space.

Our performance, when we travelled to White Hart Lane for the decider, was equally as poor. We simply weren't good enough against a quality side. Spurs won by the only goal of the game. One door to Wembley had been firmly slammed shut.

Tottenham lost the League Cup Final but won the FA Cup and got to the Semi-Final of the Cup Winners Cup. Their ranks included Crooks, Archibald, Ricky Villa, Ossie Ardiles, Ray Clemence, Steve Perryman, Glenn Hoddle and Graham Roberts.

But in the aftermath, penned inside the ground and surrounded by jeering Spurs supporters and the obligatory Police cordon, I felt downcast and irritable and not due solely to this defeat. Winning or losing are part and parcel of the game. 'Holly' our lovely, faithful Old English sheepdog had had to be put to sleep during this period. She'd grown weaker as the years rolled by and inevitably we had to call in the Vet to administer the final injection in the home she'd shared with us for thirteen so many happy years. I'm not ashamed to say that I shed tears and remained very sad for some considerable time. Not that she could ever be forgotten. After all how many fans when entering or leaving their home can gaze fondly at a hallway photograph of their pet sitting in the F.A Cup as Dot and I proudly posed with Skipper Graham Williams holding the World famous trophy back in 1968 thanks to 'King' Jeff Astle's Wembley winning goal.

Back to the F.A. Cup, and three days later the goal of the season from Cyrille Regis saw off Norwich City, and even now (thanks to the marvel of video and DVD ) I can watch that screamer over and over again and still marvel at the sheer genius of the man.

The Quarter-Final draw was most kind. Coventry City at home - what could be better? Our resident patsies looked half-beaten before they took the pitch. Goals from Regis (again) and Gary Owen completed the job. Albion had eased into a second Semi-Final. April 3rd 1982 and devastation. Every supporter that travelled to Highbury, and the team themselves, were dumbfounded as to how they could perform so dismally against the Second Division club. Losing by a single goal. The goal itself was fortunate. An attempted clearance from Ally Robertson rebounded into the net off the legs of Clive Allen. But that shouldn't have mattered. Terry Venables, the manager of QPR, had rumbled us. He had Cyrille Regis man-marked by the even bigger Bob Hazell and made sure that Derek Statham was blocked off at every opportunity. The simple plan worked perfectly. We had no Plan B. The Baggies had not only let themselves down but worse, from my point of view, had let us down. No team deliberately plays badly but on that day there wasn't a single supporter who didn't feel that a lack of commitment was inexcusable.

This match, coupled with the 1967 League Cup Final is the reason that I never now shout the odds that Albion are 'certain' to win any game. No matter how inferior the opposition appears on paper.

If that defeat wasn't bad enough, our precious First Division status was really coming under pressure. Supporters were becoming increasingly pessimistic. There had been so many comings and goings, team changes, and mediocre displays, it was hardly surprising the League form was little short of awful. Ronnie Allen was still spending, bringing in Andy King, Clive Whitehead and Romeo Zondervan. John Deehan had (thankfully) moved on, as had the very expensive signing David Mills. The ex-Boro man in particular had been a disastrous Ron Atkinson purchase. I can only recall one match (at Coventry) where he looked worth his record transfer fee and it had only been a matter of time before he sought pastures new, moving on to a loan spell with Newcastle United.

Defeat in the Semi-Final took a lot of getting over and the three days between Highbury and a League match at the Vetch was nowhere near enough. Albion players amassed their complementary tickets to make sure that most of the few travelling supporters got in without charge. But we lost. And lost the following match. And the one after that. Either side of the Semi-Final, we'd lost 7 League games in a row. Our form was so bad we even lost to Coventry, who couldn't believe their luck. For home matches, we'd struggle to get 12,000 people through the turnstiles. We had no belief, no goals and no money.

The upcoming derby at Molineux felt huge. We were bad but they were even worse, marooned in the bottom three. You'd have thought that with so much at stake Molineux would have been bursting at the seams. But such was the apathy and disenchantment all round, a pathetic crowd of 19,813 bothered to turn out for a game that traditionally couldn't be missed. Tony Godden, dropped into reserve football way since November, at last regained his place and what a comeback as he pulled off a penalty save from Wayne Clarke and then blocked the follow up from Andy Gray.

This was a tense scrappy, niggly affair, but mercifully goals from Cyrille Regis, and the only goal of the season for Derek Monaghan (after coming on as substitute) sank the Wolves and we'd pocketed the points. For me, the relief was overpowering. Wolves were doomed so it was *"stick together and watch your back time"* all the way to the station. There was a universal feeling that with 38 points and six fixtures remaining, Albion would be OK now. After all, there were three consecutive home games next.

We lost all three. Losing to Villa was bad enough but worse still (if possible) was Cyrille Regis being sent off for punching Ken McNaught. Apathy ruled and neither our big derby nor Atkinson's Manchester United could draw a crowd over 20,000.

The blunt fact was that games had to be won. With only 3 matches remaining, we needed six points to be safe. The first of these was at Meadow Lane, the home of mid-table Notts County. This was so tense. Albion did not want for support with the big, open terrace filled with several thousand hot and bothered Baggies. The bright sunshine only partly explained their condition.

As I discovered later, the senior players had got together to decide tactics among themselves and the outcome was encouraging. The work rate and determination was everything we'd hoped for and it was just enough to give us a 2-1 win. Such was the determination that Gary Owen, who normally couldn't tackle a paper bag, was sent off for a lunge. Now there was hope.

Two matches remained, both against fellow relegation strugglers. The first of them was Leeds United. The Whites were the most unpopular team in the country because of how they achieved their success and the hooligan reputation of their followers. This was their last game of the season and 6,000 Leeds supporters were thought to be inside the Hawthorns.

With United short of strikers, Peter Barnes was pressed into service as a centre forward. He was awful. The Baggies pressed consistently on the Leeds goal, who defended in their customary brutal style. The tension was unbearable. So was the naked hostility in the Smethwick End.

Cyrille's goal in the 51th minute changed both the game and the atmosphere. The United side were toothless, numbed by their impending relegation but in the away end, the mood became toxic. Some began tugging on the safety fence. Others quickly joined them. Missiles were flying onto the pitch and the Police moved in. They were abused and threatened. With just three minutes to go, Steve Mackenzie tapped in Albion's second goal to seal our status.

The reaction on the away end was immediate. The already weakened safety fence gave way under a mass assault. The thugs made it plain that they wanted to invade the pitch and force the referee to abandon the game. Superintendent Mellor's report stated *"they said that they would kill us if they got over the fence and I really think they meant it"*.

Mounted police on horseback, and police reinforcements, fought a running battle with the morons. Self-preservation came before any thought of celebration. It was a dilemma for many - were they safer inside the ground or outside? Some left after Mackenzie's goal. The collapse of the fence prompted an exodus and the final whistle more of the same. All around me, I saw people of all ages running away from the Hawthorns, such was their fear. I did wonder how many would never return. Behind them, there were 46 arrests and even more injuries. As the Evening Mail's Bob Downing described the mayhem as *"the most frightening and sickening scenes of soccer violence we have ever seen"*.

The Baggies were safe, and yet the supreme irony was that if we could beat Stoke City in the last match at the Victoria Ground, we'd relegate City and keep Leeds United up. It's very rare for Albion supporters to want their team to lose but there was a clear consensus that night. Those unforgettable memories at the wrecking of the Hawthorns shrieked for revenge and what better way than unceremoniously shoving Leeds and their supporters into the Second Division.

Stoke needn't have worried. The Baggies were playing their third game in six days, were leg-weary and frankly disinterested. The Potters were two up in 20 minutes, scored a third and then basically declared. This was much to the relief of the away contingent on a cramped, flat, fenced terrace who were content with losing but were most uncomfortable about a rout. *"We've given you the points, no need to take advantage"* was a regularly expressed, albeit cleaned up comment, from those around me.

Both home and away supporters combined to taunt the small group of miserable Leeds United supporters, heavily policed in a terraced pen on the halfway line. A certain Denis Smith was playing his last game for Stoke, and as part of a manic pitch invasion, he was chaired around the turf while the Police urged the two sets of visiting supporters out of the stadium with a distinct lack of charm or grace. They were understandably tense. Before the game, each Albion coach was boarded so that Police officers could give stern warnings for everyone to behave. For me, it wasn't the right message to give mature supporters but at the time, all fans were treated with the level of suspicion.

So Leeds had been relegated together with Middlesbrough and, particularly satisfying for many Albion supporters, Wolverhampton Wanderers suffered the same fate though mere relegation was the greatest of their worries.

Hooliganism regularly made front page headlines. A fan was stabbed to death after a game against West Ham that led to Arsenal's manager, Terry Neill, saying: *"it makes you wonder what sort of parents produce mindless morons like this."* It was impossible to disagree. Another fatality followed the Spurs v Manchester United fixture. This was football?  With such incidents, small wonder that attendances continued to fall. Many clubs had to make drastic compromises just to stay afloat. Wolverhampton Wanderers, yes the once mighty Wolves, were spared from going out of business, with just three minutes remaining of the deadline to pay their debts. As Wolves were to discover, this was merely the start of their woes, not the end. Their "saviours" being a consortium led by one of their all-time favourite sons, Derek Dougan. (who incidentally became a firm friend after I became a regular contributor on his midweek BBC Radio Birmingham programme from their Pebble Mill Studios).

For Albion, the season was truly a series of contrasts. Two Cup Semi Final defeats as Wembley beckoned, and escaping relegation by just two points. This was much too close for comfort and a vast improvement was certainly needed, despite Ronnie Allen stressing that, with the addition of a couple of new players, and freedom from injuries, Albion would be ready to go for honours next season.  Go for honours? Unlikely, unless the goal scoring ability of Cyrille Regis was supplemented by the signing of at least one other striking partner.  Albion scored just 46 goals in 42 league games with Cyrille being the only player to reach double figures, scoring 17 of that miserly total. The next highest scorer had just 5.  Sad to relate, Ronnie Allen's age was against him and there were stories that players felt he was out of touch and right out of motivation.

A sobering thought as just down the road, a certain team had managed to bring home the European Cup after beating Bayern Munich...Aston Villa. They were lucky in the accepted sense that the German side were on top. But when a team loses their goalkeeper early on and requires to bring on a novice by the name of Nigel Spink, who subsequently played a blinder, even as big a 'non Villa lover 'as I had to admit it was a hell of a performance.

Away from football, my highlight of those 9 months was a long-awaited decision to ban commercial whaling. I, along with so many others, had campaigned all over the country by marching, letter-writing and fund raising. The 'International Whaling Commission' voted to ban whaling for commercial gain. It wasn't a complete solution but this felt a major step in the right direction, a world acceptance that butchery of the world's largest mammal was plain wrong. In a world where the CD player was the hot new invention and the 'Times' newspaper named their machine of the year as 'The Internet', I was so pleased to see a place for traditional values.

Back in the early 60's, I'd created my own campaign group "the Birmingham Seal and Whale Group." There was no lack of volunteers. Realising that having backing from prominent celebrities was all - important, on theatre visits I asked well known Christopher Timothy and Carol Drinkwater if they'd be prepared to promote the cause? An immediate "Yes". Another West End dressing chat with singer Barbara Dickson made it a hat-trick. Thank you all. The icing on the cake was receiving the support from a genuine Hollywood star. On a visit to Birmingham to promote publicity for what turned out to be a Box Office smash hit, I attended the press showing. Chatted about Animal Welfare and she promptly offered to become a Patron. The film? Alfred Hitchcock's "The Birds" Her name? Tippi Hedren and her daughter Melanie Griffiths. Quite a coup.  Am I the only Baggies supporter with Hollywood connections?

## 1982 World Cup in Spain

England were back on the trail of a second World Cup triumph this time under the stewardship of Ron Greenwood. Many England observers were getting carried away after winning all three Group games. It was hard to resist such optimism, especially after Bryan Robson (how I wished he was still at the Hawthorns) scored the winner against France after just 27 seconds. England also defeated Czechoslovakia and Kuwait. The second round group was tough. Very tough. England found themselves competing in a three-team group with Spain, and - Oh No - West Germany. I didn't fancy our chances.

So it proved, Germany beat Spain and as England subsequently could only draw both of their matches against both Spain and West Germany, we were knocked out of the Championship without losing a game. Unless you win the matches that count, success will always be a long way off. The Europeans dominated the tournament throughout and on Final Day, the Italians gladdened everyone's hearts by beating West Germany 3-1. Cynical players as the Italians were, most fans rejoiced in the German defeat. Probably because deep down they were envious that apart from that 1966 Final, they'd become a thorn in England's side whenever the teams clashed.

## 1982/83

Surprise, surprise! The conveyor belt leading to the Managers office was about to deposit another new occupant into the hot seat. Ron Wylie, who'd been coaching in Hong Kong, was approached to take over from Ronnie Allen, who was moved upstairs. Wylie was handed a three year contract and in his programme notes for his first home match he stated that he'd always had a great deal of admiration for Albion and their attacking style of play.

Perhaps he had but for all that it didn't go down too well that he was an ex-Aston Villa player and coach who had eventually been sacked. So if he wasn't good enough for Villa, why was he being imposed on Albion? This was a strange move by the Board - had our stock fallen so much that only unproven novices were applying? Cynics suggested that only Wylie was willing to work for the modest salary on offer.

The only new player in for the start of the campaign was Peter Eastoe. He joined from Everton with Andy King moving to Goodison in an exchange deal. At 30 years old, Eastoe was a bit long in the tooth as a forward but needs must.

The season started promisingly despite an opening 2-0 defeat at Anfield, and after ten games, a position of joint third was better than I anticipated. Much of the improvement stemmed from the displays of youngster Martyn Bennett. He'd been linked with Ally Robertson at the heart of the defence and his performances highlighted a potential great future if he could carry on in similar vein.

Unfortunately for Martyn, he suffered a back injury in November at St Andrews. And little did he or we realise this would eventually lead to such a promising career being curtailed in such cruel circumstances. Writing in the Albion News, Jimmy Greaves predicted

*"Martyn will be England's next centre half and once there he will be hard to shift."*

In the opening games, Mark "Barney" Grew replaced Tony Godden in goal, Tony having fallen out of favour with Ronnie Allen at the end of the previous season, although in due course Paul Barron was signed from Crystal Palace to become the first choice custodian.

Team selection hadn't been helped due to John Wile missing the first twelve games of the season. He'd been playing in Canada for Vancouver Whitecaps in the summer, and didn't trot out wearing an Albion shirt until we made the journey to Portman Road. As per usual, when visiting Suffolk, it wasn't a happy day. A 6-1 hammering at the hands of Ipswich made even worse due to an injury to Brendon Batson so severe, he missed the rest of the campaign.

In November, there was a match at Wembley I simply couldn't miss, when at long, long, last Derek Statham finally gained that first elusive full England cap against Wales. 'Dekka' had received scandalous treatment from the selectors but his assured display proved that he had been well worth that International call up. Shame the game was such a miserable affair.

After the promising opening, the League performances gradually levelled out and a final mid-table position was about right. In the League Cup there was a total disaster; no humiliation would be a better word. How else can a 6-1 defeat, away at Nottingham Forest in the Second Round, First Leg, be described? Apologies were offered to the fans for such a pathetic performance and promises made that although the second leg was a formality for Forest; the players would do everything in their power to redress the balance. This they did, winning the match

3-1, and the aggregate score of 4-7 was at least a little easier to stomach.

The F.A. Cup again paired Albion with Queens Park Rangers and this time we did at last have a minor consolation for that humiliating Semi-final League Cup defeat. Two goals from Gary Owen, and a Peter Eastoe strike leading to a 3-2 home victory.

Sadly it was another London club who ended the hopes of any further progress when Tottenham Hotspur beat us at White Hart Lane. Again.

Albion goals were hard to come by and following this defeat Gary Thompson, a near suicidal hard running aggressive centre forward, was signed from Coventry City. His arrival led to speculation in the press, and among supporters, that Cyrille Regis would shortly be moving on. The club denied this, indeed Gary said at the time that one of the reasons he agreed to join Albion was to play alongside Big Cyrille.

He certainly added punch to a team that could only muster 59 goals from the three major competitions and he eventually finished with an impressive seven goals from just twelve games. Big Cyrille finished with 11 and Peter Eastoe with 9. Regis and Thommo were a remarkable physically-strong pairing and with a decent wide player to supply quality crosses, who knew what success could be achieved?

Talking of success, Liverpool won the title again. To that, they also added the League Cup and had prospects of the FA Cup as well when drawn at home against Brighton and Hove Albion in the 5th round of the FA Cup. "Imitation Albion" were in the top flight but en-route for relegation. In the shock of the season, Brighton somehow managed to win 1-0 and battled on to reach Wembley for the first time in their history Again, there couldn't have been a supporter in the country that fancied their chances of beating Manchester United in the Final, but amazingly they should have run out winners after a very plucky performance.

Continuing my tradition of attending big matches at the Twin Towers, I was stood among the Brighton fans. None of us could begin to believe the events we were to see that afternoon. Albion took the lead and were playing with style and passion.

Fighting back, United scored twice to lead 2-1. Brighton equalised with just three minutes on the clock to force extra time, and with a replay looking inevitable came the 'magic, tragic moment that led to everyone in the stadium, along with the millions watching on TV, shaking their heads in disbelief.

Brighton's Mick Robinson set up Gordon Smith with a perfect scoring opportunity a few yards from goal. The Cup was theirs for the taking. Cue the immortal line *"And Smith must score."* Yes, he should have, but he hesitated, the shot was blocked and the chance had gone. Brighton fans were devastated. They knew deep down that Manchester United wouldn't play so poorly in the replay, as the eventual 4-0 score proved. They could and should have won. Instead they would never be able to forget the miss that deprived them of enjoying the greatest day in their club's history. Nor would the player.

Hooliganism continued to raise its ugly head, notably in the quiet backwaters of Non-League. Enfield Town, then a powerhouse of the part-time game, were at home to Ilkeston Town of the North-East Counties League in the FA Trophy Third Round. Although Ilkeston had already knocked out two Conference sides, Enfield were too powerful and with fifteen minutes remaining, led 5-1. Then astonishingly in what was reported to be a planned operation, hundreds of young hooligans wearing matching green berets invaded the pitch.

The referee was forced to abandon the game, later awarded to Enfield. There had also been trouble when Ilkeston had won at Barnet in the previous round leading the FA to order an immediate enquiry. The investigation lasted a month after which Ilkeston were cleared of any responsibility. Eventually it was discovered that the gang had nothing to do with the town. They'd deliberately travelled from Derby just to cause trouble. Why, why, why? Add your own answer, if you can find one.

I had no answer and such maniacal happenings were turning me away from the game. Increasingly, I was turning to my other interests more and more such as collecting autographs.

I started my collection in my schooldays, gathering signatures mainly of footballers and cricketers. But now an adult and being a regular visitor to the Birmingham Hippodrome and the Alexandra Theatre, plus many theatres in London's West End (some after Albion matches) I got into the habit of popping round to the respective 'Stage Doors' to add the principal actors/actresses to my collection, together with, providing they raised no objection, photographs with the stars in question.

This year among others, I collared Terry Wogan, Jason Donovan, Shirley Ann Field, Les Dawson, Gemma Craven, Michael Barrymore, Les Dawson, Anna Neagle and Richard (Dickie) Attenborough. The collection required several large folders to house them all. The Jason Donovan meeting still brings a smile considering the circumstances. It was at one of the West End's leading theatres and a good friend, also in the cast, arranged for Dot and myself to meet him at the end of the show. When we arrived, there was a large crowd all hoping to catch a glimpse of the 'Neighbours' heartthrob. They scanned every car, knowing he'd be in one of them eager to scream at maximum volume. Jason did appear but on a bike! Pedalling furiously he duly waved to his fans. We couldn't help but chuckle at this somewhat unexpected mode of transport!

After the show we met, chatted, and when I asked if he knew much about football, I suppose I shouldn't have been surprised by his response *"I know about Manchester United."* He and I posed for a photograph and then Dot presented him with a box of what else but Cadbury Milk Tray chocolates. Made in Birmingham's Bournville, Jason -not Manchester!

On that amusing anecdote, I'll close these 40+ years' memories of following the fortunes of West Bromwich Albion. From good to bad. Moans and groans. Cheers and jeers. Elation and disappointments. In essence feelings that every football fan -whatever team they've grown up with and loved unless of course they're a glory hunter who conveniently jumped on the ever growing bandwagon. Adopting one of the trophy winning teams thanks to seeing them winning and more often than not, 'buying' success, thanks to influential billionaire overseas owners.

*Flat Cap to Bronx Hat'- Book Two is already on the drawing board. It will feature decades of contrasting memories. The indignity of relegation counterbalanced by joys of celebration. I joined the much admired 'Grorty Dick' fanzine giving me the opportunity to interview the club Chairman. Chats and splats (!) with Alan Buckley and Gary Megson. Meeting Preston's legendary Tom Finney. Bryan Robson' unbelievable 'Great Escape' season. Plus a reunion with the Nomads and England Captain Sir Bobby Robson. All to follow – one day.*